P9-CEZ-645

The First Time

BY

KARL FLEMING

AND

ANNE TAYLOR FLEMING

Simon and Schuster : New York

Published by Simon and Schuster
Rockefeller Center, 630 Fifth Avenue
New York, New York 10020

Designed by Irving Perkins
Manufactured in the United States of America

1   2   3   4   5   6   7   8   9   10

Library of Congress Cataloging in Publication Data

Fleming, Karl.
   The first time.

   1.   Sex customs—United States—Personal
narratives.   I.   Fleming, Anne Taylor, joint author.
II.   Title.
HQ18.U5F53   301.41'7973   75-9811
ISBN 0-671-22070-5

Contents

7

Introduction

LET US FIRST SAY that something we now care about quite
deeply, and unblushingly respect, namely this book, did not
begin as one of our more close-to-the-heart endeavors. The
idea came to us almost casually one day as we sat among
writer friends talking about possible magazine articles. And
this, a cross-section of well-known American people telling
how they lost their virginities, seemed a natural to all of us.

We felt if we could get a fair sampling of famous people to
open up and talk honestly about their backgrounds and what
effect these had on their first sexual encounters, we might
put together an interesting book—a sort of American sexual
heritage—and one which we, who take our work quite seriously, might well find more than merely commercial. We did
not set out to prove anything or to arrive at any conclusions.
The idea was simply to let people talk on their own terms
and in their own language about how sex came into their
lives.

But who would talk about it, and how could we get them
to do it? We began by making a list of some 200 prospective
interviewees, leaving off such obvious untouchables as Richard Nixon and Patty Hearst, but including such slim possibilities as Charles Manson, from whom we received an in-
decipherable postcard with one corner burned off, and Tim-

9

othy Leary, who sent us two effusively enthusiastic letters before he turned inexplicably silent.

We wanted to span a cross-section of professions but despite our repeated efforts, athletes, business people and politicians slipped through our fingers; so we ended up with a preponderance of people in the arts. We thought we would have trouble getting as many women as men, simply because there are more well-known men than women, but happily that was not the case.

After we pared down our original list to what we thought were real possibilities, we knew some of the people on it personally or, in some instances, we knew somebody who knew somebody who knew them. Often we had no connection to them at all. Whatever the case, we anticipated that it would be very difficult to get people to reveal themselves on a subject as intimate, and potentially painful, as this.

We began with a barrage of letters and discovered immediately that this approach was useless. Letters did not produce a single interviewee. Thus we relied almost exclusively on the telephone, and discovered that this approach was virtually useless too—if we had to go through an intermediary. There were a half dozen or so notable exceptions, but if an agent, manager or public relations representative was involved, either the message would be lost in translation or the intermediary would find some reason to keep us from his client. The only effective approach was to get the potential interviewee's telephone number, which in itself sometimes took several days and dozens of phone calls, and attempt a direct connection.

From the start, and all the way to the end, this was the hardest part of the project—to pick up the phone, call somebody who had never seen or heard of us, and explain as quickly and persuasively as we could that we wanted to come with a tape recorder and have them pour out the pains and pleasures of their first sexual experiences for publication in a book. Most people were polite, even while declining, but there were sinking spells of several days' duration when neither of us had the courage to pick up the phone one more time.

Finally someone we knew, actress Sally Kellerman, agreed to sit for us. She was open and receptive, and was as scared and earnest as we were—providing the first encouraging sign that people were willing to take our project as seriously as we did. From there we proceeded with painful slowness through interviews with Rudy Vallee, Mae West, Irving Wallace and Lester Maddox (who took himself out near the finish of the book), which gave enough of a sampling to get a contract, and enough of an advance to sustain us through the next months.

As we went along it became easier and easier to get people. When we telephoned to solicit their cooperation they would ask who else was in the book, and gradually we were building an impressive list of names. During one two-day stretch we interviewed Dr. Spock, Bobby Riggs, Lou Rawls and Debbie Reynolds, and then we knew we were on the downhill side of a long climb. Toward the end we even turned down a couple of people whose agents volunteered them.

Are the people in this book just exhibitionists? To say that of people who perform publicly, as do all our interviewees in one way or another, is somehow redundant. But none of them was an exhibitionist in the sense that he or she talked to us just to exercise an ego with a long, boastful soliloquy. Indeed, these interviews were all difficult, the hardest ones, in fact, that we have ever done. For the most part, the interviewees were quiet and thoughtful, if not guarded, and needed constant prodding and gentle encouragement to keep them going. It was almost impossible for some of them to talk in direct language about explicit details, and some became progressively uncomfortable as the questions cut closer to the bone. A few times people simply said they would not answer certain questions, and we accepted such stands good-humoredly if with mild disappointment. A couple of the interviews took less than an hour to do. A handful took as long as ten hours—stretched over three different sittings.

Did all these people tell us the truth? Why would they lie? The only motive would be to paint themselves as more lusty or sexy than they actually were—and we discovered few Lolitas or pubescent Don Juans in our interviews. Only one of them told us a truly extraordinary (and virtually unbelievable, i.e., twenty-six "times" in thirty hours) anecdote of sexual performance—but she adamantly insisted it was off the record. There were rare times when we felt stories were being slightly embroidered, and we trimmed the embroideries. Of the interviews we finally did, almost all survived fairly intact until the final editing phase. The ones we threw out were not discarded because of embellishment but because the people involved obscured or minimized their first beddings—either deliberately or for uncontrollable reasons—to the point of being almost monosyllabic.

Why did all these people agree to be in the book? As a catchall generalization, we concluded that people who can't or won't talk about their own sex lives can't understand why anybody else will, and people who can talk casually and without inhibition about their sex lives don't understand why others won't—or won't at least try. Specifically, the people in this book are of three kinds: 1) those who were so uninhibited that they talked about their sex lives as casually as they might discuss their swimming pools; 2) those who had been basically unhappy, if not crippled, sexually but were now in the process of "discovering" themselves and wanted to talk about what they were going through; and 3) people who had frightful early sex experiences and therefore thought that sex was a major American problem—if not *the* major one—and needed talking about.

We interviewed separately, and neither of us did all men or all women. Nearly all the interviews were taped. We explained beforehand to the interviewees that their words would be edited in such a way as to appear in the book as verbatim first-person monologues, totally faithful to the letter and spirit of their remarks. There was no attempt to smooth out anyone's language, although we tried to organize the words so that they would proceed gracefully and logically. The way each person talked about sex, the style, the words he or she used, were frequently as revealing as what was said. It was the odd turn of phrase or the odd remembered detail—the color of a dress, the feel of a room—that was and is the joy of the book to us, that and the genuine funniness with which a lot of them told of their early fumblings and bumblings.

We did not restrict our questions to the brief incident of "the first time." We asked our subjects about their parents, their churches, their schools, their neighborhoods, their friends, their fears, their fantasies, their failures, their guilts, their angers, their joys, their tears, and their morals and mores. In brief, we tried to get them to sum themselves up sexually.

Sixty-six years separate the oldest person in the book, Alice Roosevelt Longworth, born in 1884, from the youngest, actress Victoria Principal, who was born in 1950, and yet for all the outward manifestations of change that those sixty-six years have brought, for all the supposed openness, the nude fold-outs, the orgasm clinics, we came to the end of the book with the feeling that fundamentally the introduction to sex is about as complicated and difficult an experience as it has always been, and that certainly "the first time" remains an emotional, guilt-ridden, bewildering and not wildly erotic moment.

We conclude, too, that men and women have had equal damage done to them, that in their hurts and hungers they are more alike than not, that they share pretty much the same sexual needs, sexual vanities and sexual shynesses, and that our country certainly has produced far more sexual victims than villains.

K.F.
A.T.F.

The First Time

Maya Angelou *writer and poet*

Born April 4, 1928, St. Louis, Mo.

For most of a hot, dry late-summer day in Sonoma, the country town in Northern California's wine country where she and her husband have a new home, Maya Angelou talked— talked over morning coffee, talked while preparing a lunch of sausages, ratatouille and French bread, while eating, while having a swimming lesson from her husband in their pool, while drinking wine, and later, Scotch. She is almost six feet tall, a graceful, full-bodied woman with a graying Afro, whose large hands, eyes and mouth seem in constant motion. Ms. Angelou has at odd times been a professional actress, dancer and singer, and the daylong chronicling of her past was like some wonderful accidental drama. Laughing and crying within the space of a single sentence, her deep voice booming, then becoming barely audible, she resurrected some of the anecdotes from her two autobiographical books, I Know Why the Caged Bird Sings *and* Gather Together in My Name. *She is married to Paul de Feu, Germaine Greer's ex-husband, and seemed to want him near her as she talked, so for most of the day he, small, pale, but very muscular, sat beside her, lighting their endless cigarettes and refilling their glasses. He occasionally would interrupt to tell a story or a bawdy joke, and they would laugh together long and hard.*

WE WERE BORN, my brother Bailey and I, in St. Louis, where my mother comes from. When I was six months old my mother and father took us to California, Long Beach, but their marriage didn't work out. So when I was three and Bailey four, my father put tags on our arms and put us on a train to his mother in Stamps, Arkansas, a little town of five thousand which is twenty-five miles from the Texas border. Momma just took us in.

She was the mother of the town, of the black area. She had the first, the only, black-owned store in the town since the turn of the century. On one side of the town was a lumber mill and on the other side a cotton gin. When my grandfather left her with his two small children, she started making meat pies, and every day she'd run, so that they were hot, to the mill and sell them and then run across town to the gin. The next day, gin first, then the mill, for years, until she had so built up her business that she built herself a stand in the middle so they could come to her. It's still there, W. M. Johnson's General Merchandise Store. On the weekends the barber in town would come and sit and cut hair under the chinaberry tree at the store—it was just called "The Store." All negotiations were made at the store. Whites who hired cotton pickers would come in the morning to the store to pick them up. The wandering black troubadours of the South would make their way down the river to the store. On Saturdays they'd have those cigar-box guitars and sing that beautiful music, and my grandmother would say, "Sister, you come inside. That's worldly music."

She was very religious, and every week we went to Sunday school in the morning and church at six-thirty in the evening. The church was a big white wooden building, the largest building next to the school that I'd been into. It had wooden benches and fans from the mortuary in Texarkana and held 150 people. My grandmother was the mother of the church; she didn't sing in the choir; my grandmother just sang. The church stood at a fork where two roads came down and joined and made one going into the white part of town. The racial mix was 60-40 black, but there was no mixing at all. White boys and girls, neither of them really existed for me; they weren't real; they weren't people; they were white folks. You knew that white guys, if they caught you in a dark street, would violate you, and you had no recourse. I could see a movie with Clark Gable or Robert Taylor, and they weren't real. People who were real were black; those were people. When the washer women would come by the store and put their loads down on the way back from town, they'd have shorts, step-in bloomers and brassieres in the baskets, and it was just amazing to me that white women really wore the same things.

My grandmother made most of my clothes. She was really a typical African market woman; I found that out when I lived in Africa. She'd buy two bolts of cloth a year, and out of that she'd make my clothes, her clothes, my brother's shirts. She even made shoes. And she bought land. She owned all the land the poor whites lived on and most of the land the blacks lived on. We had pigs occasionally, and once we had a cow because Bailey was ill. But because my grandmother was alone most of the time, we couldn't slaughter. People who were indebted to us, families who were carried on the books over years and years, would come during slaughter time, just after the first frost, and bring us fresh meat. Sometimes Grandmother would go to a nearby place and help to make up the sausage. We always had chickens and a fantastic garden, but fresh meat usually only during

the slaughtering, the month of November. And my grandmother had all the old remedies for things. A young girl
couldn't have her hair straightened until she was fifteen and
about ready to take company, so Momma was always braid-
ing mine. If the hair fell out in her hands she'd say, "Oh, Sister, you need a mess of greens; go pick some mustard and
turnip greens from the garden." Then she'd go out—I've
pictured that so many times—she'd take off her apron and
walk down the road up past the school, she never took me
with her, and come back with just two handfuls of various
things, poke salad and dandelions, and put them in as the
greens cooked. We'd all eat them but I knew it was for me.

My grandmother was very contained, very proud. When I
was young, if I ran into the house she'd say, "Sister, that's not
to be done." There was no touching. Every now and then
when something would strike her she'd say, "Come here,
child," and then she'd touch us and, oh, that was incredible.
There was gentleness and all that, but no physical stuff. You
loved somebody and they knew it and you knew it. You were
supposed to be contained; don't run into the house, be ready,
work hard, be clean. I used to ask her, "Momma, do you love
me?" And she'd say, "You be a good girl and Jesus will love
you." That was my grandmother. But she loved us with this
brooding, abiding love.

When I was seven Bailey and I were sent back to
Mother in St. Louis. It seemed like a foreign country, everyone was so strange. Mother was so beautiful, light-skinned
with straight hair, and she wore lipstick, which Momma
would never have approved of, and she played music and
danced and was so gay. To this day she's like a hurricane in
full force—a fantastic lady! She was living with her boyfriend, a Mr. Freeman, who was big and kind of sluggish
and a lot older than my mother. Sometimes Mother would

let me sleep in their bed, and I'd wake up and she'd be gone, and there I was with Mr. Freeman. I let him hold me and I liked it and I just thought it was so fine and I'd hug him and everything. One day, it was a Saturday in late spring, I'd gone to the store to get milk and come home and was just on my way out again when he called me into the living room. Then he was holding me too tight to move and his pants were open and his "thing" was standing out and he grabbed down my bloomers. And then there was the pain and I passed out.

When I woke up he was washing me and told me not to tell a soul. But then I got very sick and was in bed, and Mother picked me up so Bailey could change the sweaty sheets, and my red-stained drawers came out from under the mattress where I'd hidden them. So they took me to the hospital, and finally Bailey got it out of me who had done it.

Then I had to go to court. My mother's parents were very well known upper-middle-class people in St. Louis, so the courtroom was packed. My grandmother was a precinct captain for the Democratic party and had a lot to say about who got jobs with the city, so she had a lot of enemies as well as friends and they were all there. So when the man asked me, had I ever let my mother's boyfriend hold me before, I said no. I carried that guilt until I was twenty, because the man was killed that evening. He was sentenced to a year and a day, but somehow he got out that same day and he was found dead that night, beaten and kicked to death. My mother and her brothers were very bad, not bad but mean. They were "bitch," excuse the expression. They were known in St. Louis, in Los Angeles, in San Francisco as "The Baxters." My mother's the oldest and of the seven she's the only one who had children, and she was so mean that when somebody would do something to our family, my uncles would corner him in a public place—and they haven't changed—and one would stand in one door, one in the other, and they'd say to my mother, "Vivian, kick his ass. And now cut him a little." And she would. That's how bad they were. So there was no way that man who raped me was going to live. If I had said, "Yes, I let him hold me," it wouldn't have made any difference. But my intellect did not free me from that guilt, not from that. I really only got over it at about twenty.

At eight, I went back to Momma in Stamps. I have no idea whether she sent for us or whether the St. Louis family just got tired of me. I wouldn't talk, I was so afraid and really shattered. I closed off people. For four years the only person I would talk to was Bailey. He used to beg me, "Please, Maya, please say something," because Grandmother would whip me. For a long period of time I just knew, I'd just go out to the peach tree—there was that bitter smell of the peach sap —and get a switch. That was less painful than talking. I just couldn't make it; I could not, it would not come out. But still every week Momma would braid my hair, and that's such an act of love. Once when I was nine or ten, a teacher hit me for not talking and I came home crying. Momma closed up the store, hung up that wooden sign and we walked to school. She said to Miss Williams, the teacher, "Now this is my grandchild and you hit her. You're somebody's grandchild," and *whap*, she hit her. She said, "Don't ever do that again." Momma would whip me for not talking, but nobody else was supposed to.

I hid in books. Oh, my Lord, what a fine hiding place. Thank God for them. Then there was Mrs. Flowers. She was quite a famous woman, the mother of the attorneys Flowers of Arkansas, and she came to Stamps for three months every year. She was a lot like Grandmother, very contained and soft-spoken, so she didn't frighten me, but she was also educated. She was short and very black and wore voile dresses and talcum powder, and if she came close she just smelled so pretty. She took me to the school and unlocked the side door—why she had a key I don't know even now—and we went into the library. She said, "Now I want you to read from here to here, from A to D, by the time I come back." So I read them. Then she'd come back and say, "Okay, now read from D to J." I read every book in that library and then she brought me more; I'd see her coming up the road from town with a bag of books. I just put it all in my head. God, I don't know what I didn't know. But to make sense of it or to apply it was another thing altogether. Like sex. I knew about it in my head because of the rape and because I read everything, but it was still a terrible mystery.

Bailey was quite aware sexually and experimenting by eight or nine. We made a teepee once, and I was supposed to be the baby sitting out front while Bailey and this little girl —I'll never forget her—went into the tent to be Mommy and Daddy. They were making all this noise; she was saying, "Do this, do that." I kept saying, "What are you doing? I'd like to see." So they ran me off; Bailey said, "Baby, get the hell out." A year later, a fellow I liked came over to play and I said, "Bailey, you be the baby while we play Momma and Papa." He just flipped. "No, no, no, no, you can't play that." Bailey's always been a big brother to me, and he's still only 5′ 4″. When I was twelve, I found a little Maggie and Jiggs comic book of his, five inches long and two inches wide. I couldn't believe it! Maggie and Jiggs that I read every Sunday, and Jiggs had a joint this big and Maggie was this kind of *woman*. Fantastic, fantastic! I read it about twenty-five times.

There were girls around who were kissing and having sex, too, at the age of thirteen. Bailey and I were always excused before the bell rang to be in the store to help when all the kids came down the hill to buy lunch, a can of sardines for a nickel, with a few crackers thrown in. And every day, I'd see these girls with their big hips and their little waists—that was the thing—coming down that hill. The way they'd walk— *chunka, chunka, chunka.* I was tall and thin and neither very black nor very fair, and I just thought, "I'll never look like that. I'll never have hips." You absolutely wanted to be one of those girls and then you'd hear people say bad things about them behind their backs. It was really schizoid.

There was one boy I liked, Eddie Lee Mathews. We were both around thirteen, and he was very quiet. Any kind of overt approach frightened me. We never kissed or even held hands—I was "good" and so was he—but when Bailey and I boarded the bus for Texarkana on our way back to Mother in San Francisco, Eddie Lee Mathews was at the station to say goodbye.

San Francisco was another foreign country, oh, my lands! My mother had remarried in 1940 and she and my stepfa- ther, Clidell Jackson, had gambling houses and pool halls from Nome, Alaska, to San Diego. My stepfather, who was my only father as far as I'm concerned, was from Texas, went to the third grade in school, and was so bright and so honest a man that when I was fourteen and fifteen gamblers would call him long-distance to ask his opinion. And he'd always say, "Maya, get on that other telephone and listen." He taught me every card game, he taught me how to hold cards and tell if they were sanded. You'd see him coming down the street in his $300 suits and diamond stick pins and you'd think he was Dr. so and so. Con men from all over the coun- try would come to our house in San Francisco and my dad would call me in the back room where they would sit—they didn't drink, my dad didn't drink or smoke—and say to one of them, "Tell my baby how you sold that bridge in Texas.

I'm educating her." I learned that the only way you can be a mark is when you want something for nothing.

Meanwhile, my mother would take us out to dinner about every two weeks, to a Hungarian restaurant, a French restaurant, a Chinese restaurant, and show us what life was like and how to order and how to tip. About every two months she made us listen to Bach and Beethoven, and every year we were obliged to go to the plays, had to see *Tobacco Road, Rain, The Drunkard* and one Shakespeare play every year— had to do that. Mom was educated and very sophisticated, while Dad, for all his knowing about the world, had no education but knew what he had to teach me.

They were beautifully happy until Dad fell in love with the horses and that was just the end. He lost a fortune; I don't think he had quite $1,000,000 but the IRS got him in the late forties for not having paid taxes on $253,000. So you figure if they found that much, then there was a lot more. It wasn't the losing of the money that broke them up; it was that Dad couldn't listen to Mother, so they just stopped talking.

At the age of fifteen I became obsessed with the idea that I was a lesbian. I read a book called *The Well of Loneliness*, a beautiful, sexually titillating book about two women, and that convinced me. I was 5′11″ and not pretty and had a deep voice. I knew I was very smart, I knew it, I just knew it, I mean, nobody told me, I had no reason to think I was, except I knew it. And it didn't help, not worth a damn. I was still that tall Southern girl with no breasts. I still couldn't get them, I just couldn't. I'd pull off my clothes and look in the mirror and it was awful—I looked like a cucumber. When the vulva grew, I thought, "That's it! Now I'm a hermorphodite." That's what we called it. I thought my life was through, finished. So I set out to disprove my worst fears.

There was a guy who lived up the street, he was around

twenty, and he wasn't interested in me but he'd always tease me, say, "Hey, when are you going to give me some of that fine brown frame?" I'd say, "Stop that; you're stupid; you can't say that to me." I was a real smart-ass. I never spoke slang and I knew foreign languages and I always walked around like my grandmother had taught me, deliberate, my head up, my hands clasped behind my back, a piece of steel right down through my head and into the ground. To this day, in a crisis I go straight there and I'm invulnerable; nothing on God's earth can touch me once I'm in my pose. So this guy was just teasing me for that reason, because I was scared. One night I was coming home from school around nine-thirty —I went to college at night at the California Labor School— and this guy was coming down the street, down the hill. And I thought, "This would be a very good time," because I didn't have to be home until eleven. So I said, before he could say it, I said, "Say, would you still like to have sexual intercourse with me?" So help me God, I said it just like that. And he said, "Uh, uh, uh." So I said, "Take me someplace and not to Jackson Street Park," which I'd heard the girls at school call "Chopping Park" because that's where everybody went to screw. I said, "Take me someplace." We went to a furnished room of one of his friends and the first thing he did was turn out the lights. I wanted them left on but didn't say anything for fear I'd appear even more aggressive. We undressed in the dark. There was no embracing, no caressing, no nothing. Just a knee forcing my legs apart and some groping, and then he got up. There was a little pain but not a great deal, because I'd been raped and the hymen was gone. It was just nothing, absolutely hopeless. With the lights off there wasn't even his body to admire. He said, "I'll take you home." And I said, "No, never mind. I'll get a taxi." I didn't feel guilty; I just felt "What a bore. What a waste of time," and really not too sorry for myself that it hadn't been great. It allayed the lesbian fears only in that I knew I could have sex. But I thought, "Well, I'm just not a sexy person. That's okay."

Two months later I knew I was pregnant. Damn! I'd see this guy on the street and he'd say, "When you going to . . ." I'd just walk right by. So I told my brother Bailey and he said, "Don't tell anybody or Mom will take you out of school, and you've got to get a high-school diploma." Then Bailey left home and went to sea, and after about four months I called this fellow, my son's father, over to the house and said, "Listen, I'm pregnant and what I'd like is just to talk to somebody. And maybe we'd go to a movie sometime." He said, "It's not my baby and I'm not going to help you." Because I was honest, and brutally so if it was necessary, I said, "Listen, at this very moment there is twenty or thirty thousand dollars cash in my father's money closet and he makes more in one day than your whole family in a month, so I didn't ask you for that." So I called Papa Ford, the old man who lived with us, and I said, "Papa, show this man out the back door."

I went to school until three weeks before Guy was born, on September 8. I didn't tell my parents I was pregnant until August 17, the day I graduated from summer school. It was also my stepfather's birthday, and V-J Day, and to celebrate he took me to one of his gambling houses. Mother had been in Alaska for a month and Dad said, "Your momma's going to be so proud of you when she gets back. You're turning into such a fine woman." I thought, "I should. I'm eight months pregnant." I was finally getting breasts and my skin looked so pretty. So that night we got to his place behind the cigar shop and he opened the door and there must have been 150 men in there. He said, "Okay fellows, I'm bringing my baby in here, watch your mouths." He took me around and introduced me to people with names like "Bettin'-'em-Back Bud" and "Steel Chest," and this was my big taking-out. When he dropped me off home, he said, "Wake me in the morning. I have to go downtown. You come and go with me. I'm so proud of you."

So I wrote this note and put it on his bed. It said, "I'm sorry to bring this on the family, but I'm pregnant." I sat up until five, playing solitaire on my bed, waiting for him to come in, and finally fell asleep. At five-thirty he knocked on my door. He said, "Don't forget to wake me up in the morning. Oh, by the way, I got your note, good night." I didn't go back to sleep. Then I woke him up and we had breakfast and he didn't say anything about the note and I was dying. Finally he said, "What's this about you being pregnant?" I said, "Well, I am." He said, "Okay, Maya, now that's going to make your momma very proud. How far along are you?" I said, "I have three weeks." He thought I meant I was three weeks pregnant. So he sent Mother a telegram and she arrived home one morning at six o'clock. Papa Ford came up and said, "Your momma's downstairs." So I went down. She'd gotten out of her traveling clothes and run a bath and she said, "Come on in the bathroom." She'd never done that before. She got in the tub and she offered me a cigarette and she said, "Now you're more than three weeks pregnant." I said, "Yes, ma'am, it's about two weeks now before I have the baby." She said, "Do you want to marry the boy?" I said no. She said, "Does he want to marry you?" I said no. She said, "Well there's no point in ruining three lives. So it's all right. I want to see it, I want to see my grandchild." There would never have been a thought about an abortion. Fatherless or no, the baby belongs to the family and particularly to the mother's family. My stepfather said to me, "Baby, any-thing money can buy you will have."

Mom delivered Guy. I woke up in the morning with the pain and she timed it and said, "Oh, nothing to worry about." About two in the afternoon I wanted some Chinese food. She said, "Go ahead and take the car." So I drove to China-town, parked the car, went into a place that had booths with those little draw drapes, ate all this food and drove back home. About eleven o'clock that night she said, "I'll prepare you." So she shaved me and said, "Now we'll go." I was scared and she told me all about the night I was born. We got to this little hospital and they took me into a room and called the doctor. The pains became severe and mother told me dirty jokes. She put my knee up against her shoulder and took my hand and she'd say "press down" and tell me the punch line all at the same time. I'd start laughing. So the water broke and the doctor still wasn't there. They took me into the delivery room and Mother said, "I can see him com-ing. Just press down one more time. Here comes his head; it's got black hair, thank God." The doctor came in just as she said, "It's a boy." So she and the doctor went out and had some drinks and Dad said that when she got home she looked like she'd had the baby.

My son Guy, to this day has never seen his father to know him. Guy always used to sniff rather than blow his nose. So I said, "You do that and one day you'll blow your whole brains right into your mouth." So we laughed. One day when he was about five I took him to the movies and somebody be-hind was snuffling and Guy said, "Mom, that guy's going to blow his whole brains right through his mouth." I looked back and there, sniffing coke, was his father, his real father, sitting right behind us. So I said to Guy, "Let's go." And we got up and left, and if the man recognized me he never said a word. Two or three years after that I started giving concerts at San Quentin, and it turned out that Guy's father was there.

After Guy was born I went around and did a whole lot of things, some unsavory, some painful, some joyful, and at twenty-one I had a car and a house and pretty clothes for me and my baby. My mother and stepfather had told me to leave the baby with them and go back to school. But I said, "I'll take care of my own." I feel that way about my life. But if you're black and female and young and inexperienced and completely untrained and intelligent and curious as hell and very independent and have a baby, there's not much you can do. I worked as a waitress and as a cook, and once I had a job taking paint off cars with my hands with steel wool. One of the differences between black American society and white American society is that the black American woman is fantastically strong and incredibly independent. She doesn't take a lot of shit from anybody and certainly not from her man. She'll say to her man, "Okay, I'll let you slide, but I'm letting you do it, no fear." A black man I know said, "It's not that I don't have the inclination to step out but, damn, I'd be so scared to go to sleep." Because what black women would use is a stove. You don't have anything, just boil some water and give him a seeing to. That's why some of the most beautiful flirting goes on in the black community. It's not that this man is going to phone you or this woman comes up to you. It's not done, it's dangerous, shit! You'd be cut in a minute. It's just recognizing that this is a male and this is a female and you're sure a pretty looking thing.

Curly taught me that. He was the first man I was ever in love with. I met him when I was eighteen and working as a cook at the Creole Kitchen in San Francisco. He was big and beautiful and very gentle, and he told me I was very beautiful and I believed anything he said. I'd had violent sex and indifferent sex, but he was lovely. It was a great thing to happen. I tried to dress, I tried to flirt, I tried to do all the nice little things. It was a marvelous gift. We were together only four or five months because he had another girl in San Diego that he'd been planning to marry. It was just as wonderful, I realized after, for him to go on. Otherwise I can't imagine what my life would have been like. It's all accidents anyway. I've been very, very blessed to live all the lives I've lived and to feel as I feel, that I'm just beginning. I tell you there's not one thing I would undo, not one. Because look at who I am. I am so grateful to be who I am. Not what—that's secondary. I laugh a lot. I am greatly loved and love greatly, and I cry and I'm pleased with human beings. So I wouldn't undo it, not one thing, not even the rape.

Art Buchwald *humorist*

Born October 20, 1925, Mount Vernon, N.Y.

Art Buchwald keeps an office at 1750 Pennsylvania Avenue in Washington, in an antiseptic glass-and-steel building that houses more than a hundred important newspaper, magazine, radio and television journalists from the national media. While his secretary fields phone calls and works on his mail and his speech-making schedule, Buchwald sits behind a profusion of newspaper clippings, magazines, books, notes and general litter, rapidly typing his syndicated column in a cloud of cigar smoke. After he finishes writing every day, Buchwald generally finds an audience of two or three reporters to try it out on—presumably on the theory that if you can make a newspaperman smile, the rest of the country will howl. Talking about his childhood, he sat coatless with his feet on his desk, his necktie askew, hands behind his head, rolling his cigar back and forth in his mouth, and answered questions in a wistfully self-effacing manner.

I WAS NEVER MUCH OF A SWINGER. I guess I was always afraid of rejection. That someone would think badly of me. The big conflict I had to fight constantly was wanting a girl to think

I was a "nice" person and at the same time wanting in the worst way to get laid. Those were the choices—either the girl said, "Isn't he a fine fellow; he stopped when I asked him to," or the girl would say after you went the whole way, "Bless you, you did it even though I said no."

For every time I got laid in my youth, I got fifty rejections. The girls had to let you know they wanted to make love or you wouldn't do anything about it. I can understand the girls' fears. They were really under the gun about sex—they feared that they were going to get pregnant and they were told that boys were dirty.

The pursuit of getting laid when I was young was very time-consuming. It was the fiction of the forties that in order to prove you were a man you had to make out every time with a woman. My biggest problem was that I wasn't willing to lie about it. I wasn't able to pretend I was in love with a girl just to get laid. I wasn't about to get involved or fall in love with any of them. I was told that when you're seducing women you can say anything, and they don't believe it, but they want to hear it anyway. But for some reason I couldn't say anything I didn't mean. The Jewish girls were the worst. They wanted a commitment. I haven't made it with many Jewish girls because subconsciously I always thought, "They're not going to, no way. They're just going to want to get married or something. They all want to become Jewish mothers, so it's just a waste of time."

One of my other problems was that I was always terribly ambitious and I figured women could slow me down. I just never had the time to devote to women, which is all it takes. So I'm not one of the great lovers, and I can't look back on my record as one of the great ones.

I guess your sex drives and habits all start in early youth and it is this period that decides what you're going to do. I was a foster child, and that has been the big driving force in my life. I'm still trying to prove to the world that I'm not a foster child. My mother died about the time I was born. My father couldn't handle me and my three older sisters so he put us in this orphanage. Then we were put in a series of foster homes. I lived in fear somebody would find out. One summer some of the kids I played with on the block went to a camp that happened to be right next to the camp for charity children where I was staying. I spent my summer hiding. Every time I saw one of their shirts I'd duck behind a tree or hide in a canoe. It really messed up my summer.

Actually we didn't have it that bad. The only real problem was that neither the child nor the foster parents would commit themselves to anything, because we all knew it wasn't for real. From the time I was born until I was five, I was put with these two German nurses who were Seventh Day Adventists, because I had rickets. Boy, we got Hell and Damnation from them all the time. Any kind of amusement or whatever, and you'd go to Hell. One of the most devastating things I remember was when my father came to take me and my sister out of there—he was getting worried about the religious thing—and we were crying because we didn't want to leave. It was home to us. He tried to make it up to us by taking us to a movie and, shit, we fought like tigers to keep from going to that movie. In analysis, I found out that from those first six years Hell-and-Damnation is still very much there in my subconscious. I'm still taking the rap for crimes that, Jesus, I don't even know half of them.

The families I lived with after that were all in Hollis, New York, a very middle-class town of five to ten thousand on the way out to Long Island. The first family I lived with, I shared a room with the maid when I was very little, and I'd see her undress all the time, and that was sort of interesting. Nobody in the second or third homes ever talked about sex, so the total of my information came off the streets and from the candy store where five or six of us boys used to hang out together when I was about twelve years old. There wasn't any information of a technical sort, but there was a tremendous amount of discussion about would she, wouldn't she, could we. There was also a tremendous amount of masturbation. Another guy and I used to jack off in back of the railroad tracks. I don't remember much guilt about it, but there were all those myths that we were going to go insane.

My real fantasies around this time were about making love to my teacher. We boys used to talk about that a lot. And then we started to have parties with girls, and if you could get underneath her sweater, man, that was something! There was one girl in the neighborhood whose mother was divorced and was gone in the afternoons, and this girl used to have parties over there in the afternoon and take off all her clothes. She was very pretty. There was no screwing or anything like that, but that was *the* place to go. She'd undress and we'd play strip poker and cop a feel. One time one of the mothers of one of the kids came looking for him and saw his dog out front and discovered us. There was a big scandal, and all the other girls in school knew about this girl—she was the loose woman of the neighborhood.

We used to play baseball down the street from where I lived and next to the ball field was this revetment where they had dug out the place for buildings but hadn't built them yet. We showed up one Saturday morning and somebody, apparently a pornographer who got scared, had dumped a ton of pornography and pornographic pictures into this hole. We went ape. We went absolutely crazy. All the kids in the neighborhood were bringing home stuff. And there was nothing anybody could do about it. Oh, Jesus, and we stashed it away because we knew the parents would try to burn it. I'm not exaggerating when I say a ton. It practically filled the whole goddamned revetment.

I used to roller skate when I was about twelve, and I hung out at a dry cleaners where there were girls working who were eighteen or nineteen, and I was really in love with them. There was this one older guy who used to pick up one of the girls and take her out, and he would tell me he could make it with this girl. He said, "I can make any girl do anything I want her to do."

Once when I was ten or eleven I went to visit an aunt in Coney Island, and I had on linen pants and I was walking in the park. It was daytime but everybody was necking, and all the girls with their tits, Jesus, I was playing with myself as I was walking along and I didn't even realize that my dong was out. I was just whacking away, you know, really public exposure. In that same area of Coney Island there were bathhouses where the women used to change, and we'd go there and look through the slats and watch them undress.

There were a couple of girls ahead of me in school that I was in love with, mainly a little blonde girl who wore sweaters and had real big tits. With any of these girls, I thought if I could get just a feel, that would be enough. I wasn't one to push it any further. I was timid, and if a girl said no, I took her word for it. But in every gang there is one guy who has it made with the broads, and in our gang his name was Elstrom. He was a little older than we were, and he was a blond kid, and he never took no for an answer. The rest of us were frustrated and frightened, so he was a kind of cult hero. The girls I knew who would let me neck with them wouldn't let me go any further, but I'm sure Elstrom could have gotten further. In fact, I think he made it with the girl who took her clothes off.

I read a lot as a kid, and one book I remember is *Of Human Bondage*. That was one of the first sexy books I read, and it was a real turn-on. The first dirty show I ever saw was *Tobacco Road*, which was playing on Broadway when I was about fifteen. At that time I was working as an office boy at Paramount Pictures from four to eight every day, so I was in the city by myself a lot. So one day I paid fifty-five cents and sat in the balcony and saw *Tobacco Road*. It had gotten terrible reviews, but it was a pretty good turn-on.

I was very ambitious and wanted to work, so the summer I was fifteen I got a job as an elevator boy at this resort hotel out on Long Island. There were a bunch of rich kids out there from West End Avenue and Central Park West who were all eighteen and nineteen and were all screwing. It was summertime and they didn't know how old I was, so I sort of got mixed up with them.

All of us employees lived on the top floor of this hotel, and there was a chambermaid up there who must have been around thirty. She wasn't that bad looking. And about the first week I was working there, it just happened: I lost my virginity. We were in her room and she had on a bathrobe over her pajamas, and I had on pajamas, too. I think she probably seduced me. I just went along. I suspect she knew I had never had a woman before. She was just a little hot. Then she took a real liking to me, but I was a little scared by the whole thing and didn't want to get entrapped, so I tried to avoid her.

Then there was another girl who was a guest at the hotel, and two of us were banging her. And I'll never forget that when I went home after that summer I was so goddamned smug that my sister immediately said, "My God, he's no longer a virgin." Funny, it wasn't that good, but I was the first one of my group who got laid so I was sort of a hero. I wasn't taking shit from anybody. But if I hadn't gone to this hotel, I don't think it would have happened for a while. The accomplishment far surpassed the physical pleasure. It wasn't a letdown, because I had made it with a dame. It was just one of the great things, me being the first one in my crowd and all.

I was afraid of getting involved with girls, of falling in love with them, or of them falling in love with me. And if I had been in love, I wouldn't have wanted to touch her at that age because we were taught that the girl of our dreams wouldn't let us do anything to her. And the sad lesson of life is that you treat a girl like that with respect, and the next guy comes along and he's banging the hell out of her.

If a girl did let me screw her I felt horrendously indebted to her, as if she had done me the greatest favor in the world. I had friends who would do very well, whose attitude—which is the healthy one—is that the girl has as good a time as you have, so what the hell is there to feel guilty about? The most successful guys with women are the ones who figure, hell, she'd just as soon be in the hay as you would. But that's my hang-up, and I never have been able to do anything much about it. That comes from your background and your relationship to women when you're young.

I've tried to please women all my life. I held women in high esteem, or was afraid of them. With my foster parents, the women were much more awesome than the men in all three homes. They were matriarchal figures, very strong, and I was afraid of them. So I've always held women in high esteem. I've had really good relationships with women, but when it comes to sex I always had the feeling that I was going to hurt them or something. I'm constantly in awe of guys who are always making it with one woman after another.

But when I got out of school and went in the Marine Corps things were better for me. I had a Marine uniform, which certified me, and I'd go to bars and meet girls, and inevitably it was much easier. The war was on, and it was sort of accepted that if a man's going off to die, and if you're a girl, that's the least you can do.

Sometimes I would wind up with the wives of guys who were already overseas. I remember one time I met a married couple in the bar of the Biltmore Hotel in Los Angeles. We were drinking and drinking and they said, "Where are you staying?" And I said, "I don't have a place." So they said, "Stay with us." By the time we got to their home the husband was really drunk and he just passed out in their bedroom. So the wife came into the guest room and got into bed with me. Just another day in the life of a Marine.

One thing I didn't do was go to whorehouses. In the Marine Corps in Hawaii a lot of guys used to go, but I just didn't want to get laid that badly. It was so antiseptic. You stood in line just like you did for the Radio City Music Hall. You only got liberty once a week, and in the daytime, if you were an enlisted man. So you'd usually go into town and buy your mother and your family presents—souvenirs from Hawaii— and then you'd go to the whorehouse and get laid or blown, then you'd have a big steak and go back to the base. I did go one time with this bunch of guys. It was a court-martial offense to get the clap, so you'd go back to the base and keep washing it. I thought I had it once when I was about eighteen. I didn't know I'd just strained the damned thing.

If you went on liberty and didn't get laid, you'd come back to the base and say you did anyhow. Mostly I didn't do very well at it. My technique was not that good. I never resorted to drinking or used many words. I just grabbed them. And most of the time they'd say no. I believed them when they said no. I believed everything they told me. Once in the Marine Corps there was this girl and the first night I took her out I tried to lay her and she got angry and said, "What kind of girl do you think I am?" She actually wanted to get laid in the worst way, but I swear to God it took me two months to get up nerve enough to do anything about it.

Another time, I was in a trailer with this gal who lived off the base at Cherry Point. She was putting up only token resistance, but like an ass I backed off. Then when I stopped, she got pissed off. And when I tried again, it was too late. I went back to the base kicking my ass and saying "I've got to be the greatest schmuck who ever lived. Nobody's as stupid as I am."

I spent a lot of time going over the game plan, trying to figure out where I went wrong with girls. When I didn't make it, I'd spend hours saying, "Jesus Christ, why did I take no for an answer when she really wanted yes?" and wondering if I had made my move at the wrong time. It wasn't very sensuous. My sexual drive was very tied up with proving myself, and that was very defeating.

I had hang-ups and guilt that didn't help. I put women on a pedestal, but fundamentally I was very hostile to them. I was trying to get even with my mother. Trying to get even with your dead mother is one of the most futile drives. There's no payoff. A lot of revenge fucking of that sort goes on. But I can't do it. I can't be cruel. I can have fantasies about being cruel, but I can't do it. I used to have a lot of rape fantasies, and my being Jewish, they had to do with fucking Wasps, country-club girls, the girls at Palm Beach or the girls at Smith and Vassar.

My fantasies were always of making it with the unreachables, and if you've got a good imagination, your sexual fantasies are always better than anyone possibly could really be.

So therefore when you do get into the hay, it doesn't live up to anything. When you have a childhood like mine, you go into fantasy very early, and the fantasies are always better than the real-life situation.

So what you do is build this wall around yourself, and you're not going to let anybody hurt you. You're not going to let anyone know what's going on inside of you. I couldn't say "I love you" to a woman, because when you do that, you're exposing yourself. And that is a really hard thing to do. I wasn't going to let them get inside me. Nobody was going to do that. Well, I handled things all by myself for a long time, but when I came back from Paris ten years ago, I had a breakdown. I wasn't getting any fun out of life, and I couldn't understand it. I didn't drink and I wasn't up to screwing around with women, the two things you usually tend to do when you're in trouble, so I just went to a psychiatrist and said, "Here I am." We worked on it for two years, and since then I've been much happier, much more peaceful. I'm not saying I'm finished with all my hang-ups, but I can now deal with the ones I have.

Dyan Cannon *actress*

Born January 4, 1939, Tacoma, Wash.

Barefoot, wearing only a bikini bottom and knitted see-through cotton top, Dyan Cannon was upstairs at her piano rehearsing for an upcoming club date. The black baby grand sat in the corner of a dimly lit L-shaped room that otherwise contained only a king-size bed, a round coffee table with a big jar of pretzels on it, several huge candles, lots of colored pillows on the carpeted floor and a display on one wall of photographs of herself with several actors—not including ex-husband Cary Grant. Her small home is on the beach in the insulated Malibu Colony, which has a manned guardhouse at its entrance. She lives there with her daughter, Jennifer, twelve. A food faddist who eats only raw fruits and vegetables, she was just coming off an eighteen-day fruit-juice fast that had left her arms and legs looking rather thin. She sat, legs crossed, on a large pillow beside the coffee table and talked at a fast pitch with mercurial earnestness, switching rapidly from almost childlike vulnerability to dogmatic aggressiveness.

I WAS FRIGID UNTIL THREE YEARS AGO. Just couldn't feel it. What happened to me was that I wasn't allowed to be who I was and what I was, so I shut down. I stopped feeling. That's what happens to you. That's why 80 per cent of the women in this country are frigid. When feeling goes, that's where women shut down first, so we can't feel, because that's the most vulnerable spot we have. I was already frigid—dead down there—when I was seventeen, before I had love made to me the first time.

Talk about Victorian upbringing! My dad used to tell me that if I let anyone touch me, anyone, they wouldn't respect me and I would be considered a tramp. So I spent many years being a professional virgin—to make everybody else happy. I was dying to be touched, but that had to be wrong, because I was told it was wrong by the people who knew more than anyone else in the whole world as far as I was concerned. My mother told me the same thing my daddy did: "You mustn't do that. Do you want to be considered a tramp?"

In Seattle all the kids used to go to the movies and neck and then walk home. So I was in there trying to get mine, but I wasn't even allowed to walk to the corner. I'd be picked up by my parents right outside the theater. I wasn't even allowed to go to the senior prom. God, I was so angry at my parents in those days! I had a fury inside of me. I was rebellious and didn't know why.

I was seventeen before they let me start dating. My mother was Jewish and my father was a deacon in the Baptist Church. I think Mommy wanted me to be Jewish because Daddy wanted me to be Gentile. So I learned to lie at an early age. Like I'd make up a name like Dick Brown, when the boy's name was really Dick Brownstein. My mother came from Russia, a beautiful woman, an extraordinary beauty, and she was raised in a very, very strict way. My father is still an incredible-looking man, still a knockout. He looks a lot like Cary Grant. But he was brought up by very strict people, too. My parents were both remarkable-looking people who were held down; obviously they passed that on to me.

I started lying to them and climbing out of windows at night. My mother climbed out of windows herself when she was a girl. After they went to bed at night, I'd flush the toilet so they couldn't hear the window being raised, and out the window I'd jump. My girl friend would pick me up in her car and we'd take off and cruise around and go to the drive-in or go with boys out to View Point overlooking Puget Sound and neck and steam up the windows and write "I love you" on them with our fingers. But I never did it in the car. I was too scared. The minute they touched anything like my breasts or anything below the waist, I'd go crazy, because I wanted them to and didn't want to say no. But I did say no because it was more important to please Mommy and Daddy. I believed what Daddy said, that it would make them want me more if they couldn't have me. That was a very key line in how I was brought up: "He'll want you more if you don't let him have you."

But there really wasn't all that much talk about sex. I didn't know what masturbation was until I was nineteen. Never heard of it. I didn't know anything. One time in school I heard some girls talking and one of them said, "Men and women kiss each other down there." I said, "Down where?" and they said, "You know. Where you go to the bathroom." I said, "What? Yech! Yech! I'll never let a man get near me." All those images used to cross my mind when a man tried to touch me—"That must be filthy, rotten dirty, and any man who would want to do that is just the dirtiest!" Oh, if they could see me now! There are still a lot of prejudices among men about that. I've been with men who really have hang-ups about it, young men, too.

My mother didn't tell me anything at all until I was seventeen, and then she told me if I ever got in trouble to come to her because there were hot baths I could take that would get rid of it. "But don't ever tell your father!" I think that came up when one of my girl friends at West Seattle High got pregnant before she was married and I went to stay with her some. Nobody at school liked her after that. Also in high school, a girl was really in trouble if she ever went to California, because if a girl left Seattle to go to California it meant one of two things: either she was Jewish and getting her nose bobbed, or she was going to get an abortion. So if a girl just went on a trip to California with her parents, she was in desperate trouble. Her reputation was gone. California meant fast living and crazy, far-out people, which many of us are.

It was difficult at times to be angry with my parents, because they really did the best they could. They just laid on me the things their parents laid on them. They did a lot of nice things for me. My mother used to can food, and cook, and make me clothes, and Daddy would freeze the back yard with water so all the kids could come over and ice skate and pop popcorn. Really nice things.

I had a reputation in high school of being very fast. I usually blurted out what I felt, so I guess I got this fast reputation because of kind of saying what I felt. But I just pretended to be tough because I was so scared. There were some wild girls in school, but I wasn't one of them. They used to cut their eyelashes to make them grow fast. We all wore pleated skirts, bobby socks, dickies and cashmere sweaters. The boys wore white bucks and white shirts and a lot of cashmere sweaters.

I guess I must have been kind of pretty, because I won the Miss West Seattle contest, but I never thought I was pretty. I never liked my face until about last year. I always had big breasts. I had to squash them and mash them to hold them down. That's why I was sort of hunched over for a long time. I'm always amazed when I go home and see the pictures of me they have on the walls. Look at those knockers!

School was a snap for me. It was a pretty big school, I guess a couple of thousand kids. They thought I was strange, and I was, because I didn't go along with the rules and laws. The minute my parents would leave town I'd go in and find the car keys—this was when I was fourteen and fifteen—and I'd skip school and have the car. And I'd get the girls to go with me. I was the leader of the 21 Club, with twenty-one girls, and we would go to these clubs where black musicians played, where you were never supposed to be. Not a white person in them, and I used to lead my pack in. I think we called it the 21 Club because I wanted twenty-one girls in it, but I could only find about four or five girls to stick it out with me. Oh, well, I was determined to make it, and I made it in school. The regular social clubs didn't want me. There was a Gentile one in Seattle that I helped them pick the name for, and they didn't want me. And the Jewish club on the other side of town didn't want me. I was dinged. If one girl didn't like you, you'd get a ding. I lived in a section of town where none of the Jewish people lived. That's where Daddy picked the house. All the Jewish girls lived on the other side of town and went to school there. But they finally asked me to join the clubs. I made myself get asked because of my desire to belong. I just ingratiated myself. I was whatever they wanted me to be. That's why I'm such a good actress. Give you any-thing you want. You want me to give you that? Sure I'll give you that. Whatever you want, I'll give you. Will you love me?

I pretended to be this really nice girl so everyone would really like me. When I say "pretended to be a nice girl" I mean just that. Because I didn't think I was a nice girl; I was doing all those things I had been told were wrong. I was letting people touch me. For sure, I was going to burn in Hell.

The religion was very strong. Get down on your knees 'cause if you don't, the Lord's going to see to it that you die and live in Hell! That's what my life was like. That's right. I mean on the way to Temple Hirsch, I used to sing "Jesus Loves Me," and I'd go into the temple where I learned there was no such a man as Jesus. He was just a figure. There was a great man called Jesus, but He was just a man. And then I'd be picked up by Daddy after that, and on the way home we prayed for my Mommy's soul because if you didn't believe in Jesus, you were going to burn in Hell, that's all.

It was a nice Jewish boy who made love to me first. If I was going to do it, it had to be with a nice Jewish boy. He was gorgeous and all the girls wanted him. He looked like Jean-Paul Belmondo, only more perfect. He was lean and dark and had a nice gentleness about him. He wore cashmere sweaters a lot, and those white collars.

We sang together in the temple choir. He was a sophomore at the University of Washington and I was a senior in high school. There wasn't any relationship between us. He just asked me to go to the movies one night. It was winter and snow was on the ground. When we got home Mommy and Daddy had already gone upstairs to bed. We sat down on the sofa and started to kiss. I guess we were both eager without knowing it. We didn't pretend anything. We didn't even turn the lights on in the living room. There wasn't any foreplay. None. We just walked in, sat down on this afghan on the sofa, and awkwardly went to it. There was nothing poetic about it at all.

Somewhere in my subconscious, I guess I knew we were going to do it, but I didn't want to know anything that was going on. He wasn't any great lover. If he had been, it might have been different. I was scared to death. I was so hungry for someone to touch me, and so frightened at the same time. We were both scared, awkward kids doing something we weren't supposed to be doing.

I knew something was going on, but I didn't know what. I didn't feel a thing. That's how out of touch I was. I didn't want to feel the truth. I couldn't do that. It was too much for me. I didn't want to be responsible for my actions. I didn't want to think that I might do something to hurt my chances with Daddy. I was afraid Daddy wouldn't love me any more. I'll tell you what it was like. We did a scene in *Bob & Carol & Ted & Alice* that was cut out, in which I was having a fantasy, a flashback, where I was walking on a stage selling raffle tickets—for me. And when I sell all my tickets they say, "And now, men, we're going to call up the lucky winner." The stage is surrounded by hundreds of men, hundreds. And at the end of this fantasy, all of these men are jumping up and down on my body and I'm screaming, "Yes! No! Oh, please! Yes, yes! Oh, no, no!" And that's exactly what it was like. "Oh, please! Yes! No! Please don't. Oh, do it! But you can't!"

I didn't know what was happening to me. I didn't even know when he left the house. But I'm sure he knew what he had done, because afterwards he kept saying, "I had no idea. I had no idea." I was a virgin, and virgins bleed, you know. After he left I looked down and there was blood all over the afghan. I went hysterical. My mother had knitted that afghan and put it on our yellow velvet couch so it wouldn't get dirty. I rinsed the blood out of it under the cold water faucet. I had to be careful not to run the water too fast or Mommy and Daddy would come out and say, "What are you doing?" That afghan really saved my life.

Next morning I called him on the phone and said, "Did you really do it?" and he said, "I really did it." And I said, "I can't believe it. You get over here and pick me up immediately."

We went to this kind of coffeehouse near the university where all the students hung out. We sat down in a booth and I said, "Listen, I have to ask you a question. Does this mean I'm not a virgin anymore?" I was very serious. He said "Yes, that means you're not a virgin."

I started sobbing and got hysterical and he was embarrassed and kept saying, "Stop. Please stop." But I couldn't. I had so many tears in my eyes I couldn't see the people in the room. I was thinking, "They all know why I'm crying, because I'm a tainted woman. I'm marked for my whole life and from now on people are going to look at me and say, 'She's not a nice girl.' " Because my Daddy had told me that if you are not a virgin no one will ever love you; no one will ever respect you; no one will ever want to touch you.

That was the last time I saw the boy. I hated him, just hated him, for making me unfit to be any man's wife! I didn't want to be responsible for my actions, so I made him responsible. I was just frozen with pain and fear.

I went on a religious kick for a while after that. I was sure I was going to burn in Hell, and the Jewish thing didn't work, so I decided I'd better go along with Jesus. So I went up into the mountains with this girl friend of mine to where Roy Rogers and Dale Evans had this religious retreat.

I didn't let anyone touch me for a long, long, long time, five or six years. And even after that, I once in a while would let somebody talk me into it, but it wouldn't be any good.

The first person to help me out sexually was actually Cary Grant. He was serious about me from the beginning, and it was a long time before we touched each other. I was the girl he was thinking about marrying, and you don't do that to the girl you are going to marry. You see, he had all that stuff laid on him too. I didn't know anything about orgasm at all, and he tried to help me with that. After we got married and I learned to trust him I gradually came to understand what orgasm meant, but only for a short time. Then I shut down again. I mustn't feel too good, because there must be something wrong about that. I felt too good, so there had to be something wrong. I was in my middle twenties, I think, when I had my first orgasm. With Cary, I think, I went out to find me another daddy. Daddy looks extraordinarily like him. But what else could I do? That's all I knew. I picked a man who would think about me just the way Daddy did. I always picked men that didn't like me. Daddy said, "If you let a man touch you, he's not going to respect you. He's not going to like you." That was the way my daddy really felt about sex. So I picked men that felt exactly the way my daddy did. All those feelings of guilt started to come out as soon as I left Cary. The last five years have been invested in a great amount of pain. I tried dope. I tried religion. I tried everything I could so I could get to where I could be with myself without that constant pain. I tried psychiatrists, psychologists, analysts, psychodrama, religion—you name it. Gestalt. Encounter therapy. I went to Esalen. I turned down movies and lived a year in the mountains in a dome house and chopped my own wood.

I tried all the dope there was except the needle. Acid.

Coke. Grass. Hash. Speed. Downers. Mescaline. I'd get up
in the morning and smoke a joint, first thing. I smoked three
packs of cigarettes a day. I was on speed for five years. I was
on speed when I met Cary. I'd take a diet pill every morning
and a sleeping pill every night. That's the real reason why I
hung out in Big Sur for a year. That's where the best dope
was. And I kept picking men that were crazy to be with, the
craziest. These men were really close to their pain, and their
pain was so great they had to shoot dope in their arms. They
had to find a release for the pain. I didn't understand that
then. But something in me knew that I was going to have to
learn to live without being dependent on anything outside of
me. So I gave it all up three years ago, totally. It's been very
hard. At one point I went up to 150 pounds. When I gave
up everything else, there was nothing left but food. It was
the only thing that would keep that pain down for five minutes.

Now my life is better than it has ever been. I'm really
alive. That doesn't mean to say that my life is without pain.
I have been in Primal Therapy for three years. But that feeling of dullness, which just means deadness, is gone. The way
I pick men has changed, too. In the last two years I have
begun to pick men who really like women, and who are
really good to me. And I'm having incredible sex for the first
time in my life, really wonderful sex. And I'm loving it. I just
love it. There is nothing . . . I mean, I just love it. I'm making up for lost time, and I just love it. I love being touched.
I'd die without being touched. I need it all the time.

Al Capp *cartoonist*

Born September 28, 1909, New Haven, Conn.

Wearing a dark business suit, plain black shoes and a blue dress shirt, Al Capp looked incongruous and uncomfortable in Bernie Cornfeld's feudal castle in Beverly Hills, where he was staying as a houseguest for three days. He didn't seem to be having much fun, despite warm days by the pool, in which sun-bronzed girls floated bare-breasted, and wine-filled evenings at a long banquet table where servants waited upon a dozen resident girls and a handful of guests. After dinner most of the crowd would retire to the basement screening room to watch movies, but Capp remained upstairs and talked and watched television. During the day, he took a solitary position under the roofed patio outside the play-room, where some of Bernie's girls shot pinball and mixed milkshakes at a long bar. Capp smoked constantly and drank diet colas and in an arrestingly lugubrious voice told stories of his early life with ironic relish, just as if he were appearing on the Johnny Carson show.

IF I COULD RECONSTRUCT my childhood sex life just the way I wanted to I wouldn't change it in the slightest way. I had it just exactly the way I wanted it. So difficult! So unsatisfactory! And yet the triumphs were enormous. The shabby little triumphs I had with girls were so great. I didn't have many of them but, by golly, when I had them, I earned them. It was always a contest with a girl to get laid, and what made it great for me was that I started in this contest with absolutely nothing.

There were a lot of kids around New Haven who had cars and clothes and summer houses, and that grated on me, because I had nothing, not a dime. No car. The toes out of my shoes and the ass out of my pants. A wooden leg. Even a clean shirt was a helluva thing to have. All I had was conversation. You couldn't imagine a more unprepossessing person to show up in somebody's living room. So I really earned it. I sat up and talked to their parents until some ungodly hour, eleven or twelve o'clock, the parents hoping I would have the decency to go home. But I didn't have the decency, so I waited until they tottered upstairs, and then, of course, it was always very nervous, for just the shifting of a piece of furniture would bring them right down. It was a slow, agonizing process. And, oh, my God, the prattle of these girls, the mindless kind of prattle that just drives a man mad, just mind-shattering prattle. Even at that age, I felt I was paying too much. Sitting and listening to this endless prattle was too high a price to pay for whatever moment of wet, sloppy sex there happened to be. Yet I liked girls and thought they were nice, and the ones who slept with me were enormously nice. I felt that to score with a girl was quite manly. There was a certain ritual to go through. You both assumed your roles.

The role of the boy was that he didn't mean to go any further. And the role of the girl was, "Are you sure?" It was a game. The girl understood it and you understood it, and she was determined to win it. Talk was part of the ritual, and since talk was all I had, I had to earn it through talk.

And no matter how many times you slept with a girl, you had to go through the same ritual every time. You would call up and ask if you could come over, and she would make you promise on the telephone that nothing like that would ever happen again. So you lied and said, "Oh, yes, nothing like that"—agree with them wholly that you could have a rousing good time within the bounds that they had quite justly set. Then you would inch your way forward. And you had to go through the talk ritual every time. You had to establish yourself as someone who was interested in her mind, so you listened to this mindless prattle until your head would burst. It was a torture beyond belief. The girls weren't very bright, so intelligent conversation was out of the question. That's why I talked all the time. I was terrified that they might say something. I remember those hours as the most painful of my life.

But I want it just exactly the way it was, because if it isn't a contest then you don't want it. Even in your marriage, if things are handed to you, you don't want them. I want to earn it.

It's very difficult to tell just when you lose your virginity, because in a teenager's first fumblings an orgasm can result and the girl may not even be in on the act. You know, you ejaculate just in the excitement of trying to find the proper aperture. Something is apt to happen.

But when I was about seventeen or eighteen—I can't remember exactly—I had a compliant and knowing girl, a middle-aged hag of twenty-one who was my father's secretary.

She was very pleasant and coquettish and I thought she was
a smashing beauty. Now she would be considered rather
broad in the beam, but then I thought she had the greatest
figure, and certainly she had the most enchanting idiot face.
It was quite a bother, though, because I had to hitchhike
eighteen miles to her house and then tramp out to the highway at two o'clock in the morning and hitchhike home.

I never went out with pushovers. I was dismayed by
them, dismayed by a girl who would lay five guys in a night.
I've always had a great horror of a spectacle like that. It's
like eating somebody's leftovers. I don't know. Maybe it was
the leg. But, my God, even the nice girls were cretins, and
the ones who weren't were cretins and nasty too. But there
came the time when I was determined to be part of the scene.
It wasn't especially because of horniness. It was just when I
felt adult enough, and when I got so I could, well, arrange
things. I could con my way with girls. It took a great deal of
conning to get laid.

The physical sensation the first time was not nearly as
important as the feeling of achievement. By God, you'd
achieved something. You'd really achieved something. And
it was great, because you knew what you were up against.
And girls at that time wore all sorts of armor, all sorts of buttons and girdles and things. I was absolutely horrified. Once
you got it all disengaged, you rolled the hose down, you
rolled that cast-iron girdle up around her waist, and there
was this unsightly bulge. I never saw the girl with her
clothes off, only flashes of her body in the dark. Thank
heaven the lights were out! It was incredibly ugly, the whole
thing, but that's the way it was. It was a great feeling of satisfaction. I really earned it. I guess I saw her for about a year
after that, and every time I had to go through the same ritual.
Good God, did I pay!

I was eighteen or nineteen before I actually was in bed with a woman, and that was vastly more satisfactory. She was a Smith or Wellesley girl, and her prattle was better than most, but it followed the same lines. I was to take nothing for granted because we were unchaperoned. I was to remember that liberties were not to be taken. I solidly agreed to all of this, and then just went right ahead. But it was a slow process, and I earned it.

Every now and then you were up against a stone wall with a girl. She just wasn't going to, and that was that. If the stone wall remained unmovable after a couple of nights you just quit and went on somewhere else. How could you stand that conversation for any length of time? Their conversation was hard to take even after you'd scored.

But you were always chivalrous. You couldn't use a frontal or boorish attack or the game would be lost. So you kept on being chivalrous. You kept being tender. You kept being a goddamned liar. You were even more chivalrous as the moment of truth approached, and afterwards you were very nice. A man should always leave a girl with the feeling that she has done a really splendid thing, that he is eternally in her debt, and that he is mad about her. Sometimes you even mean it.

You never talked about sex. It simply wasn't mentioned. The whole point was to have sex but never to admit to the other one that you'd had it. Even while you were buttoning up your fly, you just didn't admit it. Nice people simply never talked about it at all.

My parents never discussed it. My mother was quite soft and indulgent, and was very eager for us four children to grow up to amount to something. Clearly my father was never going to amount to anything. He was amusing, attractive and talented, but he simply couldn't make a buck. He was a salesman, but all he ever earned was enough to bail himself out of fleabag hotels. We lived by a series of miracles. My parents were very wise. They preferred to have me learn about sex from my friends in the gutter—which is still by far the best way.

We kids did an enormous amount of window-peeping. There were roofs of various houses that looked down on other houses, and you would catch a flash of bare buttocks and would be thrilled for an hour and a half—until the guy turned around.

When I was about eleven a kid called Cowboy Regerio said, "I'll give you a quarter to draw a picture of me screwing Miss Yale." It was a baffling commission. I could draw Miss Yale, who was a teacher, and I could draw Cowboy Regerio and although I had some idea that somebody inserted something somewhere, quite what you did I didn't know. So Cowboy Regerio told me what to do. He said, "You draw me on top, see, and you insert this in Miss Yale and have her legs stick up." It seemed a little awkward to me, but it came off very well, and then I did a landslide business. Poor Miss Yale got screwed by every mongoloid in school, until she discovered the drawings in my desk. That was my last adventure with pornographic drawing, but it did teach me that I could make money drawing, if I cleaned up the pictures a little bit.

I had an innocent upbringing, and yet I felt terribly depraved. We were all terrified and believed without any question that masturbating would soften our brains and dim our eyesight. We all knew that it was a dreadful, destructive thing to do, and anytime any of us did it we walked around hangdog and shamefaced, knowing we would never grow up to be quite the men we ought to be.

Nobody ever even heard of anything like cunnilingus in my teens. I was pretty grown-up and working in New York before I even heard about it. Now it's part of every child's kindergarten, but then the term wasn't known. I did hear rumors. I heard rumors that a really famous old-time singer did it. He was one of the most detestable men who ever lived, and possibly the worst singer, but the stories that he did something like that made him quite an exotic figure. But a contemptible one, too, because we couldn't imagine that anyone would do anything like that. It was so undignified. We heard about girls who went down on guys, and that was considered very exotic, but it was inconceivable for a guy to do that to a woman.

My first unobstructed view of a naked woman was at art school in Boston when I was about eighteen. This model came in, a rather good-looking girl, went behind a shade and we could see her taking things off. Then she came out, stark naked, and that was the most electric thrill of all time, for one minute. Then she became a problem in masses and light and dark.

I met my wife in art school. She was just one of the kids in class. She saved my life in an embarrassing situation in class, and I was so touched by this that I married her. I guess guys make up girls. You find a girl that has something for you, and you make her up. She's been completely satisfactory. Patient. Loyal. Devoted. And pretty. I'm hard about that. Catherine's my age, and I'm sixty-five, and she's a smashing-looking girl. She doesn't dare not to be.

I got quite sick recently in London. I have a wooden leg and one that works, and the one that works wasn't working. So I operated in a wheelchair. I was taken to a party, pushed in by an attendant, and as I came in there was this nine-foot-high girl, all navel, and she said to me, "I never fucked anybody in a wheelchair. Would you like to?" I disapprove of that kind of talk. I consider it very distasteful and crawly.

Sexually aggressive women embarrass me. Jesus Christ, I see them on the David Susskind show, lesbians. Well, let them be lesbians. Let them have girl lovers. But it's like talking about your bowel movements. Everybody knows you have them, but why describe them?

I'm always made quite uncomfortable by husbands and wives who discuss their sex. I don't want to hear that. I want them to pull the shades down. I like speculating, but I don't want to be told. Two people who love each other and are happy with each other, you make jokes about it, but it's all understood. It's all comfortable. It isn't any part of conversation at all. It's just part of being together. You understand what the atmosphere is at any time and this is an understanding that grows, and there's no need to discuss it. No need ever.

I have never talked to girls about sex. When I was growing up it was not considered polite conversation. It was disrespectful. You start out owing women certain credits. You owe them chivalry. You owe them politeness. You owe them rather more tender treatment than you would another human being. You mustn't be angry when they say something immeasurably stupid. You mustn't say, "You're being immeasurably stupid." A certain amount of chivalry is necessary. In speaking at colleges, I hold myself back in talking to flaming idiot girls who stand up and scream in an auditorium. When a boy does that you slice him to ribbons, but you don't do that with a girl. I find it unbearable to be confronted with a truly bright girl who wants you to know she's bright. I really prefer the professional girl who has a good mind but never quite lets you see it. The graciousness and the sweetness are there, with a computer running inside of her that you're never aware of. The atmosphere is that of a child; the mind is that of a serpent.

When I was young, the loss of my leg bothered me some at first with girls, but by and large, I eventually discovered that there was nothing I couldn't replace. After a while I found that I could do all right. You didn't have to be Frank Merriwell. If you were a raconteur, that worked just as well. And if you were thoughtful and a little tragic, that worked even better.

I had the accident the summer I was eight. My mother and the other children were staying in one room in a farm-house in the country, with kitchen privileges. I stayed in New Haven and went to summer school. One day on the way to get a haircut, I hitched a ride on this big ice wagon and when I got to my destination I backed off the end of the wagon right into the path of a trolley car and it zipped one leg right off. I was a great celebrity as a one-legged kid and got a lot of attention, and I liked that. It really didn't hit me until I was in my teens, when I discovered that it would be useful to have another leg to dance with.

I was seventeen or eighteen when somebody gave me marijuana and told me I would like it. A reefer they called it. I was so fucking mad at what it did to me! I walked and I walked and I walked and I couldn't quite make it across the room. I was terribly upset, and I never touched it again. I don't like anything in me that directs me. I don't at all like not being in control. I tried a drink when I was young, but I hated it. I didn't like having a foreign sensation introduced into my brain.

Until last year I never had a drink. Then a psychiatrist came to see me. I was very troubled, and he saw me a couple of times. He came twice, and I was appalled by him, really appalled. He is a big shot in psychiatry at Harvard, and we are great pals now although I told him, "Really, you are full of shit." He asked me the most stupid questions. I can't even remember them. The whole thing seemed to me to be a great waste of time for two grown men. I wondered what the hell he was doing there, and what the hell I was doing listening to him. I said, "There really isn't a goddamned thing in hell you can do for me." He said, "Yes, I can. I can do something for you. I'm gonna pour myself a drink of Scotch. And I'm gonna pour you a drink, and I want you to drink and sit here and talk to me for a while." So I did, and I said, "By golly, that's pretty good." He said, "Well, you just do that. Do it. If you get up feeling depressed or confused or anything, even before breakfast, pour yourself a drink." I said, "Well, now, suppose I like it," and he said, "You will like it. But I guarantee that you will never take more than two in a given day." And I never have. It does help—it's a good medicine. But he was awfully full of shit. He was saying the most idiotic things. I was jabbering away in the most startling way, so they thought I needed a psychiatrist. Nobody realized that as soon as my fever went down and the poisons were drained from me I'd be my old self again.

Bernard Cornfeld *entrepreneur*

Born August 17, 1927, Istanbul

Two bare-breasted girls were floating on rubber rafts in Bernie Cornfeld's large pool, while the international money manipulator himself, wearing a blue bikini and a madras sports shirt, reclined on a nearby chaise, his favorite of the moment, an overripe, topless girl named Sharmagne, leaning back against him with her head on his chest. A short, melon-bellied man with muscular legs and a monkish fringe of hair around his suntanned pate, Cornfeld spoke so softly one had to lean close to catch his words, and girls kept interrupting to ask him questions. Sixteen of them were living in his castle-like seraglio in Beverly Hills, some of them recent arrivals, some of them favorites who had been around for several months. They live in a dormitory-like alcove that Cornfeld built onto the house after he bought it from actor George Hamilton. Cornfeld presides over his domain from a large master bedroom done in red velvet and mirrors, with a camera and floodlights mounted on tripods at the foot of a huge four-poster bed. It took several hours spanning two visits to interview him (one session was at 2:30 A.M.) because of his casually helter-skelter lifestyle. Despite his reputation as an uninhibited voluptuary, Cornfeld talked in blandly antiseptic terms, scrupulously avoiding profane or pungent language, yielding up detail only when pressed again and again.

I HAVE FORTY-FOUR WOMEN IN MY WILL, women that I have felt close to over the years, women that I have had meaningful and longer-lasting relationships with. It's not a lot of money, nothing over six figures. Just enough to make a difference. And I've taken a few women out of my will, some I decided shouldn't have been there in the first place. My money will be divided three ways: a third to foundations and institutions, a third to family, and a third to individuals—most of whom happen to be women.

When I was about twenty-five years old I decided it would be interesting to make a list of all the women I had gone to bed with. It was over a hundred, and the list was pretty incomplete. I don't know how many it would be now. Hell, if I had to make a list even of the last four weeks it would be in the twenties. When I say twenty, I don't mean twenty different instances of screwing; I mean twenty different women. I've made love as many as seven or eight times a night in the last several years, but that's not a daily occurrence. Par for the course is two or three times a day. I can't see that my sexual appetite has waned any. God willing, I'll live out a lusty old age, much the same as I have been living. It encourages me to see that some of my older friends, like Cary Grant, who is seventy, are still very lusty.

There are sixteen women living with me now. Four or five others come to dinner every night, and some of them stay. I started living with a multiplicity of women about ten years ago. I was seeing a lot of women before that, but I wasn't living with them. I came to the conclusion that the so-called one-to-one relationship has two possible fates. Either it declines into monotony, or it becomes a sort of psychological dependency. I wanted to avoid both. I wanted relationships to stay fresh and good, and I found that the only way for that to happen was to be involved with many women simultaneously. Smoking grass adds a different kind of dimension to sex, but I have never found any aphrodisiac except variety. In other words, to fuck more, fuck more. If you're having sex with just one woman, the frequency of sex tends to diminish after a while, no matter how good it happens to be. With a multiplicity of women, the frequency with all of the women involved is greater than it would be if you were with just one woman. I mean each of the girls ends up being involved in more activity than would be the case if I were with just one of them.

There's a whole world of people who have the notion that there are all kinds of things, from whips and torture instruments to swinging from chandeliers, that make sex more interesting. And I keep running into people who tell me that they became very jaded at forty. I've never been bored with sex for one minute, and I think the reason is the ample multiplicity of sex that I have. I never needed any of these external devices to turn me on. Sex in its most basic, primitive form as it has been practiced for thousands of years is all that I require. I don't have to cohabit with a chimpanzee or have a girl go down on a German shepherd to turn me on. My taste is getting into bed with one or two girls and being involved in the basic, everyday process of copulation. Preferably with candlelight. Preferably with music, classical music like Vivaldi. When there are this many women around, sometimes it is necessary for my survival for them to make love to each other, and to the extent that the girls are into each other, not all the time but occasionally, it relieves some of my responsibility. Sometimes it turns me on to watch girls make love to each other. But generally I find the plain, garden variety of sex to be a perfect delight.

I don't think I ever slept with anyone much over forty. I've found some older women to be attractive, but it's awfully rare. I like younger girls, but just as a matter of practice I avoid having any of them around who are under the legal age of consent, especially in California. I'm much more interested in feet than I am breasts. I find attractive feet a very important sensual part of a woman. I find a small, well-formed foot very attractive. I like small breasts as much as I do big ones, which is interesting, because we live in a boob-oriented society.

I do have the feeling that a great deal of sex tends to take energy drives and divert them from other things that might be more productive. And just in terms of time, sex takes four or five hours a day. But it's worth it. How much creative energy does one man want to have? I don't have any idea how much the pursuit of romance costs me in a year. It's one of my more negligible expenditures, nothing like, for example, my legal fees.

I've never been into orgies. I've always found them unromantic. One of the girls described an orgy as where somebody is always shoving their or somebody else's fingers up your ass. That's why she stays clear of them, and I can understand that point of view. I've been in two, both in Paris. I was pressed hard to try it the second time. They assured me it was going to be glorious, but it wasn't glorious at all. Sex to me is not something you do in public with strangers. That takes all the charm and romance out of it, and to me sex really is charming and romantic.

The closest I ever came to a homosexual experience was

when I was about nine years old. I went to a little circus on Coney Island, not far from where we lived, with another kid. I was wearing short pants, and there was a man sitting next to me who kept offering me popcorn and trying to put his hand up my leg. My mother left my father when I was eight, and we lived in one room near Coney Island, four blocks from the beach, right next to the Brighton Beach El. My mother, who lives with me now, worked as a nurse, and I worked all the time, too—selling lollipops and ice cream on the beach, and delivering for a grocery store. I was even an age-guesser on Coney Island.

My father was over sixty and my mother was over forty when I was born. He was born in Rumania and was a schoolteacher. A good deal of the guilt feelings that many people of my generation have about sex is a product of the Protestant ethic, but being a Jew, I was not a part of that. I have rather strong feelings against that part of the Protestant ethic that tries to take the joy out of life. There are some elements of this in Judaism, but classic Judaism is actually permissive. There is nothing in the Ten Commandments that says you shall not fornicate. Quite the contrary—in Jewish theology, you are supposed to do extra screwing on the Sabbath. The Sabbath is for meditation, communication with God, and screwing. Judaism is a religion that is easier on the nervous system than most.

I don't recall ever having the slightest feeling of guilt about sex, although my father and mother never talked about it. There is a certain pleasure, of course, to be derived from sexual guilt, and fortunately some of the girls have it, so I can vicariously enjoy some of their guilt. I've been maintaining a survey of my own, incidentally, and I've discovered that the average age that girls start having sex in California is thirteen.

Nobody got laid when I was growing up. Nobody wanted the responsibility of intercourse. We did all kinds of petting. "Muzzling" was the term, and it referred to fondling the breasts. It was considered a big thing if you got your finger in. She might touch you inside your pants, but if you took your cock out the act was over and she would be completely defensive after that.

I knew a fair amount, because when I was younger, ten, eleven and twelve, the kids in the neighborhood were talking about sex all the time. We had a little club called the N.P.C., the Nude Picture Club. There wasn't much to choose from. Anything that even showed breasts was considered racy. What we found would be tame by today's standards. The notable exception was pornography that had to do with comic-strip characters like Li'l Abner, Dick Tracy, Terry and the Pirates, Smilin' Jack, Flash Gordon, Little Orphan Annie and Popeye. They were all alike. Somewhere about the second page Daddy Warbucks or Li'l Abner or whoever would get a tremendous hard-on. These little books were sold around school for a nickel or a dime, and interestingly enough, they did evoke erections. I haven't seen anything since that evoked an erection.

I was conscious of the fact there were girls when I was very, very young. I remember being intensely in love when I was seven with a little girl of five who lived three doors down from us. It was the kind of poignancy that is possible only when you are very young. But I've had a lot of idealistic loves in my life.

When I was young I masturbated very little, and one of the reasons was that the Boy Scout Handbook told me it was very bad for me. I was active in the Boy Scouts, and I took the Boy Scout Handbook very seriously. The Handbook took the position at that time that masturbation would weaken the mind, and that one way to avoid masturbation was to take cold hip baths—sit in a cold bathtub.

I was a virgin until I was eighteen. I figure I was about nine years behind, so I have been catching up ever since. I had one important steady girl friend between the ages of eleven and eighteen—all through high school. The kind of relationship we had consisted of going to the movies, hours and hours on the telephone and going for long walks. Occasionally we would walk from Brighton Beach, hand in hand, to her house in Crown Point. Every now and then we would stop and neck. I was a very romantic kid. I took her to my highschool prom at Abraham Lincoln High, and she invited me to hers at Tilden High. Her father died of TB while I was dating her. She was a very cute little girl, with large eyes, a remarkably tiny waist, and she already had boobs at twelve. She loved Vaughn Monroe. She was the first important girl in my life.

Right after high school I enlisted in the officer training school of the Maritime Service and she went off to be a counselor in a summer camp. I don't think I got off the base until I graduated as an ensign. She wrote me several times during the summer and then stopped all of a sudden. She met this guy there, and it wasn't until it had already happened that I found out from a friend that she married him. That was very painful for me, a gloomy period, because we had spent many happy times together. Sometimes when I hear an old Vaughn Monroe record like "All or Nothing At All," all of that pain comes back. That was a long, long time ago.

The war in Europe was over, but a lot of merchant ships were still being sunk in the Pacific. I was the purser of this Liberty Ship that hauled military supplies, and food. I was a lieutenant junior grade, and I looked quite dashing in my uniform. One day when we were in port in Bremerhaven, I met this girl on the street. She was pushing a bicycle along. I spoke a little German, from high school, so I just started talking to her. I remember her as very pretty with long hair. This was just after Germany was beaten. The town had been badly bombed. Everybody was hustling, mostly for food, and the principal commodities were cameras and sex. She was just a school girl of about eighteen, and I guess she was primarily interested in me for food. I asked her for a date that night, and we went to dinner and then to a concert in a park and then she came back to the ship with me. I was quite skinny and had a lot of hair, but I looked impressive in my uniform. We went to my quarters on the ship and lay down on the bunk, and I undressed her. She had on a lot of clothes. There was a small light on over my desk. She wasn't a virgin, and I think she would have been surprised to learn that I was one. We screwed five or six times that night, and she stayed on the ship all the five days we were in port. When she left the ship I gave her a whole suitcase full of salami, sausages and other stuff. As she was walking away from the ship, one of these German citizen policemen started toward her to take the suitcase away from her, so I ran after her and walked her home. We wrote several times, but I never saw her again. I started making trips all down through South America and screwing a lot of whores that cost five dollars.

I had this constant childhood King Arthur fantasy where I rescued fair maidens and was the lord of a castle. I guess you can say I am living my fantasy. I've always had houses that look like castles. One of the five I own now is a thousand-year-old castle in France at the headwaters of the Rhone River. It has towers, a moat and a drawbridge, and a lot of land around it with a lot of people who are responsible to the lord of the castle and pay taxes to him. I would ride my horse through the countryside and imagine it was five hundred years ago and this was my château where the people had certain responsibilities toward me, and I had the responsibility of taking care of them as the lord of the castle. I would like to have worn the costumes. The lord also had certain rights, among them the right to deflower all of the château's virgins.

The woman's role in the castle is to take the monotony and tedium out of an otherwise dreary day, and to give the scene a bit of sparkle and charm and softness. I think women enjoy that role. I understand terrible things are happening out there in the real world in the latter half of this century, where women are becoming business tycoons and nuclear physicists. This is an aberration, an ingredient that makes women less feminine, and to me that's dreadful.

The money is certainly a factor in why girls are attracted to me. But I haven't a clue as to why they are otherwise. I know one of the wealthiest young bachelors—worth about a billion dollars, has a yacht and several homes—and he couldn't get laid on a bet. I treat women well. I laugh with them. I play with them. I take care of them, worry about them, and enjoy them sexually.

I'm convinced that what Hemingway said was right, that the only difference between the rich and the poor is that the rich have money. I don't think there are any qualities that distinguish the rich from the poor, except for the money. And the only thing that distinguishes the rich from one another is the degree of their insecurity about their money. The nouveaux riches always have an apprehension that they will wake up some morning and it will all be gone. The old rich are more comfortable with their money. The old rich are very meticulous about going over items on a restaurant tab. The nouveaux riches would never do that. It would be too embarrassing. The wealthiest people in Grosse Pointe drive five-year-old Ford station wagons. The nouveaux riches always drive Rolls Royces and other status cars. The old rich take the process of having money for granted. The nouveaux riches live in fear that it will all disappear tomorrow, or next week, or next year. I'm nouveau riche.

Joseph Cotten *actor*

Born May 13, 1905, Petersburg, Va.

Home to Joseph Cotten may be a plush-and-gilt apartment in a white stucco high-rise overlooking the Sunset Strip, but he presides there as he did in many a film—as the gracious Southern gentleman, the man of impeccable manners and intimated bawdiness. Wearing a pastel cardigan, linen pants, high white socks and slender black loafers, he sat very erect, his long fingers shuffling and reshuffling a deck of cards, and talked for two hours in a patrician Virginia drawl about his upbringing, for which he evidenced a good deal of affection and little bitterness. He rarely had trouble remembering anything, and in fact his stories and anecdotes were told with the skillful ease of an accomplished storyteller, one who has as much fondness for the art form as for the subject matter. He worried only that the first-person form might make him "look like a bloody ass."

I GREW UP IN PETERSBURG, VIRGINIA, a town of about thirty thousand. It's a very historic place—where the war ended. My father was the Postmaster and wasn't particularly solvent.

It must have been quite a burden for him to feed, clothe and educate three boys. I was the oldest.

Until I was about eight we lived in my grandmother's house—my mother's mother—with my two uncles. My grandmother had moved in from her plantation with a whole family of slaves. Nobody had a family of slaves living with them anymore, so we must have seemed strange in the city. We had a stable in the back, and horses. Once a week the wagons would come in from her farm with fresh vegetables. We had a rare household—the family of slaves, my uncles, and there in the dining room sat the Queen, my grandmother, telling stories about the Civil War.

She was strict but I thought she was very sweet. She used to slip me money wrapped in toilet paper. She still had her formal manners. There was always a ham on the table at every meal. I don't know how, because we were as poor as church mice. But there it was. And the minute the knife had touched it, the ham would never reappear in the dining room after that meal.

Oh, there was another black member of the family, Tom. He'd sleep in the hayloft. He was a terribly unreliable fellow. There was another house connected to the main one by what was called an areaway, a long hallway. The butter was churned there, and the washing done by the light of kerosene lamps. The water for baths, which we took a couple of times a week, was heated, then poured into a big tub that sat in front of an open fire.

One of my uncles was the only Republican in town. When President Taft came through, my uncle was his host. He came right in the house. No bodyguards. No security. Can you imagine? They just said, "Here's President Taft."

We had a cook, a Mammy, just like in the Warner Brothers films. Her daughter Ann was my nurse until she went away to nursing school, and then her younger sister Thelma took care of me. I was brought up by Mammy, Ann and Thelma. I was happy.

The household was morally strict. Everyone was very religious—Episcopalian—except for one of my uncles. My father was named for the bishop of North Carolina, and I was named for my father. We went to Sunday school, choir practice and Boys' Brigade every week. We were in church a lot. But I think we were taught sound truths. I still believe in God. I still feel wrong about breaking one of His Commandments. They were drilled into me.

My parents were always devoted to each other. My father was a severe disciplinarian. He had a terrible temper, and he beat us fairly often. He hit me with a rifle once. Those are things you remember, things that stir up deep emotions like hate. We were out in the back yard doing target practice. He pointed to a bucket of clothespins on the ground and said, "Don't knock them over." The next minute I accidentally tripped and did just that. He hit me very hard on the back of the legs with his rifle. I guess I was twelve. Well, there comes a time when an old man gets older and a son gets stronger. I was on the football team in high school and worked hard in a factory during the summer to stay in shape. Finally one day I grabbed my father and just held him down. He demanded to be let up and finally I did. But he never touched me again.

When I was eight, Thelma, who was an older woman of about nineteen, took me out into a tent in the back yard and taught me the facts of life. Literally. If it was a shock, then it was a delightful shock. I like to think that I was her star pupil. I guess that's terribly Southern, isn't it? Particularly when Thelma might have been my cousin. She was quite light and looked exactly like one of my uncles. It was lovely.

After that, I would always say, "When are we going to the tent again, Thelma?"

My father never said anything to me about it, nor did I ask, but I sometimes wondered if that was part of the reason he moved us away. Not long after it happened, he got his own house and moved us away. In a way, the new house was stricter. In her house, my grandmother had ruled with an iron hand. But now my father had his own ship and was enjoying his own mace, which he had been denied since he was married. Sometime later Annie went off to nursing school, and Thelma just disappeared. She and Tom sort of freed themselves.

About 50 per cent of the people in Petersburg were black. And there were wrong and right neighborhoods. The "fast" girls were looked down on, mostly by the older people. The boys who went across the tracks to see the black girls, to the Jefferson Hotel, were a little bit older, sixteen, seventeen and eighteen. They were usually "college men." I still think paying for it is vulgar.

I remember the first time I ever kissed a girl, but I'm not going to tell who it was. I was fifteen or sixteen, and it was somebody I liked. I never went steady. My family discouraged me from going with just one girl. And I never went seriously enough with one girl to exclude myself from the other members of my set.

When I was fourteen, fifteen and sixteen we'd ask a girl to go dancing at the country club on Saturday nights. Some of us would take swigs of bootleg whiskey on the sly. That would have shocked my father. He was a teetotaler until he died. He was quite alarmed when I was reported to have been tipsy at one of these dances. The nosey old man who was my Sunday school teacher reported me. It was one of the few times I ever lied to my father. I denied it. And a man who was a friend of my father backed me up.

There was a lot of necking in the back seat of the car or in the front porch shadows, particularly during the summers we spent at Virginia Beach. It was very sophisticated to say, "I can't see you. I have a late date." That meant the girl had to sneak out to see you. There were also a lot of house parties. We'd play the Victrola and drink nonalcoholic punch.

A little went on between the boys and girls of my high school, although less than the boys said. Nobody ever denied that something happened last night. We boys were a bit caddish. I don't remember hearing a boy actually boast about something he'd done with a girl, but we did exaggerate and allow for some very unfair implications. There were girls whose reputations suffered, who got the reputation of putting out because the fellows they had been kind to mentioned it. Not to be harmful, but because of that fake masculine braggadocio. I remember doing it once, and it's the thing I'm most ashamed of that I ever did with a girl. I let on that something had happened on the night of the fifteenth with such and such, and the minute I said it, I wanted to bite my tongue off.

Did I sleep with a girl during that period, before I left home? Let's just say I had a few rather happy moments in town, particularly during the Virginia Beach summers in the shadows of the dunes. I assumed that other fellows were doing the same thing. I guess our families pretended no such thing existed, and I pretended also.

If we had had the benefit of psychiatry, then we would have seen how all that stuff about *nice girls don't* could really screw a person up, particularly if you think that nice girls don't and then you find out that your mother *does it*. It's all very confusing. But I never felt guilty about fooling around with girls. My conscience didn't pinch me that deeply, and I don't think I ever thought too much about *nice girls don't do it*. That philosophy floated around among us, but I never took it very seriously. My simple desires toward nice girls were too strong to admit reasons for denying temptation. But I never went to a whorehouse in my life. That to me was vulgar.

The worst thing I ever did was to accompany one of my friends to rob the attic of his uncle's farm. We stole a case of bourbon whiskey. I can't imagine what we did with it all. I was about sixteen, and at that time you could buy a pint of corn for a dollar. And at parties we boys would sneak out to have a sip. We never drank in the presence of ladies. We used obscene language, but only when we were off by ourselves. For boys, sowing their wild oats was seen as a necessary part of their evolution.

I remember that when my father died (I was already a movie star then, in my forties) my mother had a whole new life. She said to me, "See, I wrote a check, all by myself." She was so proud that she was able to write a check. My father had always done everything. She was that innocent. Most of the women were. But each generation has been a little less innocent.

In school, I was interested in carpentry and what they called public speaking. My teacher was a frustrated director, so we were always putting on plays. I never quite understood why my parents let me go north to acting school—to Washington. I always thought maybe they wanted to get me out of town, away from the "fast" set they thought I was running with. It's a bit of an incongruity. The old rector of our church had gone to Chicago (have you ever noticed that when they get a "calling" it's always to a bigger and better church?) and when he heard I had gone off to acting school, he came back to Petersburg and tried to persuade my parents to bring me back—that they were sending me to Hell. Looking back, I can't see them agreeing to let me stay, in the face of this reverend. They must have seen that I had some promise, some higher hopes.

The minute I left Petersburg I stopped going to church. On Sunday in Petersburg you didn't lift a finger unless there was an extreme emergency. You couldn't pick up a screwdriver if the front gate fell off. The drugstore was open, but you couldn't buy a Coca-Cola or a cigar. And everything else was closed.

After acting school in Washington I went to New York— where I was met with something less than a ticker-tape parade. I don't know any rich people who go into acting. Dina Merrill. Sonny Tufts. But they are the exception. I went to New York, and then I went broke. I sold paint in a warehouse. Then I went to Florida and sold advertising for the Miami *Herald* for five years. I'd go to New York every summer because that's where they were casting everything. Belasco gave me my first job, and I quit the *Herald* the next day. I came out to Hollywood about the time Orson Welles was making *Citizen Kane*. I liked the summer climate. I never fell in love with my leading ladies. I did more pictures with Jennifer Jones than with anybody else, and we ended up very, very close friends.

Patricia [actress Patricia Medina] and I were married twelve and a half years ago. It was a lovely, solemn, romantic occasion. Before that I had been married for thirty years. My wife died.

I'm proud to have manners, social grace. There's too little of that left really. The South is becoming less Southern every day. When I was young I always thought I was in love with every girl I was with. I was always terribly romantic, got romantically involved with damned near every date. I was always brought up to be a gentleman, to stand up when a lady came into a room, or take my hat off. But I never could figure out what was the difference between a gentleman's manners in bed and anyone else's. It's like this silver cup that I was given in 1972 by the governor of Virginia. On it is inscribed: "Joseph Cotten, a Distinguished Virginian." That's a redundancy, don't you see. A Virginian is distinguished by definition, and I never felt undistinguished.

Nora Ephron *journalist*

Born May 19, 1941, New York, N.Y.

She was gamely fighting the frustrations of trying to find people who knew something, and would talk, for a magazine article on Rose Mary Woods, who was Nixon's secretary, not long after the eighteen-minute Tape Gap was discovered. Lunching in the huge, noisy dining room of the Hay-Adams Hotel in Washington, around which were scattered a half dozen other well-known reporters, she self-consciously picked at a salad and fingered a glass of white wine, somewhat discomfited at being on the other end of an interview. She was simply clothed in a beige knit dress—a delicate, thin figure with a large, serious face. She talked with great description and insight, but uncertainly and with nervous care, as if she were trying to envision how the words she spoke would look in print.

THERE WAS A LOT of talk back and forth about whether we should do it, and I remember we were riding somewhere in his car and I told him we should. But he said he wasn't sure. The first person you went to bed with—which was when I was nineteen and a junior at Wellesley—was usually someone you were engaged to and that you practically had to talk into going to bed with you, because he really didn't know if he wanted to do that with someone he loved so deeply. But even before that, something appeared to me to be true—that men were much more puritanical than women; they wouldn't take the next step; you always had to talk them into it. I think the men were stuck with the nice-girls-don't-do-that thing much worse than we were, although we were stuck with it, too. Also, of course, I don't think they had any idea of how sexual women are. This boy was much more scared than I was. He wasn't a virgin, but he didn't have much experience, and I don't think he knew any more than I did.

We finally did it in his dormitory room at Harvard, on his bed. It was over very quickly, and I don't remember much physical sensation one way or the other. It didn't hurt and it wasn't terribly pleasant. Just a kind of nothing feeling. I remember thinking, "My God, is this it? Is this what I've been going through all this torment about?" It was very disappointing. And then, to make matters even more ridiculous, he accused me of not being a virgin at all. I didn't have a hymen—I don't know anyone who had a remotely athletic adolescence who did—and he assumed that because I didn't, I must be an old pro. It hardly seemed fair to have finally done it and then not even get the credit for its being my first time.

I think I believed really for quite some time afterwards that you didn't sleep with people unless you were in love with them. So I went through a period of trying to fall in love with people just to go to bed with them, and then a period of thinking I would eventually fall in love with whoever I was going to bed with. It was a terrible crisis when I finally came up against the possibility that sex might be something that was just fun. Until I did, I had a lot of guilt about it. The syndrome of the false pregnancy, which is somewhat less universal than it used to be because of the pill, was an outgrowth of this—you felt guilty about the sex, and you had to punish yourself with three days of suffering for having gone to bed with somebody. I had a friend in college who had been going with someone for years and had been screwing him, and in fact carried her diaphragm in her book bag, which I always thought was wildly devil-may-care. She got colitis at Wellesley, and I was always sure it was from the tension of four years of having a pregnancy scare every month.

It was a long time after my first experience that I started having good sex. In fact, it was about five years. I sometimes wonder why. It would have helped if I had been more at ease and more confident. And also, I knew very little. I don't know what my parents would have had to tell me to make it better. I think about that myself. I don't have children, but I don't know what I would tell them about sex if I did. I really don't. I'm sort of fascinated now by the number of people who feel that you tell your children everything. I have a friend who just recently tried to explain to her four- and five-year-old children that she was having an abortion, and you just know that there's no way a child is ever going to understand that. And her daughter went to school and told everyone her mother was having a baby. That's how successful the conversation was. So I suppose in a way it's better not to spell it all out. At the point at which I lost my virginity, what I would have required was someone sitting down and virtually explaining sex to me, and I don't know whether I believe parents ought to do that.

What my parents seem to have done, I find as I've gotten older, is simply straight out of Spock and Gesell. I mean, including things like when the child is three or four having

him or her take a bath with each parent, and, oh, yeah, I remember doing that. Whenever I would ask where babies
came from, my parents gave what I suspect was a standard
fifties answer, which was that Daddy gives Mommy a seed.
And naturally at some point I said, "How?" at the dinner
table, where most of all this went on, and my mother said,
"I'll talk to you about it later." I must have been nine or ten,
and we went to her bedroom and she told me how, and I was
appalled. She explained intercourse to me—she said, "Daddy
puts his penis into Mommy's vagina." Right, that was the way
it was explained. Of course, it had never crossed my mind
that any of those parts were used for anything but going to
the bathroom. It was quite a shock to me. Menstruation,
that wonderful word, was all part of the same discussion. But
of course she left something out. A penis going into a vagina
is not an explanation about sex at all. And neither were any
of the books she gave me. One I remember, which was called
Being Born, started with the fertilization of the egg. So gradually when I began to find out about sex and got into things
like petting, I just couldn't believe it. I mean, it had never
crossed my mind that sex had anything to do with desire or
bodies or that you did it except when you wanted to have a
kid or something.

I don't know when I first was aware of boys as sexual beings. The first person I went steady with was in the third
grade. It lasted six days—then he came up to me and said he
had to have his I.D. bracelet back because he was giving it
to someone else. We didn't have any sex, though. I don't
think we spoke the whole six days of the relationship as a
matter of fact. I remember necking in the sixth grade, but it
seems to me I didn't have anything beyond that kind of car
thing until I was a senior at Beverly Hills High School—
which was a good deal more sheltered than it is now. I mean,

I talked to a lot of my friends about petting, that was all. The question of whether you would go to bed with someone wasn't a question, it was out of the question. There were a handful of girls I now know who were doing it, but they would never have admitted it.

My family had moved out to California when I was quite young, and I grew up there feeling very out of place. I didn't feel at all pretty, and I wasn't, by the way. I always felt that when I left New York and came to Los Angeles at four and a half I went immediately into an awkward stage, which lasted until I got back east to college. I mean it. My arrival there coincided with drastic physical changes where I turned from one of the most adorable children to one of the most gangly, awkward, gap-toothed, scraggly-haired kids. I sort of knew if I could just get out of California everything would work out, and it did. I mean, my skin cleared up when I went to Wellesley. And the funny thing is, when I go back to California my skin still breaks out.

I don't think the competition in high school was sexual or to have boyfriends; it was to have one boyfriend who would take you to the dances. In my senior year I started going with this person who was part of the crowd I wanted to go with someone in, and we went to the dances and our names appeared hyphenated in the school newspaper gossip column. That was my first experience of being a couple, my first experience of the first person plural. The sex was inside the clothes above the waist. Once he touched me outside the clothes below the waist and apologized profusely. "How could I have done this; how could I have done this to you of all people," blah, blah, blah. It was funny. But I would never have told him it was okay, because essentially it wasn't. I mean, I didn't want to be with him for my first person. He was just too stupid, and there was no way I could have convinced myself I was going to marry him, which was what I thought was necessary. Nice girls didn't do it. The girls who did it, that the boys talked about, were kind of dumb, bovine girls. I also think that the fact that the boys talked so much was a little inhibiting. But actually I look back on all those early sexual experiences with a great deal of nostalgia. There's something very silly, and heady, about that period of adolescent agony, of coming home with that stomachache I always used to get after three hours of God-knows-what at this person's parents' cabana at the beach.

I think people are a lot better about sex, a lot more open now than they used to be. The women's movement has helped. It's possible now to talk to women, to find out that your experiences, rather than being unique, are cliches. I don't know many women who didn't take a bit of time getting used to sex, but everyone was always pretending to be having great sex. You kind of had the feeling that you were the only one who wasn't. People have a great deal of difficulty talking about their shortcomings, particularly when they don't know anyone else has them. Men are much worse than women about admitting to any problems at all. Women are able to talk much more easily. But even so, sex was an area we knew so little about. We forget, twelve years ago we all had a book in college called *The Power of Sexual Surrender* by some woman Freudian analyst who defined frigidity, not as not being able to have an orgasm, but as not being able to have a vaginal orgasm. No one knew anything about orgasms. I don't know where the world would be without Masters and Johnson anyway. And the funny thing is that I think all of us secretly hope nothing has changed. We would hate for younger people not to go through all the agony and pain and stupidity that we did. It's unfair how mean we are about sparing people that. Please, God, don't let anyone have a good sexual experience the first time out.

I muddled through. I could have been spared a lot of pain somehow or other, I guess, if I had known more or if I'd gone to bed with someone who knew what he was doing. That would have helped. At the same time, I think the awful thing about being a writer is that you have a kind of vested interest in your own pain. You think that you would not have become the person you became without overcoming a certain amount of unhappiness. So you think, "Okay, I had to go through that. Now let's get on with it."

Charles Garry *attorney*

Born March 17, 1909, Bridgewater, Mass.

His office at the foot of Market Street in San Francisco was lined with autographed photographs of clients, among them Huey Newton, Bobby Seale and Angela Davis. Such clients are his "family," and he made it plain that work is his raison d'être. Halfway through the interview he got an urgent call from one of his clients, a convicted arsonist who was about to be jailed, and Garry, wearing a shiny green suit and brown boots, his white hair brushed straight across his head in the manner of Douglas MacArthur, dashed out to try to arrange a bail extension. En route to the Oakland County Courthouse, he had no trouble going on good-naturedly with the interview, and at the same time joking with his client.

I GREW UP IN SELMA, CALIFORNIA, a little town of about three thousand people in the San Joaquin Valley. I had two brothers and one sister, all younger. My father was a farmer, then he worked in a shoe factory. We were very poor. My mother worked in the local canneries. During the summers I worked in the canneries, too, from the time I was about ten. I'd say it was a happy childhood.

My father had come from Turkey in 1898, my mother in 1895. They didn't even become American citizens until twenty years ago, so they couldn't vote. But my father was always a rebel. When he was back east he lived with his brother in Cambridge, Massachusetts, and worked in his brother's wood and coke plant. But when my uncle found out that his own brother was heading the strike, he threw him out of the house.

My father was religious in a philosophic sense. He was not church-religious. He never went to church. My mother was religious in a conventional sense. She taught Sunday school. I'm an agnostic. If I'd been able to accept a belief in a divine deity as God, I would have been a minister. But I couldn't. I still think the Bible is tremendous. I often quote it in my jury trials.

Selma was actively religious—Protestant. Even dancing was held in disfavor. And there wasn't liquor because it was during Prohibition. The town had one theater and one pool hall. Some chickenshit betting went on at the canneries, and I could always make a couple of bucks playing snooker at the pool hall.

I was always a loner. Before and after school I worked in a grocery shop—waiting on the trade—for five dollars a week. Then I worked in a delicatessen–butcher shop where I made all the cole slaw and potato salad for seven dollars a week. I was the only kid in my high school who was working. I was lucky. There weren't any jobs to be had. None of the other kids lived on farms. And we were the only Armenians in the community. I didn't start school until I was seven because I couldn't speak English. We always spoke Armenian at home. I was graduated salutatorian in grammar school. I was an

oddball. Every night from the time I started school until I
finished eighth grade I had a fistfight. I kicked the shit out of
more people. All I needed was for someone to call me a goddamned Armenian, and we'd go. He'd say, "See this chip. I
dare you to knock it off." Instead I'd knock him down.

The town was made up of poor white trash turned elitists.
The Ku Klux Klan was very active around there. Later they
asked me to join, and I told them to shove it up their ass. But
my father was very well liked in the town. He had a sense of
humor. He always wore overalls, and somehow one of the
straps would always be off his shoulder hanging down. People would come along and yank that goddamned strap. One
time somebody even cut it off.

I remember the Christmas following my fourth birthday.
The entire family went to bed hungry. When my father had
come to Selma he had bought a ten-acre ranch. He didn't
know his ass from a hole in the ground about farming. All
he saw was ten acres of the most beautiful trees. He didn't
know it would be two years before any of them would bear
fruit. For two years he worked for fifty cents a day in a factory. He'd pedal his bike eight miles each way, and if a rain-
storm came up he'd sleep under a bridge for the night. It was
rank, unadulterated poverty. Three years later he traded the
ten-acre farm for a forty-acre one where we raised grapes,
which we sold to the Sun Maid plant and peaches, which we
sold to Libby. I never liked farm life.

I'd always been a reader. By the time I was nine I'd read
Les Misérables three times. My father put that on an equal
dignity with the Bible. He had a good library, but it was all
in Armenian. I read every book in the local library. I used to
bring books with me when I was plowing. We wore those bib

overalls in those days, and I'd put a belt around them and stick a book under the bib. When I'd stop to let the horses rest, I'd pull it out and read. At night I'd go to bed around seven-thirty or eight. We had those kerosene lamps, and I'd often read for three or four hours until it went out.

Dirty books never appealed to me. When we were about twelve or thirteen we'd sit in the back of the church on Sunday reading the book of Ruth. There was a lot of begetting going on in there. We thought that was plenty dirty. That's the closest I ever came. We never discussed sex at home. I didn't even know what it was. I thought to knee someone was fucking. I guess I got that straightened out by the time I was twelve.

When I was fifteen, my sister, who was three years younger, died of cancer. My parents went to pieces. My dad went bankrupt. We moved back to Amesbury, Massachusetts. For two years I supported the family, first by working in an auto plant, until I got lead poisoning, then as an apprentice tailor, pressing and cleaning clothes. I dated a lot when we were back east. I had never even kissed a girl before we left Selma. I did it the first time in Massachusetts when I was fifteen or sixteen. It was with some old woman of twenty-nine. I double-dated with some guy from the tailor shop. He was up front. We screwed in the back in the rumble seat. It was probably a Hudson—the plant was in town, and that's what everybody drove. I pretended I had all the experience in the world. She probably didn't get any satisfaction. I never saw her again. I didn't have any guilt. Afterwards I just worried that I might have gotten her pregnant or gotten the clap or something.

I dated mostly on pickups. In Amesbury there was a main street about one and a half blocks long, and there'd always be girls out looking for someone. You didn't have sex with all of them, only if there was a meeting of the minds.

When I was coming back from Boston to California—I was around seventeen—I ran out of money and decided to stop in Chicago and work for ten days. There was this gal on the train, ten years older, and she liked me, so we got off the train and got a room together. I got a job pressing clothes, and when I had enough money and told her goodbye, she said, "If I can't have you nobody can," and whipped out an automatic and fired the fucking thing at me. Luckily she missed. The bullet landed in the wall behind me. I took it out with my knife and carried it around for many months after that as a reminder. You might say I was gun-shy for some time after that.

When we moved back to Selma and I was finishing high school, I was already older than the other kids—eighteen or nineteen—so I didn't date local girls. Instead I came up to San Francisco to meet girls. When we were young in the city we'd do the same things people do now. You'd date out. I went to plays a lot then. I couldn't stand silent pictures. You'd have dinner somewhere, neck awhile, sometimes fuck. Unless I was interested in a girl I didn't bother. I fell for one gal in San Francisco before I was married, but it was adolescent, puppy love. If you went out with one girl for a time, she'd get serious, and I wasn't looking to get married at that point—far from it. But then I met my wife and had no choice. I fell in love with her. Whatever love is, I had it. She was visiting out here from Hood River, Oregon. We'll have been married forty-one years on November tenth. That's a long time in anybody's market.

In 1929 I had taken the English A exam and had saved thirty-five hundred dollars to go to Stanford. I'd always been an honor student, did my second and third years of high school in one year, and had scholarship offers from a number of schools. But I wanted Stanford. Instead, I invested the money in the stock market and lost it all. So I went to work in a tailor shop in the city. Given the year, I was lucky to have a job at all.

By 1934 I was married, working—at my own place, Garry's Cleaners and Tailors, 312 Eighth Avenue; it's still there—and going to San Francisco Law School at night. I always wanted to be a doctor or a lawyer, but a lawyer more. I wanted to do something about capital punishment—be in the forefront of the fight against it—which I have. I helped organize the Cleaners and Dyers strike of 1934 and was on the general labor council. After I got my law degree, I was in the army— PVT That was my choice. I just didn't like the idea of being an officer.

The first time I went to court I said, "Okay, I'm here for the arrangement." "The arraignment, you mean," said the judge. "It's all the same to me," I said. My favorite trial was probably Huey Newton's first. It had all the human aspects, the whodunit, the political, the scientific. Two years ago I was defending Bobby Seale in New Haven for his life. Two years later he's running for mayor of Oakland.

I've always related thoroughly to every continuing struggle of youth there is. The dating and free love today are probably healthier, although I don't live in a small town any more, so I don't know what it's like. The larger cities back then I don't remember as being very restrictive. After all, human beings are always the same, have the same impulses. There are probably just as many virgins today as there ever were—women in their thirties who have never been fucked, men in their thirties who have never fucked, even with all the so-called enlightenment.

I have a lot of clients, women, who come in and say, "my husband's chipping around." I say, "You mean fucking. So what's the problem? Why don't you try it? You go to lunch with a man, don't you? You dance with a man and it gives you a thrill. Why not take it one step further and fuck once in a while?"

Marriage is fine, if we could just eliminate the ownership in it, the he's-mine, she's-mine shit. It's like we're dealing with chattel—that's shit for the birds. I don't regret having been married forty-one years. I have no regrets. I don't look back. I don't think I missed a goddamned thing. My wife never worked outside the home, and we never had children. I never wanted any. They're a pain in the ass—all diapers and bellyaches. Isn't that what W. C. Fields said? Any man who hates dogs and children can't be all bad. I've been my own boss for a long time, even after I was married.

I've been accused of being a male chauvinist pig. I'm sure I have a lot of male chauvinism in me. I am a lot more advanced than most of my sex, but it's almost impossible to eradicate male supremacy. The question of women and the question of race are synonymous. No matter how liberated we are, we're still white racists. No matter how liberated we are as males, we're still male supremacists. It will work itself out only if this generation of women asserts itself on merit, not through rhetoric. That turns me off.

Bob Guccione *magazine publisher*

Born December 17, 1930, Bergenfield, N.J.

The publisher of Penthouse, Viva *and* Forum *magazines was hosting a catered cocktail party for seventy advertising clients the next evening, so crates of hired glasses, crockery, silver, whiskey and chasers were stacked around the first floor of Bob Guccione's floridly furnished brownstone in Manhattan's East Sixties. Dressed in soft white boots, blue slacks and a cherry sports shirt with a wide zipper up the front, he emerged into the long dining hall from the front of the house, where he had been shooting color photographs of a nude for* Penthouse. *His black hair was combed forward in a Napoleonic curl, which gave his strong-featured face a mildly sinister look. His blonde secretary fetched him a diet cola from the kitchen, and Guccione slumped lazily in a chair at the end of a twelve-foot marble dining table, over which presided a green chandelier shaped like a cabbage head. He spoke in a muffled, nasal voice and tried to keep the thread of conversation going between business calls and chats with his secretary. In an almost casually flaunting manner, he talked unashamedly about his experiences for forty-five minutes, but at 6:30 his secretary came over and told him he had four more people waiting, and they all had appointments.*

WHEN I WAS FOUR YEARS OLD my parents put a playground—swings, a seesaw and a slide—in our back yard. All the kids in the neighborhood were excited by the fact that I had this playground. I used to let all the little girls come and use the swings and other stuff, provided they came into the garage with me and showed me their little things. I can still see visions of those little girls, four and five years old, standing in the middle of this concrete-floored garage with their pink bloomers down around their ankles, and holding their dresses up.

So I started off as a sort of entrepreneur voyeur. That's how I merchandised my swings. And it worked beautifully. I learned a very primal lesson in life: if you've got something to offer, something exclusive, you can exact some sort of payment for it.

I grew up in a small town of six or seven thousand in New Jersey, called Bergenfield. Guccione is Sicilian. My father was an accountant for the family business. My mother's brothers had a very successful neon business in Union City, New Jersey—they were the biggest in the world at one point —before they went down, down, down and then lost everything.

Sicilian morality is very structured, very inflexible, and the woman plays a very important role in the family. In my family, which was very large, the real head was my grandmother, the only one of the four grandparents who was still living. She became the focal point, the head, and we respected her as such. There is terrific respect among Italians and Sicilians for women in the family. One looks after one's sister, one's mother, one's female relatives in a special kind of way. I was conditioned very early to respect this family concept, to re-

spect the fact that all women belong to somebody. There was
no such thing as an isolated woman who had no background
and no roots. Once in grammar school I accused a girl sitting
next to me of being fat and ugly and stupid. She went screaming to the teacher, and the teacher sent me home, and my
mother was very upset by this, and more upset that I had
been unkind to the girl than that I was sent home from
school. She said to me—and I'll never forget her words—she
said, "You have to remember that every girl is some guy's
sister." Since then I've gone through life having that sort of
attitude toward women. I have great respect for them. I love
women. I love the idea of women. I love women quite apart
from sensuality, just as people. I've a great fondness for older
women. I like looking after old women, like the proverbial
Boy Scout who helps the old woman across the street—
whether she wants to go in the first place or not.

Sexually, I developed the attitude very early in life where
it became important to me to see that the girl was properly
satisfied and properly looked after. I would never get into a
sexual relationship with a woman without having clear-cut
intentions of seeing that she's satisfied to the greatest possible extent of my ability, and I can't trace that feeling to anywhere, except that I always had this attitude—respect toward
women.

My first real bounce was when I was fifteen, with a girl
named Violet. She was dark-haired, very delicate and feminine looking, very sexy, very white skin. I met her through a
friend. One Saturday afternoon me and some of my friends
and she and some of her friends went to the public swimming pool in a nearby town called Paramus. She was sixteen
and was driving a car, so she came by and picked me up. We
sort of lay around in the sand—this pool was a little artificial
lake—all day, touching, and I knew we would try something

before we went home. My luck was on. The rest of them went home about four o'clock, but we stayed deliberately so that we could be alone. I had been wrestling with an erection off and on all day. Then we got over into the back seat of the car, fumbling and feeling and scrambling for each other, and I couldn't get it up. I knew nothing about impotence, and not knowing what the hell had happened, I made all sorts of stupid apologies. I didn't understand. I mean, I was masturbating about three times a day, literally—I've always had a vigorous sex drive. Screwing once or twice a day now is not unusual for me. Anyway, this girl had patience, or a terrible need, and finally at the end of a couple of hours I got there, lost my virginity in a blaze of glory, like a meteorite flashing across the sky—hot, ferocious and fast.

She was good, not a virgin, and we had an affair that lasted six or seven months after that, an affair full of brilliant experimentation. Sixty-nine. Everything.

I had my first whorehouse experience when I was sixteen. I went to Blair Academy prep school in Jersey, and for Easter vacation I went down to Palm Beach, Florida, where my grandmother had a winter home. I asked this taxi driver where the action was, and he took me to this whorehouse on Clematus Street. I went into a room with this girl, in her early twenties, and she was very, very much a woman. I had never faced anything so blatantly sexual in my life. This was the face of infinite sex, unlimited promise, total sexuality wrapped up in this one woman. She was very impressed by my size and shape. I was a very well-built kid. She filled a little basin with warm, soapy water and she started to wash me off. While she was doing it she brought me off. I came in the soapy water, and she said, "Oh, that's good. That's nice." And she started getting dressed.

"Wait a minute," I said, "What's nice about that?"

"Well, you're finished," she said. "That's all. You came. That's what you paid for."

"I'm not paying twenty dollars to come in a bowl of soapy water," I said. A big argument ensued, and the madam came up. I explained what had happened, but they threw me out. I never went back there.

I had a not dissimilar experience when I was living in Rome after the war, in about 1949. I went with an Italian friend of mine to an Italian whorehouse and had another similarly tragic experience with a girl and refused to pay. A big fight ensued, and my friend went out and got a cop, and he closed up the whole place. This was an Italian cop, called upon to operate in his fullest official capacity, and he called everybody together, interrogated everybody, miles beyond his authority, wanting to know all the details, and all this time the girl was screaming that I owed her two thousand lira, which in those days was maybe two dollars. The reason I refused to pay her was that this girl only liked being screwed in the ass, and I didn't want to screw her in the ass, so I thought I had been used. I said, "I'm not gonna pay for it, because that's not what I wanted." The cop absolutely gobbled all of this up, because it gave him a chance to deal with abstractions that didn't even exist. Finally he padlocked the place and took us all—me, the whores, the madam, my friend—down to see the captain, who was very pro-American and fined the madam and the girl and let me off.

The summer after high school I had a route where I drove a truck picking up and delivering clothes for a dry cleaners. There were all kinds of great-looking women on my route, terribly frustrated women, great-looking housewives who would come to the door in a kimono. If you happened to be a good-looking kid and were available in the mornings and afternoons it was amazing how many women were ready and played the part. This one woman, very beautiful, a knock-out, wanted me to come and read her poetry with her one night, so after dinner I went back. Her husband was out of town. From ten o'clock that night until ten the next morning I screwed her eighteen times. I couldn't do that again, I don't mind telling you.

When I was a kid, finding a girl who screwed was like finding gold. It was a great piece of news if you heard about a girl who screwed, because it was extraordinarily unusual for a girl to screw without a lot of problems—having to take her out, court her, spend money on her. When you did hear about one, she was inevitably the object of many a gang bang. I remember going to see a girl in Teaneck, New Jersey, and there were four or five carloads of guys, and we picked this dame up, drove her to the schoolyard, and one by one, twenty guys screwed her on the grass.

I'm not terribly promiscuous now, but I went through a period of terrible promiscuity when I was living in Italy. I was like a satyr. I was getting laid four and five times a day. I was living with a Pan-American ground hostess and screwing her two and three times a day, and as soon as she left for work in the morning I was out on the move looking for something else. I had a terrible inferiority complex and screwing was a way of compensating. I didn't think I was worthy of the girls I was going out with. Whores turned me on, and they still do to some extent, and I must have screwed more than a hundred of them, but I never paid. I got it for what they called *simpatía*, friendship. I was a great-looking kid, very desirable-looking, and I never ever paid.

After that bout in Rome I went through a period when I was impotent for three or four years. I picked up a couple of minor venereal diseases, and they got to me psychologically. I didn't like the idea of my body not being clean, carrying germs around, not knowing where the hell I got them from. It frightened me deeply, and I wasn't able to perform. I'd get fantastic opportunities, great women, and then not be able to perform at all. It was a terrible, disheartening, shattering experience. Then suddenly I met an American girl on a boat from Genoa to Tangier, and it all came back to me.

I live with a woman I've been with for ten years, and we're perfect together. I have no real need for anything else now, unless it's something very exceptional. I'm a solo performer. I'm not a swinger. I don't go in for group sex. Me and any multiple of women, I'm all right then. But I don't like the invasion of another male. I don't take kindly to the competitive situation. Two women and me, that's fine. But two guys and two girls, that becomes a competitive situation, and I don't like that. I'm just not capable of sharing my woman with anyone. I'm really not. I wouldn't have it, and I make that feeling known. I said, "Look, if I ever have to fool around, I probably will. I don't know that I'm capable of being totally one girl's man. But I'll promise you one thing: if I do it, I'll tell you about it. But if you ever get the idea that you too are interested, if you feel you must, then you must. But don't come back. It wouldn't be the same for us any more. I couldn't see you in the same way. I realize I'm asking for an unbalanced situation, but that's it, and if you accept it, great."

I still believe that despite the liberated-woman syndrome men are naturally more aggressive in a sexual way than women. And I've drawn many conclusions from my life, not the least of which is that women are much more sexually liberated than men. There is a very small group of very vocal, very militant women's libbers who are not normal women who want to become as good as men, but are dykes and man-haters who want to replace men. This bullshit stuff about women being sexually liberated is just that—bullshit. Most women already have been sexually liberated. Women have a much greater capacity for sexual experimentation than men. I've found that almost all women have an inclination to want to go down on a guy. I've seen women in many orgies—me not taking part, because of my own inabilities—and they take to group sex with much more flair than men. A man will always shy away from a sexually aggressive woman. Men are great when a woman is shy and needs protecting and wants to be seduced. But when a woman starts to demonstrate her own strength, her own power, her own ability, we suffer and become drained of our power. The stronger she becomes, the weaker we become, whereas the weaker she is, the stronger we become.

Clifford Irving *writer, convicted con man*

Born November 5, 1930, New York, N.Y.

He had been paroled just the day before, after being in prison for masterminding the Howard Hughes book hoax, and was staying temporarily with a woman friend and her grade-school daughter at the decaying Chelsea, a residential hotel filled with writers, artists, poets, dancers, junkies and welfare mothers, in Westside Manhattan. Wearing a white dress shirt, dark slacks and black shoes, Irving walked down to a corner deli for pizza and wine when an old writer friend appeared, and in between reminiscing with him and catching up on gossip, he talked easily, with a writer's eye for construction and detail and with no embarrassment whatever, about his childhood, his writing career, the Hughes fiasco and his prison term. He had a quiet, seductive voice and an engaging manner, and though broke, on the brink of divorce, and without any prospect of immediate income, he was imperturbably charming and optimistic.

MY PARENTS were lower-middle-class, second-generation Jewish immigrants brought up in New York City. My father was one of four children and his father, my paternal grandfather, was the first Jewish captain of police in the city. Then he went into the insurance business. And my father, who was really destined to be an insurance agent, to follow in his father's footsteps, unfortunately for him, he had a talent. He was an artist. He began doing several kinds of cartoons for the New York *World* at around the age of nineteen, secretly, ashamed to tell his parents. It just wasn't what a Jewish boy in New York City did—they didn't go to work for a newspaper doing sports cartoons.

Eventually my father became a fairly successful cartoonist. He also became very frustrated, because my father dreamed of all this glory and success in the world. It came to him briefly, in his thirties, I would say, and then forever after eluded him. But he'd had a taste of it; he knew it was there. And it affected my life enormously because he transferred his own ambitions and needs onto me. I was an only child and I became the repository for all his broken dreams. Oh, I bridled at it; I couldn't bear it. I didn't want to be his heir in that sense. I remember when I was about twenty-seven, he said to me, very bitter, he said, "By this time, I thought you would be out in Hollywood sitting by the side of a kidney-shaped swimming pool with producers, with a telephone on a long cord that was ringing all the time." Twenty-seven—and I was a bum in his eyes. I was upset. No, angry's the wrong word. I was hurt. I really didn't feel I deserved his disappointment. I felt in a sense that I had lived a very independent life and a good life and that I deserved the approbation of my parents.

My mother was very quiet, dignified—to some people a very cool, removed, detached woman. I got along very well with her. She was not very demonstrative, but she was very witty. And I always felt that in relation to me she was warm-hearted, though perhaps not to my father. He needed things

from her which he didn't seem to get. I began to sense in my
teens that they were unhappy together. And my father would
often in a kind of fumbling, crude way try to discuss it, or at
least he would be driven to complain. I didn't want to hear
any part of it. I defended myself as best I could from being
drawn into a conflict of that sort, by withdrawing to a great
extent. I had my own room, and I spent most of my time
reading or doing homework or whatever. My father was a
great reader. He read less and less as he grew older, but at
the time I was starting to read, he read a lot. He was particularly addicted to adventure stories, and as a kid that suited
me perfectly. I started reading Tom Swift and those Baseball
Joe books and the Oz books. And gradually I started reading,
you know, anything.

Religiously, I think he would have preferred not to be a
Jew. It troubled him; it really bothered him. Most of his
friends were not Jewish. He used to love to talk with an Irish
accent. He had that peculiar syndrome, I think, which was
far more operative in the thirties and forties, of being a Jew
who everybody knew was a Jew but who practically passed
as a non-Jew. It wasn't that he was ashamed. He just would
have preferred not to be identified as someone who was different from everybody else, and different in a way that people might look down on.

He didn't drink. What I mean is that he rarely drank. He
would go out with the boys to a cartoonists' meeting and get
drunk every now and then, but he didn't drink at home. It
wasn't that he was so straitlaced, he just wasn't by nature a
drinker. I guess he probably was puritanical, though not
in comparison to his peers perhaps. He would never even
admit to me an interest in another woman. I was brought
up with the idea that there was no sex life whatsoever exist-

ing in people over forty, because I was convinced my own parents didn't screw, and there was never even a hint of admission that my father might have looked elsewhere. And of course my mother—the same thing only more so.

Sex was never talked about. I didn't try to bring it up. I didn't want to discuss it with them. I didn't think they knew a damn thing about it. I don't know if it's the same way today, but by the time I was fifteen or sixteen, at which point my parents were in their middle to late forties, I was convinced that they no longer had any sex life at all. I certainly never saw or heard any evidence of it in the house. It might have been very healthy for me to have heard something.

I was fascinated by sex, of course. It was the major topic of conversation among my friends. I had a lot of friends. Growing up in New York City, I was part of a gang. We roamed the streets, busting up things or playing sports like roller hockey and stickball. We lived on the Upper West Side —92nd and West End Avenue. I used to work Saturday nights folding newspapers at the newsstand at 91st and Broadway. When we were around eleven or twelve we started going to kissing parties on Saturday nights. I was always the youngest of the group because I'd skipped in school, so when the kissing parties started I must have been around twelve. The other guys must have been thirteen or fourteen. We'd play spin the bottle or five minutes. Five minutes was a very sophisticated game where the boys drew lots and the girls drew lots, and whoever had the same number would go into the bedroom together for five minutes. The evening would always end, as I recall, with a kissing contest. Each girl would go into the bedroom with each boy and be kissed, and then the girls would vote as to who was the best kisser and we would do the same thing. One guy always won those contests, and it was only years later that I found out why. He was kissing the girls on the lips. That's what it was like at the age of thirteen.

The first topic was, I suppose, how do you do it. I remember—I can't place it in time—being told once that you shoved your dick up some hole that a girl had down there. That was on a terribly theoretical level. I didn't know what it was all about. Oh, and then one day when I was about eleven somebody said, "Listen, there's a way you can practice it—sex." He told me about jerking off. So I thought *wow*, and I got into that very quickly. I was ashamed of it. I knew it was wrong because the climate of opinion in those days told me it was wrong. My father once said to me—I think he knew what I was doing—"Don't do it too often and don't worry that you're going to grow hair on your palms or go crazy, but," he said, "don't do it too often."

I had a lot of sexual problems as a child. I was younger than my peer group because I skipped the first or second grade. And my pubic hair was late in growing in. Oh, I suffered the agonies of the damned. I remember going to summer camp when I was ten or eleven and all the kids in my bunk were starting to grow pubic hair and I had nothing. And we had these communal soap-ups and showers two or three times a week, and I'd hide in the corner. And then sometimes they'd soap up in the lake, and I always pleaded a headache or I went somewhere else. I guess it struck me that the growth of hair was a sign of oncoming manhood, and I just didn't have it. I felt I was a freak, that there was something wrong with me. The other kids obviously knew I was hiding. Some of the kids from my neighborhood also went to the camp, and when we got back after the summer, we had a poker game one night at one of their houses and they wanted to play strip poker. I didn't want to play, and eventually they ganged up on me and stripped me; all the boys just stripped me, you know, and made fun of me because I had no pubic hair. I was horrified. I was maybe twelve. Looking back on it now, I don't remember it that vividly. But I guess it was awful. Oh, and we wound up the evening pals and buddies again. Naturally I had to forgive them.

I had one little private homosexual experience when I was thirteen or fourteen with one of the guys I had grown up with. It was a Saturday night and we'd been hanging around a bowling alley and a Ping-Pong parlor, you know, desperately looking for girls, ever hopeful. We never once picked up a girl, but we always looked. My friend said, "We're never going to get laid, but this is the next best thing." So we went back to his apartment and jerked each other off. And that was the one and only time it ever happened. It didn't do that much for me.

I was taking girls out from the age of twelve onward. After a couple of times there would generally be a kiss at the door. When I was thirteen or fourteen I began kissing the girls on the lips, generally closed-mouth kisses. A French kiss was a big thing. You were on your way then. And in New York City at least, we had this shorthand which we used to describe sexual progress. If you could kiss her, that was a single. If you could feel her breasts, that was a double. If you could get a hand on her pussy, that was a triple. And if you could fuck her, that was a home run. There were two fellows who claimed home runs. And the way they described it—it was during the summer and they were bellhops and she was a waitress—we would have been able to believe them.

By the age of fourteen, I had already found a couple of girls who let me feel their tits. I wasn't really getting much. I always felt I was kind of backward with girls. I was amused because at the time of the great notoriety about my case a couple of years ago, all sorts of people were saying what a whiz kid I used to be with the girls in my teens, which was a lot of bullshit. I never was. Maybe I was a smooth talker. And maybe I presented a slick appearance, but what was going on was zero. I never pretended to hit a home run. I was as frustrated as any of the kids, and I always said so. I mean, it was an agonizing process. It was the interior dialogue that was so fantastic. You'd sit on a couch with the girl after you brought her home from the movies, and you'd talk and then finally, preparatory to the first kisses, inch by inch, your hand would creep around till it was around her shoulder, if you were going in from that angle, from on top. It was such a big goddamned thing. Most of the dialogue was meant to cover up what was happening. Then inevitably she would say, "Stop. Please don't." Then you would go into the big argument. "Why Not? Let's do it. We won't go any further. I really like you and I know you really like me." To me it was always a genuine struggle. I felt—and this of course is, I suppose, sad—I felt that I was basically doing something against a girl's will by simply trying to feel her breasts. And further than that I knew would be against her will, would be a question of seduction, a question of some sort of incredible snow-job. It was the prevalent attitude of society that a woman gave herself to a man and a man took her. The girls always said, "If I let you do this to me you'll think I'm cheap." We always protested. But in fact we believed it. We did think it cheap. We all wanted a virgin when we eventually married. I can't remember whoever told me this. Not my father or mother. The "they" are there, but they don't identify themselves.

Not one of these girls that we were taking out to the movies was putting out, not a goddamn one. There was a girl in high school who lived in Brooklyn—this is terrible—and the rumor went that if you went out to Brooklyn and were nice to her you could feel her up and maybe she'd take off her panties for you. That was the ultimate. I went to one of the most progessive high schools in the city, the High School of Music and Art, and I realize now there must have been kids in that school getting laid. But I didn't know them. They weren't talking to me.

I wasn't tormented at all. I wanted it, and I was willing to accept the guilt and the guilt be damned. I would proceed full steam ahead. I just didn't know how to succeed. I wasn't clever enough or attractive enough or, you know, I just wasn't a man yet. I was a boy playing boys' games. From the breast phase I jumped right into the home-run phase. First of all, four or five of us, my gang, went out and got laid a couple of times with a whore who used to work the neighborhood bowling alley. I was fifteen the first time. We picked up this girl, a woefully thin little creature, in the bowling alley and went to a rooming house on West 95th Street. We had seen her around. We knew who she was. Somebody at some point must have said, "Look, there's a whore." I seem to recall her name was Terry. On this particular night, one of us—and it wasn't me—went up and propositioned her and said there are three or four of us, and how much, and will you, and he came back and said it's on. And my heart went *boom, boom, boom,* because this was it. I think it was three dollars or five dollars each. It was an investment for me, but I had it. I worked and I had earned it. And, well, this was going to be a major breakthrough in my life—a big door was opening for me that night.

So we took Terry to this rooming house. She didn't have a place, and apparently none of us did either at the time. She took us to a second- or third-floor bathroom in the rooming house. That's where I lost my cherry, in a bathroom, seated on a closed toilet seat with this bony creature, you know, impaled on me. With a yellow light bulb staring down. One single light bulb. I sat on the toilet seat and slipped my pants down to my ankles, or she did it for me. And she pulled up her skirt. She had nothing on, no underwear. And she put a rubber on me. She provided it. That was part of the deal. I had one in my pocket, but she provided it. A Trojan, it must have been a Trojan. God, the name comes back. And it was pretty dreary. It was over very quickly, and I remember I wanted to kiss her and she looked at me like I was nuts. I mean kiss her mouth. And she thought that was a very peculiar urge on my part.

As I said, I was anticipating a major breakthrough in my life. I was going to find out what it was all about. I didn't particularly like the atmosphere of the bathroom though, and it was a disappointing experience. But I can't say it was a horrifying experience. It was just disappointing. I thought afterwards, "That was lousy. I've got to fuck someone else." It was not traumatic. And we did find someone else shortly after that, and this time we were able to go to one of the guys' apartments and it happened again, this time on a bed. But again I was disappointed. The woman was so unattractive. I can picture it right now. Thin—both of them were thin and kind of mousy-faced as I recall, you know, ratty hair, tangles. I'm sure I felt sorry for her, because that was part of the bourgeois image that you had—the poor whore. But it didn't get in the way of my lust; it didn't stop me from getting a hard-on; it didn't stop me from having an orgasm. And the method was always the same. You know, she always jumped on top of you and called you honey.

Then I met a girl named Lois, a real Jewish beauty. She really was lovely, a tall, very full, large-lipped girl with

larger-than-average, beautifully shaped breasts—everybody
said so, so it wasn't just my own opinion. Blue eyes, brown
hair, high-pitched voice but very pleasant, very clean and
very affectionate. Just, you know, every boy's dream.

We were sixteen and we were in love and we finally made
it one night on her parents' living-room couch in Washington
Heights. After a real siege. I worked on it; I thought of nothing else day and night for months. I maneuvered. I swore un-
dying love. "I'll marry you when I'm old enough. We'll go
away together." I must have lied to her like a son-of-a-bitch,
but I think I believed it at the time. And I adored the girl. I
also recall that my parents didn't like her, which naturally
strengthened my feeling for her. My father thought she was
a cheap little tart. For all I know, she might have been. But I
can't remember—oh, sure, she was a virgin. And that night
was painful for her—the blood—which troubled me, but it
didn't stop me. And the awkwardness. I think I took off all
my clothes except my socks, and the image of it still haunts
me when I think of it. I was far from a gentleman. I was
just a fumbling kid. But I was in such a state of mind that
that was my only object in life at that age. I was going to go
to college and all, but that seemed somewhat secondary.

What I recall most about that night was her tears, her pain.
She was mortified. She was losing her virginity at the age of
sixteen, and in 1946 that was a big deal where we came from.
I guess she also suspected that I wouldn't marry her in the
end and that she was going to be damaged goods after this. I
felt like a rake, a son-of-a-bitch and a man all at once. And I
also suspected that this really was not what it was all about
sexually. Fucking on a living-room couch with the parents a
couple of rooms away, with my socks on and the lights out—
somehow that wasn't the idea that was working around in my
head. Probably my ideas were shaped by Hollywood more

than anything else. I suspect that was it. I was in love with Jeanne Crain. Remember *State Fair?* She was so fresh, my ideal woman at that age.

Well, we kept it up for a period of about a month or two, by which time I was bored with the whole thing. It wasn't that good, what we were doing—there had to be more. It was such a strain, that kind of sex on the living-room couch. The concept of a female orgasm was totally foreign to me. I mean, I don't think Lois was getting anything out of it. She was doing a lot of huffing and puffing and panting, but I can't see that she was in any way satisfied except perhaps in some romantic idea that she had.

Then the summer came and it was my last summer before college and I didn't see all that much of her. I worked as a bellhop at some lodge up in the mountains somewhere, so I only saw her at the beginning and the end of the summer. Then I went away to Cornell in Ithaca, New York. She came up for one house-party weekend and she was a knockout as I recall, because I remember the comments of my fraternity brothers when they saw her walk in the door. It was a long weekend, like four days, and it ended our relationship. She said she didn't want to sleep with me any more. That's the expression we used—"sleep with me." And I said, "You've come all the way up here to tell me that?" And she said, "Yes, that's the only thing you want from me. You wouldn't love me if I didn't sleep with you." And I said, "No, no, that's not true," all the while suspecting she was right. I guess I wanted to believe that there was something honorable about my intentions even though I knew that the basis of the whole thing was that I desperately wanted to get laid. Eventually we did sleep together on that weekend, but it was very unsatisfactory and she cried. There's nothing worse as far as I'm concerned than being in bed with a woman and having her weep underneath you, or over you—no, then it was always under. She left that weekend and we both knew it was over and I don't think I ever saw her again.

Sometime later in my first year I was walking back from the boathouse—I was rowing with the crew—and I just started talking to this girl who was walking near me. She turned out to be a waitress named Ginny and, Jesus, she laid at the drop of a hat. And to me that was just marvelous, not to have to go through the bullshit. I remember the second time I saw her, I said, "Would you like to come back to my room in the dormitory?" She said, "Sure." We went back there. I started kissing her, then peeling off her clothes and she didn't protest and I thought, "God, you've answered my prayers." But God is ever a joker. When we got into bed—the big moment, I've finally found a girl who wants to fuck and there's no bullshit—I said, "Would you mind stopping chewing that gum?" And she said, "What for? I always chew gum in bed." What a disaster. I can smell it now. That girl smelled of chewing gum the whole time. I saw her every now and again. She was very practical. She just lay there to get laid. I suspected there was something wrong with that. I was used to the huffing and puffing and the guilt. There was no huffing and puffing but there was no guilt either. I just knew I hadn't gotten to the right woman yet. She was just around the bend.

At the end of my first year of college I met a girl who was Jeanne Crain incarnate and I fell in love and that was the real thing and we eventually got married. Her name was Nina and she was a lovely blonde girl. She was still in high school when we met on a double date. She was then very active politically. Her parents were New York Progressive party people. Her mother had had a play produced on Broadway, and her father had been divorced and remarried. It was a new world for me to be in.

I was mad about her and she was mad about me and we really turned each other on sexually. We used to go through rituals that when I think back on now I shudder. She was a virgin and would not sleep with me. No, no, no. But since she loved me, she would do just about everything else. We went through some of the most contorted sex. We'd get stripped down and be body-to-body and naturally I had a hard-on and I was between her legs and I'd say, "Let me go in you, darling." And she'd say, "No, no, no." And she kept to the no, and I would just rub myself off between her legs like that, which she thought was fantastic because she always had an orgasm. Naturally I did. And that's what we did. The first time was on her living-room couch in Greenwich Village. I bought a car just so I could have a place to be with her.

That's how it went with us. I remember going with her to the Yale-Cornell football game. We drove with some fraternity brothers of mine, we were in the back seat with one guy and there were three in front. And both going and coming from Ithaca to New Haven, in that back seat we were working away like buzz saws on each other and I think we each must have come two or three times. I don't know how the hell we managed to keep it a secret from the guys in the car. Maybe we didn't. Maybe they were having a fantastic time at our expense. When I think of what we were doing to each other it horrifies me, just horrifies me.

Once I persuaded her to spend the night with me at Binghamton on the way to or from school—she was at Cornell by that time. We registered in a hotel as man and wife. What a thrill. She turned her garnet birthstone ring around so it would look like a wedding ring. I remember doing the husband-and-wife shit in the elevator. "Oh, darling, I'm so tired" —who knows what the hell we said. Anyway, we didn't screw there either. Later on she taxed me with that weekend and said that was the time she would have if I'd really pressed hard enough. This was at a moment after we were married when we were mutually agreeing that the only reason we'd gotten married was because we were so sexually frustrated. And I said, "Well, why didn't you sleep with me before we were married?" She said, "Well, I would have but you stopped trying after a while." Maybe it's true, maybe I did.

We got married in 1951. I was still in school. Both our parents were against this marriage. They said we were much too young. But the Korean War had just started and I thought I was going to have to go off, and her mother said, "Well, you better marry him. He might get killed." A night or two before we were married—it was a big wedding, you understand; all the presents had come in and all the guests were invited to the Hampshire House—we were sitting in the car and there was a strain between us and she started to cry. She said, "I know you don't want to marry me." I protested naturally, although I didn't want to marry her. She said, "Why don't you stop lying?" She said, "We're only doing it because we wanted so much to go to bed together and we didn't do it." And I said, "Well, then we've got to call it off." And she said, "We can't. All the presents are in, and what about all those guests?" I tell you there was no cliche to it. It was very real.

Essentially it ended that night before we got married. We stayed together on and off for about a year and a half. I decided soon after being married that I didn't want to be, and we finally split up and she got an annulment on some trumped-up grounds. I was already in Europe when it came through. I left this country in 1954. A lot of the details of this are very clear to me because I wrote about them once. It's unpublished, but I decided to write about it. That conversation in the car and the whole experience with her I tend to think of as one of the more significant episodes of my life in the sense that it engendered incredible guilt in me. By the time we separated I felt I had ruined her life, or was in the process of ruining it. She begged me not to go. She was mortified and humiliated that she couldn't make the marriage work. And I was suffering horrible tortures because I knew I didn't want to stay married and yet I felt I was destroying a person by going. She cried, she wept, she thrashed. So I left that marriage with a terrible sense of guilt.

I hope I've gotten rid of it by now, but I think I operated under guilt toward women for a long time. But I was lucky. I met some sophisticated, sensitive women in Europe when I was still in my twenties, and they taught me a lot. One was an American and one was an older German woman (I was twenty-five and she was in her mid-forties) and they both educated me. They made me aware of things that a woman wants and needs and made me aware of my own selfishness in many respects. Not that I was able to cure myself of selfishness, but at least I knew it was there and I could sometimes keep it in check.

Europe to me was the ultimate foreign exciting experience. After my marriage I went off there to write a book. I had almost a thousand dollars in my pocket when I went. I blew half of it in Paris in the first two or three weeks. Then I headed south and wound up on Ibiza by accident. I got on a ship bound for somewhere else and when we wheeled around into the bay of Ibiza, I fell in love with the town before we even landed. I love fantasies. To me, if you can live these fantasies, then you're really on the road to who you are. In many ways, getting involved in the Hughes thing stemmed simply from an enjoyment of risk. I got into it by a step-by-step process. It just seemed like such an exciting idea. It was as if someone said, "Hey, how'd you like to sail through the Dardanelles to Russia?" You say, "Gee, that's a terrific idea." And they say, "Well, there's the boat right down there. Let's go down and take a look at it." And I say, "Great. Let's go," except in this case I'm the one who's saying "How'd you like to?" There's the boat, and I say, "Let's get on board and see how she sails." We get out of the harbor and we can put in at the next place, pick up supplies and just keep on going. And you survive all the storms en route. And each storm you survive, you feel more excited, more confident, and in a sense look forward to the next one, knowing you can lick it too.

At some point the whole thing also stemmed from simple financial greed. That was something I didn't want to admit two years ago, but now I think I can say it with impunity. Now, money had never been a problem for me—I had always spent it freely in the pursuit of what I wanted. And it wasn't a problem when this thing started. But maybe I thought, "Oh, well, wouldn't it be nice if I had all that bread and I could do whatever I wanted." Who knows. Maybe I wanted the money because it would make it that much easier to manipulate my sexual life. I was leading a double life at the time. I had a wife and a mistress. Who knows what it is that God has given us—sexual desire, appreciation, ego, whatever —that makes us need more than the simple reproductive act, or more than one woman.

I never had the reputation of being a ladies' man as a child or youth. Well, Lois was a good-looking girl and Nina had been a Kansas beauty queen, literally. And I guess that did it. I always went after the best-looking girls that were around, provided I liked them. It wasn't a slavish kind of thing— "There's a beautiful girl and I'm going to have her even though she's stupid and doesn't speak English." Sure, the male ego's part of it, but there is just a great pleasure in walking down the street with a beautiful woman. I'm not going to dedicate my life to walking down streets with beautiful women.

I don't really dig the young women today. I don't find them very sexual. That's a hell of a generalization because surely out there there are some fantastic young women, but I find that mostly they're bored with sex, that there isn't that explosive kind of wonderment any more. The first time this came home to me I was thirty-four or thirty-five, and I jumped into bed with some young girl in Spain one night. She spent the night at my place and the morning came. She got out of bed and was getting dressed and I lazily got up and said, you know, "When will I see you again?" We'd had a good night, nothing wild and and exciting. We liked each other, nothing more, no promises. "When will I see you again?" And she said, "Like, man, I'll be around." Wow. I was crushed. I think first of all my ego was crushed. Secondly, I thought, "Well, what's it all about?" Then I realized that I'd been affected and touched by all the events of my youth. Because I would never get over the feeling that there is a commitment involved, that I am taking something from a woman, and that sex, even after all the experiences, is something very special.

Erica Jong *writer, poet*

Born March 26, 1942, New York, N.Y.

The photograph on the back of her best-selling novel, Fear of Flying, *shows Erica Jong to have a round face, a full, sexy smile and a long mane of thick blond hair. Her face and mouth were indeed full, and her body was small and round, but she had cut her hair to shoulder length "because people were recognizing me on the street," she explained in the comfortable living room of her apartment on Manhattan's Upper West Side. Dressed in blue jeans and a loose navy-blue overblouse, she at first seemed shy, almost awkward, quite without the moxie and bravado of Isadora Wing, her book's heroine. But what appeared to be awkwardness was merely a careful writer's carefulness: she wanted to know how the interview would be done, how it would be edited, what would be deleted, and whether she could see and approve the final version. Sometimes she would stop herself in midsentence with a "that's inarticulate," then resume in a slow, firm voice, as if she were writing every phrase on an invisible piece of paper.*

THE FIRST YEAR of having a best-selling novel was one of the most stressful years of my entire life. People who wouldn't give me the time of day the year before now wanted to fuck me. Suddenly I was a trendy cunt. It made me feel very insecure. I wondered, "Okay, what's happened between two years ago, when I couldn't get him on the phone, and this year, when he's wooing me sycophantically and wants to take me to lunch, to drinks, to bed and so on?" It gave me the sense that everything was ephemeral, that nothing had any stability, and that tomorrow I might be in the garbage can. Also, I felt barraged by other people's envy of me. And anger at me. Old friends would call and say, "Well, now that you're rich and famous, how about . . ." And I'd say, "Well, I'm neither as rich nor as famous as you think." Marilyn Monroe, who certainly was much more famous than I'll ever be, said what I think is the last word on fame: "When you're famous, people come up to you and say things as if they were saying them to your clothes." Fame is supposed to insulate you against feeling hurt.

As a "successful" woman I am admired by other women as a role model (I hate that word; it always makes me think of bagels and croissants and things) but men tend to fear me before they get to know me. I guess I can empathize with that. When I was in college I always ran from the big man on campus, the good-looking super-achiever, because I thought he would make me feel so small and nebbishy and nothing. And maybe a woman who seems successful and talented and hard-working and attractive is threatening to men in that same way. I think men are really very confused about what they want. On the one hand, the creature of male fantasy is the willing dream girl, and on the other hand, a woman who comes on sexually is terrifying. Most men, often unconsciously, still divide women into two groups: whores and madonnas. It took me a while to understand that to many men my writing, which is very up front about female sexuality, was a come-on already, and that if I answered their letters, I'd inevitably get their complete unpublished works and/or invitations to dinner or bed or both. Not wanting to be a cock-teaser, I stopped answering the letters. Certainly all of this was very hard for my husband. I've been married eight years to a child psychiatrist and it's been crucial to my work that he has always supported my desire to be an artist. But it's very hard for a guy who's living with somebody to hear the phone ringing all the time and people calling me up in the middle of the night saying, "Hey, Isadora Wing, I'm coming over for a Zipless Fuck."

Success is not without pleasure. Once you've had it and have experienced it you don't have to be hungry or envious any more. It makes you humble and generous rather than pompous and selfish, I think. There are no more stingy people than embittered failures. I myself no longer care about going to parties where there are stars. I did once. Success has also brought me a degree of freedom, freedom in a lot of ways. There's a lot of shit I don't have to take because I can pick up and go. Even within my own marriage I feel I can now say, "Look if we can't work this out, goodbye."

It was always clear to me from the time I was very young, twelve or so, that I had to have a career and become something in my own right. I don't know exactly why I was so sure of that. Some aspect of the standard female brainwashing completely passed me by, although other aspects remain on a very deep unconscious level that I still haven't even dealt with. I never ruled out marriage and children; I wanted to do *everything*, but it was all going to come together. And the men I chose were men who accepted my ambition to write, and if they didn't I didn't choose them.

I can't imagine life without writing. I can't imagine life without some sort of work that you care deeply about, even if it isn't writing. For a long time I thought I was going to be a painter. My mother is an extremely, extremely talented painter and so are my grandfather and aunt. My mother is no dabbling Sunday painter or anything like that; she was somebody who won all the prizes in art school as a young woman. But I think she found it hard to resolve the family–career thing. When she was painting she felt guilty about not being with her children, and when she was with her children she felt that she wanted to be painting. So there was this sense of having an enormously gifted mother who was tugged between career and children and never quite made her peace with it. My father was also in some way a frustrated artist. He's in the importing business now, but in his early twenties he was a musician, a self-taught pianist and drummer. He was in Broadway shows and played nightclubs and wrote a couple of quite popular songs. He always wanted a theatrical career but, for whatever reasons, either felt it wasn't the right thing or couldn't advance far enough. My childhood was absolutely surrounded by painting and music. Though I have almost no talent for music myself, I do have a lifelong passion for Cole Porter (which my father used to play on the piano when I was a kid). So there were two parents both of whom had talents and aspirations. I took art lessons from the time I was twelve and went to the High School of Music and Art in Manhattan. But in my first year of college I gave up painting rather abruptly when I decided to dedicate myself to writing seriously. I guess I gave up painting because there were so many talented people in my family and I wanted something that was completely my own.

My parents have been married forty years and I think they have a happy marriage—a stormy one, but a happy one. They have a strong sort of pleasurable bond with each other. I sense it that way. I can remember violent fights, but I can also remember them reading aloud to each other in bed and sharing the same activities. My family life was characterized by an incredible level of noise, people screaming and arguing across the dinner table about practical matters like what to eat, or intellectual things like Marxism, Leninism or the nature of modern art. I remember myself always running off to put my nose in a book to get away from this incredible decibel level, but obviously the fact that my family was articulate, well read and vociferous had tremendous influence on my being a writer today. Through all the yelling I had the feeling that my parents were affectionate with each other. I cannot remember my father pinching my mother's ass, or vice versa, but there were always sexual vibrations in the house. I felt my parents were sensuous people.

Some of these vibrations came from my older sister. When she was fourteen and I was nine, she had breasts and pubic hair and was menstruating and had reached her full height, and was a woman! She looked like a twenty-five-year-old Gina Lollobrigida and was already going out with boys. They seemed like men to me. She was very sexy, and she would be off necking with her boyfriends in the house, or at least I thought she was. Sex was something forbidden, dangerous, and something that my big sister did which was terrific and exciting, and I (being flat-chested and dying to have a period) wanted to imitate her. I had the feeling that my parents disapproved violently and tried to stop her. All blessings on my sister, maybe she wasn't doing anything at all, but in my mother's head and in my head there was all this exotic stuff going on. My best friend and I snuck around reading her mother's copy of *The Ideal Marriage* by Van der Velde. When I was nine or ten my older sister sat me down in the kitchen one day and said, "Now it's time for me to explain to you how sperm meets egg." She had all these anatomical charts with a cross section of the male organ and a cross section of the ovaries and all that jazz, and she made it all seem very positive. I think maybe it disturbed me that my mother hadn't leveled with me. Not that she'd lied, but she never sat down and gave me that crucial information—and I think I wanted it from her. Around this same time, a friend of my sister's who was reputed to be very fast told me about diaphragms. She said, "There's this thing that a woman can wear and you can get fitted for it and a man doesn't know you're wearing it and you put it inside." I didn't really understand, not really.

We started having spin-the-bottle parties in sixth grade, and I remember one episode where a boy kissed me, sort of wetly. I went to P.S. 87 in Manhattan, that old, smelly redbrick building built around 1870 that used to be on the corner of 77th and Amsterdam Avenue, just one block from where I now live. I first got felt up at the Beacon movie theater at 74th and Broadway. Boys used to put their arms around you and sort of dangle a hand in front of your boob as if they were unaware of it and then *wham*, right down on the boob. What subterfuge!

My first real boyfriend was a terrific painter. He was tall and dark and had a big nose and was a junior at Music and Art when I was a freshman. He used to send me these wonderful drawings of his and valentines which he would letter in gold with a poem by Yeats or Blake or Shakespeare. It was a very sentimental, gift-giving, romantic relationship with a great deal of sexual experimentation. But of course he was madly in love with me and wanted to marry me—otherwise I wouldn't have done it, right? We started petting below the waist (to use that ridiculous expression) when I was thirteen. We couldn't take off our clothes because we were doing it in the living room with my parents sort of lurking around. So there were furtive unbuttonings and unzipperings and fingers being inserted between clothes and things. And there was quite as much pain and pleasure. There was the pleasure followed immediately by, "Oh, my God, what have I done?" and the thought that even though this was a boy who loved me and whom I loved and with whom I shared everything, my best friend and my half-lover, he wouldn't respect me. And I'm a bad girl. I felt terribly, terribly guilty. I think I felt more guilty about our sexual play than I ever have about anything in my life. And I don't know why. It wasn't that anybody had said you'll grow warts on your nose from finger-fucking or something like that. But I believed that we were the only two kids in the entire world who had ever discovered this. I really believed that—I cannot tell you the intensity with which I believed it. I eventually broke off the relationship, after about two years, purely because of the guilt. And he was of course baffled, hurt, didn't understand, and felt rejected. I just couldn't stand the guilt any more.

Then I got the idea that I'd purge myself by starving to death. I went on a diet and got thinner and thinner and thinner and stopped drinking water and started going through all these funny food rituals, and my parents sent me to my first shrink, an experience I've given to Isadora Wing, my heroine in *Fear of Flying*. I'd stopped menstruating and had gotten skin problems and had a mild case of anorexia.

The shrink's analysis was that I was starving myself because of some fantasy of birth, equating feeding with pregnancy or something like that. I was better within a year.

My last years of high school were marked by very little sex. A lot of dating and goodnight kisses, what we then called French kisses, but no real body sex. I started seeing my old boyfriend again when I was sixteen and it was a relationship that lasted until I started college. But the sex never resumed. Those early experiences were very traumatic for me; I wasn't ready or something. I remember too that it was terribly important to me that a boy hold correct beliefs. I was in a car once with a boy I really kind of liked and thought was attractive and we were going to kiss and make-out, no petting above or below the waist or anything like that, he just wanted to kiss me. Then he told me that he thought Richard Nixon was America's hope for the presidency. This was in 1958, and I simply said, "Take me home." I, of course, was pro-Stevenson, as was my family, and if this boy thought that Nixon was America's hope I was damned if I was going to kiss him. At the very end of high school I did meet a boy with whom there was some petting and breast fondling, but I was just sort of off sex. Funny. My guilt did not extend to masturbation. In fact, when I was sixteen and not fucking boys, I remember feeling that masturbation was keeping me pure and chaste, that I could get my body taken care of without submitting to the evils of male domination or worrying about getting pregnant. The Kinsey Report came out around this time and I was very comforted to know that *everybody* masturbated. That made me feel very good. The other, quote, dirty book that was very important to me in high school was *Lady Chatterley's Lover*, especially the part about him putting violets in her pubic hair. I was always wondering why no one ever wanted to put violets in *my* pubic hair.

My first fuck was with somebody I was in love with and it was tender and romantic. He was a sophomore at Columbia when I was a freshman at Barnard, and he was short and dark and intense and brilliant and garrulous and manic, and we were in love. That was the excuse for everything in 1959 —"But we were in love." We met my first week at college, went together for three months, went to bed, were together four years after, were married when I graduated from college and the marriage lasted one year, then fell apart. But my first experience was very tender. I was very scared about losing my virginity and said, "Oh, no, we mustn't; I don't want to." But I really *did* want to, and then it was clear that it was time. It was in his apartment off campus, and there was candlelight and wine and nice music and considerable fumbling. He'd had some abortive attempts with prostitutes in high school, but it was his first experience, too. I don't remember it being painful or bad, but nor do I remember the earth moving either, not like Dottie Renfrew in *The Group,* who experiences orgasm her first time. It was scarcely like that for us. But the emotions associated with it are very tender because we saw it as making a commitment to each other. It took us a while to learn how to do it. After I slept with him the first time I was very guilty. Then about a month or so after, I was jubilant and I thought, "Oh, God, I've lost it. Terrific! Wonderful! How Great! I'm not a virgin any more." And I've never regretted it.

I would go out with other people from time to time and we were always apart in the summers, and though there was quite a lot of fooling around, I don't think I ever slept with anyone else. I felt a tremendous sense of fidelity to this one guy and guilty even when I just went out with other people. Then we married. A year later it broke up because he went crazy. I shouldn't say crazy. He had a psychotic episode that dissolved the marriage effectively. It was a really painful thing to live through. We were very, very close, the kind of closeness you almost only have in an adolescent relationship. We used to study together in the library, go to movies together, we did everything together, we lived inside each other's brains. I still have on my shelves many books that he gave me. One day I came across the collected essays of W. H. Auden, which he had given me on my twenty-first birthday. It said. "For my Erica on her 21st birthday: May we love to see the 31st and 41st." I read the inscription and I really wept.

After my marriage broke up, I was twenty-two, I was a baby, and I went off to Europe with a friend. That's where my generation went to get laid, particularly Italy, where every guy you wound up in bed with told you he was a principe or a marchese. The idea was that if you didn't speak the same language as the man you didn't have to feel guilty. I had a friend who also felt that if you just went down on each other you didn't have to feel guilty. If you actually fucked, that was *really* taking someone into your inner sanctum, and I do think that for a woman to take somebody into her body in intercourse is really a kind of deep commitment. I guess I've been lucky in one regard, that sexual responsiveness has never been hard for me. There are times when I've absolutely frozen and felt invaded, but that's because I was conning myself into doing something that I didn't want to do. With somebody I cared for, it's never been hard for me to relax, feel easy with my body, with the touching, stroking, cuddling, warmth, and if you're free and easy that way, the other things usually come along. I'm not saying I've had an orgasm every time, but more often than not, I have. I've certainly had my times of feeling, oh, it doesn't matter whether I come as long as he does. I mean, we've all had that brainwashing about trying to pleasure a man and show him what a sexual virtuoso you are.

Because I wrote about the fantasy of the Zipless Fuck in *Fear of Flying*, I've been asked whether I believe in casual sex, one-night stands, sex with strangers. I think it doesn't usually work except as a fantasy. I scarcely think it's a viable kind of sex for a mature woman, although maybe, from time to time, it's fun to do when you're feeling a little bit crazy and Bacchic and abandoned. It was a fantasy of my early twenties, but it is not a fantasy that obsesses me now, I must say. I don't look at men on trains and buses and say, "I'd like to fuck him without knowing his name." At this point in my life I feel that somebody's sense of humor, somebody's friendship and warmth are what really make him sexy, not just his body. We all need stable relationships in order to grow and do work and raise families and do all the things that keep civilization going. But we also need adventure, women just as much as men. One day you can't think of anything nicer than hearth and home, and the next day all you want is to break free. In America we don't deal with this split in the human spirit. We don't have a one-day-a-year Dionysian festival where everybody can go off into the woods and fuck everybody else. We believe in romantic love and in monogamy, so we end up with serial monogamy. I don't know if it's such a good solution.

I've not had a lot of casual sex in my life. There have been periods of crazies, but most of my relationships have been

very long-term and pretty monogamous and pretty stable—
in high school, in college, and now I've been married eight
years. I have friends who believe in honesty and openness
and tell each other all about their peccadillos. And I have
friends who believe just as strongly that you never tell. I
don't really know which I believe at this point. I must say
I've tried both and both have been painful in different ways.
I treasure the ideal of a good companionable relationship
between equals, but you've got to work very, very hard and
you can never sit back and say, "Well, now we've done it." I
think we're living in a time when women are outstripping
men, in levels of consciousness, in maturity, and in their ability to deal with the world. So many of the men I see are boys,
and so many of the women are women, and there are boys
and women and naturally the women are going to be frustrated. I think we're going to have to be very strong and very
tough and maybe even go through periods in our lives when
we live without men.

At this point in my life, if I were not married, sex would
take on a much more relaxed quality for me. I would not feel
that every sexual encounter had to be preceded by great de-
votion or a romantic earth-moving commitment. Friendship
and mutual attraction would be enough. It doesn't seem like
a big deal any more. That has to do with getting older. I must
say that now I feel better about my body than I ever have before. Oh, I still alternate between feeling I'm the ugliest
woman around and feeling at times pleased with myself physically. I can't make sense of it. I know that the outside world
considers me to be an attractive woman, though I'm certainly
not to everybody's taste. Sometimes I make myself look horrible, dress like a slob or put on more weight than I should,
as a kind of self-punishment. I have a big thing about punish-

ing myself for being more successful than my mother, for being a recognized artist whereas both my parents wanted that and never really got it.

I think I will not allow myself to pass the age of thirty-five without having a child. Somewhere in my unconscious I had sort of made a bargain with God that if He (or She) would let me become a successful writer I would give up all else. Now I feel that's ridiculous. It's like saying, "If you let me have success in my work I won't seek life, love, or children." But you never reach a point where you want to live without love or affection or friendship. You need those things to feed your work. I've been very lucky. When I look back on the men I've known, sure there have been some bastards, but I have the feeling that there were a lot of men in my life who really cared for me, and that I was not unloved.

Sally Kellerman *actress*

Born June 2, 1937, Long Beach, Calif.

Her sunny, comfortably furnished two-story wooden house sits on a steep hillside lot overlooking Beverly Hills, and friends like Richard Benjamin, Rob Reiner, Anjanette Comer and screenwriter Carol Eastman come on Sunday afternoons for brunch and spirited volleyball games. The asphalt volleyball court and a pool take up nearly the whole back yard. Ms. Kellerman is a warm, affectionate, large-framed woman with a throaty laugh and a somewhat self-effacing manner. Barefoot, wearing a long halter-dress, she sat on the carpeted floor of her large living room and talked with almost painful candor about herself, explicitly frank except about one particularly traumatic episode, which she could only describe as "a bad experience with a man when I was a little girl."

I HAD A BOYFRIEND, Chicky Bardot, his name was, even before grammar school. They lived in a back alley. I think I was titillated by him. We sneaked up to a closet and ate candy canes. But then he swore or something, and so he had to go home and I don't remember seeing him much after that.

Then I had a boyfriend in Granada Hills who beat me up. That was in grammar school. I was in the third or fourth grade. I definitely liked him.

I necked with someone who lived down the street later on. But I didn't have a serious boyfriend until I was eighteen. Oh, I'd love to be able to say that such and such happened when I was ten, or eleven. But I didn't let anything happen. I didn't let anyone get close to me. I think my own sexuality scared me. Sex scared me.

And I certainly understood that one was not to make love with a boy in high school. I don't know where I got that idea, because I don't remember my parents talking much about sex. My sister was three years older, and when my mother sat us down and said, "Do you girls want to know about sex?" we said, "We know that, Mother, we know that."

God, I've made so many experiments into this thing—to get free of my background. Certainly my mom and dad had a terrific sex life. She told me in older years, when I was old enough to ask and was in analysis. But in my young life things were fairly ruled at home. "Sit up straight! Stop that! Put your napkin in your lap!" My dad was an oil broker, a Republican. When I see men seventy-four years old today, I see in their faces what was in my dad's—you know, of that generation, golf and work, decent and proper. Suit and tie. A briefcase. A Buick. A lady doesn't do this or that. There were those kinds of rules. My mother played the piano, and there was humor. But he had a temper. She was from the South. Baptist. Arkansas. They came with a lot, both of them. High-charged. Attractive. We were well-off and our background was, you know, stressed. My dad was from St. Louis. A good family. It meant a lot to them. But they weren't able to open up their feelings a lot, and so we didn't. That was what they were taught. You didn't talk about things like that.

And I was full of feelings like, you know, what about me? What are you feeling right now? Later on I had a big breakout, you know. I just spent so many fucking years rebelling. I practically rebelled my life away, from this rather restrictive atmosphere.

Anyway, so then I met this girl and she said, "Try this," and showed me, and I discovered masturbating and orgasm and things. We were in junior high. And then I moved away and saw her at the beginning of high school and I said, "Do you still do that thing?" You know, we didn't even know what it was called. "No," she said. And I said, "Neither do I." And then when I was older I used to say, "I'll never do it again." You know, to God. I thought I probably wouldn't be able to have children, that I would be punished for it, or that I was terribly bad or wrong to do it. Every time I masturbated I said, "Oh, God, I'm never going to do this again." I don't know where that guilt came from. It was never talked about. When I first started analysis the first thing the guy asked me was, "Do you masturbate?" and I just burst out crying and cried for an hour and a half. I went over the hour. So humiliated. "I confess!" The Catholics are so lucky. They've got someplace to go. My God, the burden was heavy! Heavy!

My dad was very private in his bathroom. Wanted me to always have on a slip, underpants and a brassiere. I'd go from my room across the hall to the bathroom, you know, this far, and he'd say, "Who do you think you are?" So I showed him. I took off my brassiere at eighteen and never put it back on. Sorry, Dad. I wasn't going to be gotten down, you know. I wore a girdle in high school in the late fifties. My mother wore a girdle, so I did. A tight girdle. Tight. Tight. Tight. A big rubber Playtex. Can you believe what they did to our bodies? Real comfy. You felt so gorgeous. "Look over here, but don't touch me. I've got this shield, this magic shield on me." That certainly was confidence-stopping. I mean, I backed out of rooms for years, and still enjoyed the sex and everything, but backed out of rooms until my husband, of all people, said, "What a great ass!" He was crazy about my seat. Now I back into rooms.

My niece, nine, well, we were shopping for clothes in New York and she was saying, "Oh, I don't have any waist." We'd eaten a big lunch and I looked and said, "No. You don't. But what do you expect? You've got great legs, a great ass, a beautiful face and hair. So you don't have a waist." My husband once said, "You've got the worst legs in the world, but I'm not a leg man. My last girl had skinny legs. Well, you can't fuck a leg." So none of us are perfect 8 x 10 glossies. There's just no way. But what's the big deal? And once I caught on to that, that men, or my man, was just going to find me irresistible, you know, 'cause that's his taste, well, it's funny, funny, how we all want to be perfect. But that's a point I never understood in those days. I thought you had to have a girdle because you had to have the slimmest hips.

I've grown to respect my parents a lot, though. My mother always said, "You never said a nice thing about Dad and me until after your father died." And it's true. And even when I did, nobody wanted to write about that. Hey, I love my parents.

We moved to the Park Le Brea Towers and I went to good old Hollywood High. That's why Sally became a movie star. It was a shock, coming from the San Fernando Valley. There was a girls' club called "The Models" that, I mean, you didn't even deal with. They were all so gorgeous. Dressed to the nines—makeup, high-heel shoes, when we wore saddle shoes and a butch haircut. I sat on their bench one time and one of them said, "Evidently someone doesn't know whose bench she's on." They were much more advanced. There was no competing with these girls. They had their own clique and their own superior rating. They may not have been feeling it, but that's the way they seemed to me.

My club was the pretty girls from, you know, the good families. Cute, you know. But no makeup. But natural. Cheerleaders and school officers. But I was never a school officer. We talked about boys and wore circle skirts with crinolines under them, bobby socks and saddle shoes. I always looked so terrible! After I got out of high school I thought, "No wonder I had such a hard time being attractive." When I realized that one could dress with what was becoming to one—well, you weren't allowed to do that in those days. There was one girl in our club who wore makeup. My parents weren't too crazy about her. And there was one in our high school, you know, that already knew about boys and married one right out of high school, and she said, "Aw, he's always farting in bed." You know. Real loose. I giggled. I found it enormously amusing. But I realized she was much more developed than I was. We were sent to our rooms once for, you know, "All right, who did it?" until one of us confessed. God, I didn't want to knock my dad. (Mother would die. That's the last thing I'm ever gonna say about him.) Dad was a sexual man. It was just that he didn't want us girls to know it. I didn't want to get into it analytically, but my dad probably did find us attractive. And didn't understand. I mean you can say, "I'd just like to eat that child up," and it's normal. Mothers get turned on to their babies nursing. It's normal. That kind of thing. And as long as you know it's normal it won't hurt you.

And there was one girl in school who was supposed to be the hooker. There was a good-girls' club and a bad-girls' club. I belonged to the good-girls' club and ran around with the bad girls. The bad girls were the ones who drank and smoked and probably slept with their boyfriends. I was the square. They'd say, "Boobs—oh, mammary glands to you, Sally." Then they'd teach me how to swear and then when the boys would come around I'd swear and they wouldn't. I never did catch on to that game. Later on in acting class we'd go out and we could say "fuck" and I thought we were, just, free! Wide open! Soul Sisters! Well, I was definitely the original beatnik.

I went to college for my parents. But then I quit. Because I never wanted to do anything but act. And then I lost my virginity because of something somebody said in acting class.

It was in Los Angeles, a theater-in-the-round. Someone in the class said, well, you'd be frigid if you were a virgin past a certain age, like going on twenty-two. So I lost my virginity when I was twenty-one. Listen, I know twenty-two-year-olds who are together like nobody I ever knew was together. But I didn't see them back then, or I hung out with people who weren't. But I was not together at twenty-one, twenty-two, twenty-three or twenty-four. A late-bloomer maybe. And you know, I'm not sad about it now. I mean I'm grateful. Because I'm getting a lot of gravy now.

It wasn't a guy I'd been going with. It was just someone that I knew liked me a lot and I thought wouldn't tell anybody. So I wouldn't be hurt, or some marvelous motivation like that. It was controlled, my control, in that I felt like I wasn't going to let him hurt me. I just wasn't able to get close. It was fear. He was an older guy, older than me. I was a struggling actress and in acting class and lying on the floor waiting for my parents to come through with the $200 to help pay the rent. I had all kinds of jobs. I'd moved out from home because some girl said, "You ought to move out and get an apartment." I wasn't even crazy about the girl. But I said

okay. I was too intimidated to say wait a minute. So I moved
out and got a job as a waitress. Was fired. Then taught swimming. Elevator operator. Secretary. General office work. And
then I finally landed a job I loved other than acting, which
was waiting on tables at a coffeehouse for two years, where
all my friends came every night.

I don't know what the guy did. I met him somewhere. I
was working as a waitress. Everybody knew everybody. It
was no courtship. Just friends. I knew him as a friend. We
talked about it. We discussed it. I told him I was a virgin.
He had a house in the Valley and we went to his place. I was
frightened. Emotionally. Physically too, probably, because I
didn't know what was coming. I was scared to death to be
close, to want to have sexuality in myself and to want somebody. I think I must have wanted him some way, because I
ended up with him and I'm not the kind who gets together
physically with a lot of people I don't want. But he was not
the dream of my life. It was weird.

I was panicked. I was horrified, horrified. Afterwards he
felt like being close, and I said, "Oh, please, don't talk about
it."

He was saying warm things. "I can't believe you're a virgin." But my guilt was so great I was saying, "Let me out of
here. No." Oh, I never wanted to see him again. I was just so
panicked. And I must have hurt him, which I didn't mean
to do.

It took me a while after that to have it be personal, to actually have a boyfriend connected with it. In those days,
early twenties, you know, it took me a long time. It was bizarre that I'd be with somebody. I had a lot of boyfriends
who wanted to make love to me, and, "No." You know. "No,"
for days and then, finally, the deadline. I didn't want to be
frigid, you know, and I'm glad somebody gave me the dead-

line, 'cause, God, if I went that long, imagine . . . I could have gone on forever if I didn't have a cause, you know. Panic.

I have a girl friend, my age. Very close. And she says to me, "You mean you went out to dinner with him and you didn't make love?" "Well, we just met," says I. And I have another friend of mine who's about six years older, and she says, "I know the minute I look at a man if I'm going to sleep with him or not, and if I am I go home and make love to him."

I was wait-and-see. With the first few men, I thought the object was that you were to lie there until the man came or something. We were obviously inexperienced. I thought the man was supposed to fuck you, to have intercourse, until he came, and that was it. I don't know where I got that notion. And the guilt!

My deadline with guys varied. It was seldom on the first date. Burt Reynolds says people fuck too soon. You don't find out if you have anything in common. But you don't find that out anyway 'cause you're always wanting the other person if you're not making love to them and you really dig them. Because that's the only way we think about somebody. If I'm really digging them it has to be the second time. I mean, I don't mind the tease. I don't mind dragging it out. I don't know. I'm never an easy jumper into bed, unless it's just overwhelming. And then it's probably not the first time. But my friend says—oh, that's so absurd of her.

Hey, I had some affairs. A lot. A little. I don't know. Maybe somewhere in between. Sure, I had the idea virginity was of some significance. Are you kidding? One time I knew Marlon Brando, and at the time, I had bleached blond hair and weighed thirty pounds more and I talked nonstop. And he likes those quiet—whatever. One night we ended up in a situation where we could have made love and I spent the evening saying, "No, no, no." He was my hero of all time. But I said, "I want it to be special." What an idiot I was. Then I met him two Christmases ago with the friends I'd known him with before, and I was just separated from my husband, and there he was. "Sally, this is Marlon. Marlon, this is Sally." And he says, "How do you do." And Sam says, "Marlon, this is Sally Kellerman." And when Sam said "Kellerman" Marlon leaped up and embraced me and said, "I didn't recognize you. How you've changed!" But then passed the warmth of hello. Luckily I've lived past that. I wanted to be special. God!

But I love it now. Somewhere along the line I met a man that I had an affair with and I loved him. I quickly realized the, ah, beauty of the act. This too happened to me in my early twenties, so I was lucky. He lives right around the corner now, very happily married. He really does.

I was certainly an emancipated woman who wanted to find a full sexual life, have a normal sex life and not be stiff. And once I met this guy, the one I had an affair with for about a year or so, it just broke me loose. Since I've been single most of my life, I don't mind that there's been more than one man. I think that's healthy. I'm not promiscuous. I'm not somebody who sleeps with everybody I meet, but in my growing years I certainly had more than one lover. And I'm glad I did. I'd like to be as healthy in other areas. You know, now that I've worked that out, I wish I were a whole human being. Yes. I didn't want to be tied up. I wanted to love the human body and love the experience of that union with someone that you care about. Be available, you know.

Florynce (Flo) Kennedy *feminist lawyer*

Born February 11, 1916, Kansas City, Kans.

*A kind of dense jungle of law books, papers, periodicals, dirty
dishes and filled ashtrays had grown up in her mid-Manhat-
tan apartment, but Flo Kennedy, the author of two women's
lib books and an influential founding member of both NOW
and the Feminist party, waved it away with nonchalant dis-
dain: "Listen, honey, I'm a better housekeeper than I used to
be," she said. She was expecting guests; a pot of macaroni
from the deli up the street sat on the stove. She wore blue
jeans, a white T-shirt and a rough leather vest, yet her finger-
nails were very long, very red, and impeccably manicured.
She wore a myriad of gold chains with whistles and other
baubles around her neck, and both wrists were festooned
with big clear plastic bracelets. An inverted v of tiny Indian
beads disappeared from her forehead into her tight gray
Afro, and at her waist was anchored a chic Vuitton pouch.
She sat down in her darkened living room, where the drapes
were pulled tight, and talked rapidly and fluently in a thick,
high-pitched voice, as if she were repeating a familiar litany,
about her childhood and sex. A woman friend sat through the
interview with her, but that did not inhibit her at all.*

I KNEW WHEN I WAS eight or ten or twelve that sex was over-rated; I knew that no matter what you did in the middle of the night, you woke up, the rent was due and everything else. So I was pretty cool about sex because I understood that there was an attempt on the part of the Establishment, though I didn't use that kind of language, to make you believe love and sex was a great super thing, and it was really just a trap to get you married, and nobody with taste and brains wanted to be married. In 1946, when I was thirty, way before I ever dreamed of having anything that would approach a serious love affair, I wrote a little piece called "The Case Against Marriage," in which I suggested that you wouldn't lock yourself in the bathroom because you had to go three times a day, and you wouldn't sign up to eat your favorite delicious meal for breakfast, lunch and dinner every day of your life, so why get married. Marriage was for the birds, and if you didn't have web feet and feathers, you shouldn't bother. I was always political enough to understand that the sex thing was oversold and overrated and that society for some reason wanted you to get entangled and enmeshed in it, and to the extent that you did, you were cooperating in a big con game. I was always leery of society's reasons for wanting me in it. Why are they giving me all this orange-blossom shit when I know all it leads to is dirty diapers and smelly milk-throw-up shoulder? I knew I didn't want no kids—they were heavy, they peed, they screamed, they cried, they bit you. What in the hell did I want that for?

I realized that most people didn't, don't, feel that way, but I just wasn't into the romance scene. Sex led to marriage. Forget the children. The thought of marriage was worse than the thought of pregnancy. So, to me, you didn't get sleeping with people because you might want to marry them. See, the thing I always worried about was that I might want to marry them; I didn't care what they wanted. I might get swindled into this scene and want to get married. But if you made your own money you had no need for marriage. My theory was that marriage had no romantic basis, that it was purely an economic arrangement; it was a money matter and you did it to change your life rather than because of love or sex or kissing or hugging or hard-on or hard-off or any of that crap. My sisters and I used to go to the dances in high school and laugh about the boys with their hard-ons. To me sex was always much more a question of gamesmanship. He's trying to get something from me that I'm not about to give him and why should I? I'm going to trick him out. There wasn't that much outrage at the fellow; in other words he was supposed to go as far as he could and you were supposed to not let him. Let's say you had an income of $150 and you knew people were going to try to rip you off for it, and you just had to be very, very careful that nobody was going to rip you off for your bread. It was a power trip.

I don't need to trade off pussy for a dinner, okay? I just don't need to deal in that shit. I always felt that when women would say, "Oh, does he take you to a good place or a cheap place?" that that was prostitution of a sort. I felt that nobody was really that into sex but they used it as a bargaining point. I just put it on a totally rational basis. To me a fuck was a fuck and if you wanted to go fuck somebody, go fuck somebody. You didn't have to get into all this business of morals and love and marriage and having kids. If you want to fuck the guy, fuck the guy. But I could never see what was so great about making big pools or small pools or spots in sheets or clothes. It just seemed like drinking coffee, which everybody did, which wasn't good, or drinking liquor, which everybody did, which didn't taste half as good as lemonade or grape soda pop or even grapefruit juice. It wasn't that I thought that romances weren't fun or that kissing and petting and sex wasn't a great thing, but you see, I never saw sex or love as anything that I could afford. I couldn't afford it. It was something that could really take up your time and really get you entangled. For me it would be like taking up golf or taking up flying—just taking up something I wasn't interested in.

The difference between me on the sex thing and a lot of people is that I was never deprived so it was no great adventure. I had a sister Evelynn (we called her Lynn) a year older and a sister Grace (who we called Gay), who was a year and a half younger than me, and we were a trio of little hellions. My mother was crazy about us and we were really cool and we really had a ball and we were into a whole lot really early. I mean we were really crazy. For example, after the church meetings—and we could go or not go; my parents never did a church number—we'd go around and smell the different seats to see what the women smelled like. We thought that was funny as hell. And my mother was never outraged in a moral sense at anything we did. We'd tell her dirty jokes and she'd laugh. When we told her how the kids would smoke in the basement she'd say, "Don't ever smoke in the basement; you smoke up here." My mother was smart and intelligent, with taste and brains and very cool and very smart; she'd gone to normal school, which would be the equivalent of a teachers' college, which for a black person at that time would be like getting a Ph.D. And she trusted us. I never remember any kind of punishment over sexuality. It was her feeling that if she hadn't dealt with us appropriately we would do inappropriate things; and if we were going to do it, she couldn't follow us around, so she just had to trust us. She never hit us and she never interfered or got into our shit. She was very much inclined to respect a person's privacy. To show how permissive she was, she once gave us castor oil and I threw up and she never gave us castor oil again.

I never hardly saw my daddy sit down at dinner or anything like that, because he was a taxi driver and he always had to be getting up to the stand at 2 o'clock in the afternoon. Before that he was a waiter; see, he couldn't work for other people because he had a bad temper, so he had to be where he was sort of semi-independent. He was from Alabama and my mom was born in Kentucky; both their moms were born into slavery, and I guess they met when he was a waiter somewhere, but who in the hell knows. They really got along great. He and Zella—I call my mom Zella because it's my theory that people kill their mothers so calling them Mother doesn't mean you care, and mine was special so I called her by her name—anyway, he and Zella were not terribly demonstrative, but they never argued. I remember they had a big argument during the Depression because she was going to work and he didn't want her to, and that's one of the few times I ever saw my daddy cry. He really treated her good and he was kind of a cranky type and she was more demonstrative than him, but we weren't a kissing-hugging type group. They really did definitely like each other and it was very obvious, but I don't remember if they kissed each other much. He would probably kiss her whenever he came in or out, but I never in my life saw them sitting anywhere with his arm around her or something like that. But you know we knew they were cool. And we were cool.

The main thing was, Daddy would come almost every day and take the three of us around the block before he went to work. He always had a big sedan, because that was his work, but it didn't have a sign or a meter on it. It was like having a small plane now, because for people, black or white, to have a car in the twenties was a big deal. The reason I have this scar on my face is because Daddy was watching somebody in a Model T who was black and he was so amazed that he wrecked the car—not a bad wreck, but I went through the windshield. Then of course I got a toy, a bicycle or something, because I didn't cry when they sewed me up. So every day before he went off we'd get in the car and scrunch in the corner, because we would act like he didn't realize how long he was taking us and if we didn't say anything he would drive us that much farther. We'd be quiet like mice and we'd look at each other and we wouldn't make a sound. Then when we got home we'd say, "Oh, Daddy, thank you so much, we had such a wonderful ride." Then we'd run into the house and tell Zella. We'd always run to the corner to meet her; we were just really, really crazy about her. I used to wake up in the morning and it would be sunny and sometimes there'd be a fly, but most often it would just be nice.

When we were like five and six Mother took us to California and we were horrified when my older sister, Lynn, told us our parents were separated. We thought it was a terrible disloyal thing. We couldn't even believe it. They'd write letters all the time; he was very, very smart but wrote a kind of dumb letter. He always wrote in pencil and he'd capitalize the first letter of the sentence and put a period at the end but if an "I" was in the middle he would just have a small little baby "i," and we thought that was really cute. I still don't think they were separated in the classic sense. It was just that she wanted to get away from Kansas City, where we lived, and he had this taxi cab and the Depression was coming on and he was very conservative, not in his politics but in his personal thing. So we came to Los Angeles and she had boyfriends and we thought that was hilarious. We weren't upset. We were proud. It was so swinging to have a mother who had a boyfriend, shit! She was very good-looking by black people's standards. She sort of had high cheekbones and a thin face and she was a little heavy in the waist—she was what she called short-waisted. She had nice legs and probably weighed about 135, and when she died at age fifty-three she wasn't as gray as I was at forty-five.

We stayed there for a couple of years, then my daddy came out because Mom got ptomaine poisoning and he brought us all back to our very same house on Walren Street, in an all-white neighborhood in Kansas City. In fact, he had never changed the sheets and they had to be thrown away. We lived in a tacky, tall, straight-up-and-down frame house very close to the sidewalk. You walked up seven or eight stairs and it had a wooden porch and then you walked into this hall, which ultimately was my grandmother's bedroom at some point before she died; then you walked into our room, which had the stove and a big double bed for the three of us; then you walked into Zella and Daddy's room. We just had a drape that hung from a pole between those two rooms, but they were fairly good-sized. At night in the wintertime we'd all pee in this bucket, which would be half full of water, instead of going downstairs to this cold bathroom.

My mother was determined to make the house look attractive. So every season she'd go to the Jones Store Company in Petticoat Lane, downtown Kansas City, and she would buy rosebushes, five for a dollar or maybe six for five dollars, but they never grew because there was a big maple tree in the yard that killed all the sun and we didn't have brains enough to prune the branches. Nobody cared but my mother, and every year she would go buy more, and it was like a standing joke and we would just be hysterical and she'd laugh too.

See, my mother believed in fun, so even though we didn't have much money we had an atmosphere of having a ball. She would automatically call all the creditors around October and tell them, "You won't get the November payment and you won't get your December payment; I have to have Christmas for my kids." Nothing kept us from having big parties. My daddy would go to a place in the black community where you could get soda pop for twenty cents a gallon —they didn't drink; my dad got lit occasionally, but very, very occasionally—and we would have sixty people over and music. And sometimes we'd get somebody from the orphan home and give them a dollar or something and they'd be nearly our same age and they would pick up the glasses. So we did things that poor people normally don't do. Maybe twice a week Daddy would bring home frog legs or he'd be on a barbecue binge and he'd bring home barbecue. He didn't get off until two in the morning, so he'd come in and wake us up in the middle of the night and we'd all sit in bed and eat all this food.

Mother was very much into trying to keep us not looking depressed or oppressed. We didn't have the money, so she was always making us clothes. When we were in California she made each of us a little black sateen slip. Mine was bordered with apricot and pink maybe, Gay's with green and peach, and Lynn's with lavender and green. On each side there were appliquéd flowers of the same color and they would be slit up to the thigh and we'd have little black satin bloomers underneath. We were "fly" as hell.

Zella was very honest. She was very depressed during the Depression because she almost had to take welfare. She wanted them to give her a loan so she could pay it back. Once a woman accused her of stealing—this was when she was working as a domestic. She just got furious and she stripped down to zero. She had the curse and they didn't use Kotex if they were poor, so they would have these cloths or towels; I don't know if they washed them over or soaked them or what. Anyway, she took this sanitary cloth and shook it in this woman's face to show her she didn't have anything of hers. And she said, "Give me my money and let me get out of here." So in other words, at no point, no matter how low our circumstances, we never took shit. When we were very small I remember my big sister, Lynn, who was and still is very conservative and very timid, came running in because Gladys Hiromus had hit her and Gladys Hiromus was smaller than my sister. So my mom made Lynn go out and hit Gladys Hiromus back. We were taught not to take any shit. The principal of the Wendell Phillips School, the black school—we had to pass two or three white schools to get to it—was about to hit me once and my daddy was on the way down to pick me up and the Browns told him I was in Mr. Cox's office and he went home and got a gun, honey. We were polite and made fantastically great grades and we weren't to take shit from nobody.

I remember once Gay had a fellow that slapped her and she just dropped him cold, absolutely cold. And I did have this uncle and once I was in his car and he just sort of moved his hand or something and, boy, I didn't ever mention it to anybody but, boy, I just never felt the same way about him.

But there was absolutely no prohibition about sex. My mother didn't get into that scene at all. We were having kissing parties when we were six and seven and we'd just giggle our asses off. I don't remember the first time I was kissed, because it wouldn't have been a big thing. I think the

reason a lot of people remember it is because they got into
trouble. We did not get into trouble at all. We were heavy
into necking and petting by the age of twelve and thirteen.
They would touch our breasts, under the sweaters, everything short of actual fucking. We weren't much into feeling
below the belt; you know boys were a little scared, too. Hell,
we'd be doing it with fellows on the front porch, but my
mother completely absented herself. She might have fainted
if she'd known how many guys we were kissing. We kept kiss
lists of everybody we'd kissed all summer. And of course the
idea was to kiss as much as you wanted but never put out. It
was a very definite game. I mean you never fucked anybody;
you just didn't get anywhere near that. We had such freedom
and we didn't take shit, see. Well, here's the thing, when we
were old enough to drive we had access to our daddy's car
and we'd go hang out at the swimming pool or sometimes
we'd drive over to a club or a carnival in Topeka and come
in at two or three in the morning. I knew Mother was very
agonized and very worried, but she never told us when to be
in. Sometimes Dad would see us talking to guys up on
Twelfth Street way late at night—you've heard of the
"Twelfth Street Rag"? Because we had the car and were
into clothes—King Tut sweaters, pleated skirts and black-
and-white shoes, Carol Teen–type clothes—nobody thought
we were as young as we were. See, the three of us all went
out together and we usually ended up with older guys and
when we'd get home we'd compare notes if there was anything that the other ones didn't already know. I was very
small for a while; in fact, Uldine Johnson and I were the
littlest ones in the grammar school graduation, and I used to
stuff Kleenex in where the tits should be. I also remember
wetting a handkerchief with liquor so it seemed like I drank.

What we let them do would depend on how cute they

were and whether we really dug them. In terms of the games-manship we'd be pretty questioning of somebody who was going to start getting fresh on the first date, but it was much more that we weren't going to let them take advantage of us. We were slick; we were smart; we were hip. It was not a question of morals. It was just a question of this creep tried to be cute and we weren't about to let him get away with it.

Lynn was kind of romantic; Grace was a hard bargainer but seemed sweet; and I didn't try to appear nice or sweet, I just laid it out. We knew we had what it took for other people to want to be around us. We had the car; we had parties; we had a lot of friends. We knew a lot of people so that we really didn't need them and we knew they needed us. We were more interested in adding names to our list and in finding a circle of friends we could have fun with than in trying to get some kind of big deep relationship. We were much more into a power trip. Nobody was smarter, nobody was better, so we didn't need them. If people went to proms and we didn't have the kind of connection to get us to the prom, we'd know of something better that was happening that night, like a public dance at Fifteenth and Paseo where Georgie Lee or Fletcher Henderson or Duke Ellington was going to be. Sometimes we didn't have money to go in and we'd stand out at the windows.

We really, really, really played the field because we understood that there was no way you could not have to put out if you got with one single person. It was almost like we played Scrabble. I was bragging just before I got married that I'd never had three dates in succession with the same guy, and I didn't get married until I was forty. Before I married Charlie, this half-drunken Welshman, the only half-serious affair I'd had was with Earle when I was like nine-teen. He was the first guy I slept with, I guess because he was better looking than a lot of the guys and even slightly more intelligent. He had freckles and a kind of reddish mustache and sandy hair, and I think he drove a truck and maybe played a trumpet or something. Anyway it didn't last long at all, and I don't know what happened to him. It was not a big love thing. The demarcation between petting with just dozens and dozens of guys and making it with one was not a big thing. I would not be able to tell you the first time I made out with Earle. I couldn't tell you where it was and what was going on. I just know we were never anyplace where we could undress and take our clothes off, I mean I just never was in that circumstance, so I'm sure the first time was some kind of tussle in the back seat of a car. I just can't bring back the circumstance. I wouldn't think I was that crazy about him. I think it was much more a question of opportunity and of course the fact that he was cute and the fact that there wasn't a hell of a lot you could do with him because he always wore these overalls and you couldn't take him anywhere.

I would say that Charlie was the first person I ever just took off my clothes and went to bed with. By then I was in my late thirties and he was ten years younger. He was the first person I spent the night with, and we ultimately married. I would say he was the only guy I ever stayed overnight with. He was keeping the place of a friend who was a homosexual; Charlie was about half-fag himself, a drunken science fiction writer. I smelled his breath about the third time I ever went out with him and I just knew because he had that saturated smell. So my theory with him was just let him do anything he wants, because I figured he wasn't going to press the marriage thing. But I think he was just so desperate; I think he was in much worse condition psychologically and physically than I realized. He was so badly off that he couldn't cruise any further. So we married—to me it was like going to Lausanne although you hate cold weather—and three years later he was dead. The only other person I sort of had an affair with was a client later on, and that was like twelve or fifteen years ago.

I've never had a lesbian experience. Except on one occasion, a very, very wealthy woman whose place I was staying at let me know—nothing overt, she never said a word—that if I'd wanted to I could have moved into a person-to-person relationship with her. I'm sure she had many women lovers and didn't particularly need me. I have some theories about lesbianism, that very often women are together because they've had bad marriages or bad heterosexual experiences. Most women I know that would love a woman would also love a man; if a man they really dug came along they would go heterosexual. Of course, the women in the Movement now have a political commitment and feel it's a betrayal for a woman to have an affair with a man or get married; it would be like a white person going with a black person. Well, how many of these women would turn down a guy—whether they thought he was the sexiest creep in the world or not—who makes forty thousand a year and has halfway decent political commitments and is nice and sweet? Not many!

A lot of lesbians have had children themselves, you see, and been married, and have acted much more like a wife than I ever did with Charlie, because frankly, if there was a wife involved, he was more like a wife than I; he did so much of the cooking and he was neater. So in other words, I feel that I'm less sexual than a lot of women who are committed to making love to women. An appetite for sex would mean you'd be more likely to have a lesbian relationship than you would if you weren't particularly into the sex itself. A lot of women who go to school do a lot of exploration with girls and women. But we weren't into that. I don't know, I think in many ways my sisters and me, we were really quite puritanical. We weren't religious or anything, but we had pretty definite ideas about getting into sex so I would say that we were pretty heavily indoctrinated. Well, for example, when I was married to this drunken Welshman he would always laugh because I would close the door to the bathroom and even lock it sometimes. He couldn't understand that. Even to this hour I do it, and I still flush the toilet when I take a flying shit.

Personally I don't like people to massage my neck. I have a terrible back and it might be better, but I'm not into that. I would never get into masturbation and never have, no, no, no. In the first place my nails are too long; it would just be uncomfortable. My main reason for not masturbating is that I don't like touching things. In other words, some people like to touch their hair and their bodies. I don't. To me sex is like an interruption of my life and I guess it always has been.

Jack Lemmon *actor*

Born February 8, 1925, Newton, Mass.

There was an upbeat mood at the expensively paneled office of Richard Carter, head of Jack Lemmon's movie production company, for Save the Tiger *was getting rave notices, most of which said that Lemmon ought to get the Academy Award for it. Shortly after 2 P.M. Lemmon returned from a lunch date, excused himself to go to the bathroom, and then settled into a big squashy chair in Carter's office. He wore a knit sports shirt and a tweed jacket. His eyes were sad and a little bloodshot, and his voice was timid. He sipped red wine and smoked a long cigar as he talked, sometimes with a great deal of pain, about his early years, while Carter was on the phone four feet away talking business. There were frequent long periods of silence when Lemmon would stare out the window, then jerk back apologetically and say, "Oh, yeah, where was I?"*

I GREW UP IN NEWTON, Massachusetts, a nice middle-class suburb of Boston. I never thought about the deprived. A ghetto—I wouldn't have known what the fuck the word was.

Ecology or the state of the world around me or anything like that, just forget it. I think the whole background was something you took for granted as your way of life. I didn't have the awareness to start thinking about other communities, other worlds. All there was was you. I lived a normal middle-class life, running around with the other kids, doing the sports and going off to my private school each day.

It was not a religious school. I was born Catholic. By the time I was confirmed at the age of thirteen, I was already quite disillusioned. Both sides of my family came from Baltimore, but my mother's side was nowhere near as religious as my father's. I think she was Baptist. I say "I think" because she didn't really practice very much as far as the overt going to church. My father, on the other hand, came from a very strict Catholic family where they had the statues and the candles burning in the home. But he never really pushed me and I just got turned off. I was being told at Sunday school what I was supposed to feel rather than being able to feel something without feeling guilty. And I never could quite understand that no matter what I did, as long as I went into a booth and said so, I was forgiven. Once I was confirmed that ended it. I think that I personally am a very religious person. I don't overtly pray or anything like that, but I believe in something that's bigger than us, and I'm very aware of how I feel we should treat each other. So it becomes semantics as to whether or not I'm religious, but I feel I am and that's the most important thing.

My parents were rather strict but I'm not sure that they felt they were strict. My father was more the authoritarian. In retrospect, I think it was because of the image I had of him. I was very aware, possibly too aware—which was maybe not his intent—of measuring up to my father. I never got over that until I was quite old and had kind of proven to him, but mainly to myself, that I was on my own two feet and what in his terms would be successful. Then I could relax with him and we became very close, thank God.

But before that there was always the fear that I couldn't measure up. He was a pretty successful guy as we use the word. He ended up as vice president and general sales manager of something called The Doughnut Corporation of America. Actually it made more than doughnuts. It was a large company which made all those machines that they used to have in windows, you know, where the doughnuts were coming out. And they made dry mixes for bread and cakes and cookies. He wanted me to go into this company even though he knew damn well that I didn't want to do it. I always knew what I wanted to do and I would never be dissuaded from that. But he asked me nevertheless. He would have loved it. And that's a very normal thing—for the father who has made it, the self-made man. His family was not wealthy at all. He had worked his way up and he loved it. And when I said, "No, I don't want to do that and you know I don't. I want to be an actor because as long as I can ever remember I wanted to be an actor." And he said, "Do you really mean it and do you love it?" And I said yes. And he said, "Well, okay, Godspeed, because the day I don't find romance in a loaf of bread I'm gonna quit." And I've never forgotten that. In other words, do what you have to do or at least give it a crack.

My father was a very imposing man, pretty puritanical, I think. He had a code of behavior that one should behave a certain way. But he was a very popular guy, not cold at all. He was a marvelous, handsome man with a rather military bearing which made him look an inch or two taller than he really was. He was six feet or barely under but he looked like he was six-one or -two. And a handsome guy—the proper dress, extremely polite, a marvelous sense of humor, could tell a great story. He'd get up in nightclubs with Bill Robinson and do a soft-shoe with him. And yet he never lost that kind of bearing, that dignity that made him kind of awesome to me in a way. Also, I was the only child. I remember once when I was a kid I got into the tub and it was full of gin. I didn't know it. I put the goddamned hot water on and he could have shot me. I thought he was going to kill me. It was one of the few times I thought he was going to spank me. He tried to spank me once. On the way home from school—I must have been in the fourth or fifth grade—I was with some kids from the neighborhood, and one of the kids started throwing rocks at an old abandoned Victorian house. We went ape and busted about forty or fifty dollars' worth of windows. And the caretaker spotted us and told our parents. That was it. My father pulled me into my room, put me over his knee, and started to spank me. But he really couldn't do it. It never really hurt and finally I said, "That's twelve. Isn't that enough?" And he said, "Yes, I guess so." He just couldn't do it.

My mother was a wild, crazy, terrific broad and the two of them together were one of the great, great couples. For all his innate dignity and military bearing, my father had a marvelous sense of humor, which saved him, because my mother had a sensational one. She would be the one to say, "Screw his business. Be an actor." She had wanted secretly to be a singer when she was young but one didn't do that. One didn't go into show business, Jesus God. My old lady was pretty wild. She damned near destroyed herself with her wild living—late nights, booze and then a sleeping pill to go to sleep. She did pull herself together. She woke up one day in a hospital with a whole bunch of things sticking in her arms and suddenly said, "What the hell am I doing?" They had separated when I was eighteen and I think it kind of threw her. It was a mutual thing. They really should have done it. They made the mistake of thinking they were staying together for me. But a kid knows, and I knew. It really sort of disintegrated. They were two terrific people, but the marriage was not good.

I was not aware of their physical life. They apparently kept that rather private. I was more aware of the fights. You could hear those. You can hear mine too, I'll tell you. I inherited that. I was aware of the fact that they slept in separate rooms from the time I was like four or five on. I didn't think much about it until I was older. My mother always said it was because of his snoring. She did have a point. The kid could be heard for a city block. It was incredible. Nobody could sleep as soundly as that man. He had an uncanny thing which I've always admired. If we'd be driving, he would stop and pull over to the side of the road and say, "I'm a little sleepy." And he'd look at his watch and say, "I'm going to sleep for four minutes." And I'd sit there and within twenty seconds he'd be snoring, and four minutes later he'd wake up. He had a built-in alarm clock. He'd wake up, feel refreshed, and we'd drive on. That incredible control—one always felt that. It was another thing that unsettled me, because I ain't in control of myself, never have been.

I was a little slow about sex. I didn't have a full-fledged affair until I was eighteen or nineteen and in college. I remember one scene with my father about sex and one with my mother. When I was fourteen and going to Andover, my father and I were driving one day to the country and finally he said, "You know all about those birds and bees and all that jazz?" And I said, "Yeah, oh, yeah." And he said, "Good, well, as time goes on, if you're going to, well I mean, if, ah, always use a rubber." And that was all he ever said. Period.

Ever. Hell, I was four years away from the chance at that point anyway.

And once my mother—the only words she said to me about sex—came in and sat on the edge of my bed as I was lying down ready to go to sleep. I was around thirteen. And she said, "Do you ever play with your thing?"—or whatever she called it. I'm sure she didn't say cock or something like that. And lying, I said, "No. Why?" And she said, "Well that's good, because it can make you crazy." The age-old bit. I didn't believe it. When she left the room, I remember saying to myself, "Oh, well, I'm going to go crazy and I'm going to have a ball." The first time I masturbated I was twelve or thirteen; just like Portnoy, it flew across the room and hit the far wall. I wasn't conscious of feeling guilty about it. But I think that when I was a young man I still had strictures imposed by outside people—my parents, the church, who knows. I think that certain things without question have a profound cumulative affect. And it's one thing to fantasize; it's another thing to do. And I was very inhibited.

My first dates, if they can be called such, were around eleven, twelve, thirteen. We'd go to dancing school once a week. It would be a car pool. One of your parents would drive and let you pick up the girl on the way to the dance. I was nuts about all of them—every fucking one I ever picked up I thought was adorable. And sometimes I'd close myself in the closet where the phone was downstairs and call a girl and talk to her for a half hour. That was a big thing. All you did was talk. And then if you'd go by to see them—you had a big crush on them—on your bike, you'd sort of lie on the front lawn, and you'd lie side by side and talk for as long as you could. But you'd never try anything. We were very physically aware of each other, but nothing happened. And usually in my teens it was the age-old thing—holding hands in the movies. I'd get in a trolley car and go out to a girl's house in the suburbs somewhere, get her, maybe go all the way the hell back into Boston, see a movie, bring her back, talk for a while on the front porch, and hope to hell I'd get kissed good night.

The first time I got more than a kiss I was up in New Hampshire in the summer. We were lying out in a field at night, talking, leaning against an old well, and it was chilly. Even though it was summer it was chilly, the breeze was coming in off the lake, and she had a kind of light fur coat on and, I don't know, we were kissing and I just suddenly, just went *womp* and I grabbed it through the fur, the coat. I couldn't feel a stinkin' thing but I knew my hand was there. You couldn't have moved it with a bulldozer. And I remember thinking to myself, "She isn't trying to move it, she isn't trying." And then I gathered all my courage and before we left I had it under the coat and, boy, wow, for days I kept thinking about that. It was not under her dress; I wouldn't go that far.

When I began dating seriously at the age of eighteen or nineteen, I'd go just so far, you know, with the petting and the necking, but I was very reluctant to even intimate that we should do it. That was unattainable. I was very scared by the whole goddamned thing. When you heard that a guy had gotten it, that was terrific. I was very interested in how you do that, I mean, you could get your head knocked off. I guess maybe there was a lot more going on then than I thought. You'd hear about bad girls now and then. That goes back to the old double standard. It's okay if you can, but you wouldn't want to marry a girl that did. I had those stupid strictures. It may be okay for the fellow but in the meantime the girl has done something wrong. I don't know how the hell they thought they were going to do it unless it was with a girl. It's a transference of guilt I guess. I think people are much less ingrained with it today. I don't think my father ever played around; I truly don't think so. I never had a thought or an inkling that he was philandering at all. Not that it would be that rare. But I just don't think he did. I have a feeling in retrospect that the marriage deteriorated physically as much as anything. The attraction was gone between them. The bloom wore off.

The first time I had an affair I was in a parked car in a parking lot in Harvard Square. I had just gotten to Harvard and had ended up that evening with a girl I had met several times. She was older—twenty-two or twenty-three—not a student, working in the bookstore. We'd been to a movie and had a couple of beers and somehow got into this car in the parking lot around one A.M. It wasn't my car. It was an old Model A or something, a convertible with the old stick gearshift. We're in the seat and I can't get over this shift and I'm trapped and I'm going fucking crazy and I'm sweating and it's just the most uncomfortable goddamned thing you can imagine. Finally, I'm upside-down and my feet go through a rip that's in the goddamned canvas and one of them gets caught. Now—this is the God's truth—we're in this car, we don't know whose car, in the corner of this parking lot and there's such a commotion going on and I'm saying "My foot's caught," and she's saying, "Wow, Oh, Ah" because I'm moving around to try to get my foot out. She thinks I'm terrific, right? I'm just trying to get my stupid foot out. And all of a sudden, a voice and a flashlight in front of us: "Who is that? Who's in there?" And the attendant, who I didn't think was even on at that time of night, was coming towards us. My foot was still caught and I said to her—now get this—I said to her, "Someone's coming." And she said, "Not yet." I'll never forget it although it really didn't hit me until afterwards.

And the guy came and shined the light at us and, oh, Christ, it's a wonder I ever did it again. If that didn't turn me off nothing would. That's probably what slowed me down for ten years. Anyway, the guy was hollering things like, "Get out of there; I could have you arrested," while we tried to pull on our clothes. She just had her panties off and I had my Navy bellbottoms—I was in the Reserve—pulled down. We got out and I walked her back to her boarding house. I was really repulsed. Physically it was such an impossibility; you had to be an acrobat. I never came. Jesus Christ, it was not at all touching. I didn't feel guilty, just disappointed. You had visions, you know, of the deep thrust. But instead— up, down, up, down. I had enough sense to realize that it would take King Kong under those circumstances to stay cool.

The next time was a little while later with the same girl. She understood. She was an oldie; she'd been around. And a very, very sweet girl, bright girl too. This time was in her boarding house, which was more pleasant, but still a little quick as most of them were at first.

I had one other unfortunate experience when I was very young in which I thought that a girl I had had an affair with was pregnant. And she was locked away in some private boarding school in New Hampshire and four months went by during which time nothing could be done about it. By then I was an out-of-work actor in New York and I was petrified. An abortion? No way. We wouldn't have known how to do it or where to get it. And more time was going by and we could only talk on the phone on Sundays when she was allowed to go down into the town. And then, *boom*, it suddenly happened. She sent a telegram which said everything was okay. I have never breathed a bigger sigh of relief. She turned out not to be pregnant but, Jesus Christ, I know the whole thing had an effect. I was inhibited for a long time, I think even in my first marriage.

I tell you truthfully I don't feel that I ever really opened up until my second marriage, and that's been terrific. It's violent; it all hangs out, which I think is very healthy. Nothing is held back between us, which is a switch from the way I spent my life until then. I was thirty-eight when I married Felice [Felicia Farr, the actress]. We had gone together four or five years. I had always had great self-doubts—the male ego, were you satisfying them, all that crap. You worried about how great a lover you might be even if you were running around with all these gals. A whole generation was prey to that. And it's funny, because I could let it all hang out on the stage. I was much readier to take chances and expose myself up there, in the sense of opening up, than I could individually as Jack Lemmon. And to this day I will still feel more exposed by far when I'm on a show as myself, like on Johnny Carson, than when I'm playing a part. Now it may be that psychologically you hide behind the part, but actually it's not that unhealthy. I think it just exists in actors, that they are more comfortable very often when they are somebody else. And there are some actors who become actors, I'm sure, because of a real need to be somebody else, I mean a real need. If they didn't have that outlet they'd become real basket cases.

I guess I was frightened of women, of doing something wrong, of being rejected. There's that age-old story about the guy you can't believe, who'll go up to some woman and say, "You want to fuck?" And he gets his face slapped but every now and then he gets fucked. Well I could never do that. I might get slapped. That, coupled with the age-old fear of inadequacy and everything else that afflicted us at that time, that made it all too bloody important. Kids today don't think of it that way. If they're attracted to each other, that's that. It seems to me they don't have the hang-ups to anywhere near the extent we did.

I think I was self-centered when I was young. You sort of have to be in this crazy business, in which you've got a chance in a million anyway. You may have talent but you have to have luck, the right place, the right time, the right part. And you're going to have to have a drive possibly beyond the norm because the odds are rather slim. If someone had said to me when I was in my early twenties and through with my education and the Navy and in New York, "You know, you really have one chance in a million," I'd have said, "Don't worry, I'll make it." It took me a long time before I could stop thinking and worrying and start living just for me, before I was mature enough to become aware of things in life that might be more important than how the hell I'm reading a line.

Liberace *entertainer*

Born May 16, 1919, West Allis, Wis.

The huge Las Vegas Hilton showroom was packed with Middle Americans, short-haired men in short-sleeved shirts, churchgoing women in their night-out clothes, many of them looking mildly stunned at the prices (medallion of salmon, $16; prime rib, $17, all plus 13½ per cent tax). But their faces lit up when the glittery curtain ascended, a chauffeured pearl-gray Rolls landau rolled onto the stage, and out stepped Liberace, draped in a floor-length ermine coat, his hands ablaze with diamond rings. The crowd roared its approval, and Liberace proceeded into a medley of familiar piano songs before giving way to a teen-age banjo prodigy and a troupe of Korean folk dancers, saying as he exited, "Excuse me while I go slip into something even more fantastic." The crowd loved him, and there was a long flood of applause as Liberace, resplendent in a dazzling sequined suit, finally sailed aloft and into the wings on a wire hoist, waving his arms in a burlesque of Peter Pan. A few minutes later he appeared in the spacious parlor of his sub-basement dressing room, still heavily made up, wearing a powder-blue jump suit—and looking not even slightly fatigued. He sipped a gin and tonic and smoked several cigarettes while chatting in a completely uninhibited and cheerful manner, pausing

only to speak long distance with a real estate agent who was
trying to sell one of his two Palm Springs houses.

I'M NOT A PRUDE or a puritan about sex, because it's a part of
life. I've always been adventurous, and I believe in experi-
encing things. I'm good when I'm supposed to be good and
bad when I'm supposed to be bad. I'm no angel. I've done
everything and I'm proud of it. I have nothing to hide.

Sometimes people come up to me and say, "Do you know
what so-and-so is doing to so-and-so and who's in the middle?" I always say, "Sounds great!" I believe that as long as
you don't hurt another person, whatever your bag is, if that's
what you dig, great!

When I was in London I worked at the same studio as Tom
Jones and the word around the studio was that he pads his
pants. So people kept saying to me, "You have the same
dresser, ask him, ask him if Tom Jones pads his pants." So
finally I said, "Keith, tell me the truth, does he pad his
pants?" and he said, "Yeah." So I said, "Great. He's smart.
He's found out what the people like and he gives it to them.
So he uses padding in his pants. Why not? Girls use silicone
in their boobs."

I hate it when people whisper things and think they're
giving me a juicy bit. Like, "I just heard something about
someone you know. It's so-and-so. He sucks cock." I say,
"Great! Fantastic!" It's all a lot of shit. Who cares?

That story in the papers not long ago about my announc-
ing that I was not a homosexual was completely false. What
happened was a very simple, innocent thing. I won a big
trial in London in 1959 against this columnist who accused

me of homosexuality in something he wrote in 1956. So not long ago I had this press conference in San Francisco to announce my autobiography and talk about my show, and this son-of-a-bitch says, "Do you feel the same way about homosexuality that you did when you fought your trial in London?" I said, "Whatever I said in the high courts of London, I meant, and if I said it then I mean it now." So he took this one line out of twelve days of testimony and quoted it completely out of context without any explanation at all.

For me to say something like that today would be stupid. It made it appear that I'm down on gay people. Shit, I resented it. I never said it! For me to spend the rest of my life dwelling on that article is absolutely ridiculous. If it were written today I'd probably go out and buy a hundred copies and send it to all my friends and say, "Isn't this the funniest thing you ever read?" But in 1956, people were destroyed by that accusation. It hurt me. People stayed away from my shows in droves. I went from the top to the bottom in a very short time, and I had to fight for my life. And I won, and I came back. Now people couldn't care less about that kind of thing. I kid about it on stage in my shows, talk about my balls and all that kind of thing. People love it. They couldn't care less how I swing.

I had a past and had sown my wild oats by the time I was fifteen years old. And I don't regret it, because I was burned up with the desire to be a success by the time I was twenty-one and leading a wild life would have hurt me. I played the Palmer House in Chicago and the Waldorf Astoria in my early twenties and I played with the Chicago Symphony when I was nineteen, and all this glory so early in life could have really spoiled me for later things if I hadn't matured some. I've never been turned on by drugs, and I'm an absolute teetotaler when it comes to work. It's almost a religion with me. I never drink before I work. I had a couple of bad experiences early in life with drinking, and I learned that I can't do it. I played in a lot of those speakeasy roadhouse places during Prohibition and one night when I was about fifteen they were passing the bottle around and I wanted to be one of the boys so I took a drink and passed out and threw up all over my brother George's uniform. He was eight years older than I was and was playing in name bands. He'd bring these uniforms home and hang them up in the closet and I'd snitch them. Oh, God, was I sick. I was the star of this little group. It had a saxophone, drums, trumpet, guitar and a piano, and we did what they called "casuals" at these roadhouses around Milwaukee, where I grew up. They didn't have microphones or anything, so I sang through a megaphone. I did all the vocals.

I was making maybe twenty-five dollars a night and that was good money during the Depression, more than everybody else in the family at home was making put together. We always had food on the table, but we were poor. My younger brother and sister and my mother and my father all worked. At the end of the week we'd sit down at the kitchen table and pool our resources, and then I got an allowance. My father and mother were very simple, middle-class and conservative, but they were very happy people. My father was a classical musician but he had to play in the American Legion band to make money. He also worked in a factory. My mother ran a grocery store and worked at the Johnston Cookie Company. They were Roman Catholic and very religious. There was liquor around the house and I had wine with meals when I was a kid, mixed with water. But my father felt very strongly about smoking. He used to take all my cigarettes and painstakingly put pinholes in them so they wouldn't draw.

We didn't get any of that birds-and-bees talk about sex. I learned it the hard way. I started playing in these speakeasies and strip joints when I was thirteen. In a tuxedo I looked a lot older and I was big for my age. When I was fifteen I was playing for strippers at these stag shows where they would also show fuck movies. They would go out and round up these strippers in a bus, and nine times out of ten the girls wouldn't have any music. They'd say something like, "Well, when I come out the first time play some waltzes, and then the next time play a foxtrot, and the next time play something peppy." I could understand why, because each time they came back they had less and less on. I'll tell you how innocent I was when I started. The first time I saw a lady smoke, I stopped playing. I'd never seen a lady smoke before. So when I saw that for the first time, I stopped playing, and the girl said, "Hey, you son-of-a-bitch. Keep playing."

But they all loved me, and to this day I like strippers. They're very sensitive, misunderstood people. One night we got raided and I was busted and put on probation. My probation officer had an artificial hand. He sat me down in his office at the courthouse and said, "You know, you have a great gift. Don't burn it up. Don't sell it short. I would love to do what you do. But I can't. I have only one hand. Now you can go either way. You can go on with this drinking and wild company or you can put that behind you as experience and start thinking of your future. You've sown your wild oats." He was a fantastic guy.

One of the conditions of my probation was that I couldn't work if my grades didn't stay up. I was a very unusual case at the West Milwaukee High School, because I was the only one allowed to come to school at eleven-fifteen. That was because I was working at night. All the boys in school wanted to talk about their conquests and sex, and they would come up to me in the locker room and say, "Where did you go last night? Who were you with? What was she like? How far did you go? Did you bang her?" I was having some pretty weird experiences and I'd tell these kids about them and they'd sit there and be my audience. They said, "Oh, you didn't do that. Did you really do that?"

Like, I lost my virginity, if you can call it that, when I was about thirteen. I think I was raped. I was playing piano for my brother's first wife at this place called Pick's Club Madrid, which was a very fancy club for that area. All the Chicago crowd would come down. She was a soubrette and did those cutesy-pootsy kind of songs. Every major nightclub in those days had a prima donna who sang operatic things like Jeanette MacDonald, and then they had soubrettes who did these flirtatious kind of songs. They were table singers. I had a little piano on wheels, and we went around from table to table and the girls would sing and I would play. Sometimes we would get a five- or ten-dollar tip to sing a song, and at the end of the night in the dressing room the girls would split their tips with me. They also had a kind of big production show twice a night, and in between them I would hang around the Twenty-Six game, which was a dice game they had in those clubs. If you won, you got a coupon for prizes they kept in this case. I was a shill for the dice game. I would stand around and look very longingly at this Charlie McCarthy doll until some big spender came along and said, "Heh, kid, do you want that doll? I'll see if I can win it for you." He'd play all night and finally win it and give it to me. I'd say, "Thank you very much. I really appreciate it." Then I would take it to the dressing room, and at the end of the night it went back in the case.

Anyway there was a girl who worked in this place who was a friend of my brother's wife. She was a big, chesty broad who sang blues songs. She was a very good-looking woman, and kind of wild, but she was old enough to be my mother—in her thirties. My brother played in the orchestra and his wife sang, so every night we three all rode home together. One night this singer said to them, "Look, I've got a couple of hot customers. I need him to stay and play. I'll drive him home, and I'll divide the tips with him." So I stayed and played and we went around the tables, and she was having drinks and all. After we closed, she started driving home. It was about a twenty-mile drive. It was a warm summer night and she was driving some kind of covered hardtop car. After a while she pulled over and stopped on the side of this dirt road and all of a sudden this hand started coming up my leg and she said, "Oh, you're a big boy, aren't you?" Then she took it out and started gobbling it. I didn't quite know what was happening, but I liked it, I liked it. I was all ready in a few minutes for a repeat. Then she crawled over on my lap and screwed me. It was very fast, like, would you believe about five strokes?

And, oh, God, I had lipstick all over my white pants. I went home and tried to wash it off, because I was afraid my mother would see it. The next day in school I said to the kids, "You'll never believe what happened to me last night," and when I told them, they said, "Aw, come on, you're making it up."

I made George promise he'd never tell, because she was his wife's best friend, and then I told him what happened. I thought it would be a big revelation, because I had never had anybody go down on me before, but George really put me down. He said, "Is that the first time you ever had that happen to you? Christ, you're really a kid."

"None of the boys at school ever had anything like that happen to them," I said.

"Well, they're just babies," he said.

"They're the same age I am," I said.

"Well, then you're a baby, too," he said.

But I was ready for it. The only part I didn't like was trying to get the lipstick off my pants. I screwed her a few times after that, under better conditions. She had a place. My brother kept his promise. He never told his wife, and she thought I was the sweetest thing in the world.

I think I found out about masturbation from my brother. I caught him doing it. So then I tried it. I must have been about eleven then.

I was closer to my father later in life than I was as a boy. He was very strict with me, mostly about the music. He wouldn't let me play any popular music, no jazz, no nothing. He was a strict taskmaster. If I didn't know my school lessons he'd punish me by locking the piano, and I would beg him to let me play it.

My father's ninety-one now, still living, but he's next to being a vegetable. He's in a convalescent home in Sacramento, and my brother and his wife look after him. The last time I went to see him he didn't recognize me, and that hurt me. He told my brother George, "That's not him. I know my boy, and that's not him."

George said, "Did you look at his rings? Who else would wear all of that?" but my father said, "It's not him." I made my brother promise not to ever force me to go again. I don't want to remember him that way.

We were a very close-knit family. My father loved classical music and he was very serious about it, worshiped it. When

I was about nineteen Leopold Stokowski came to Milwaukee and I bought two tickets to the concert for him, with my own money. They cost fifteen dollars apiece. I went to my father and said, "I've got a surprise for you. I have two tickets for Leopold Stokowski."

He made up a whole bunch of excuses.

"Take one of your friends," he said. "I really can't go. I have to rehearse."

So I went to the concert, and there sitting two rows in front of me was my father with another woman. That's how I found out he'd had a mistress for years. My mother knew about it, but she tolerated it. It was a terrible shock to me. To think that my father was living with two women! I couldn't conceive of that. It made a tremendous mark on me at the time, because I really took it very emotionally.

But I loved my mother and father, and I think there are great advantages to being brought up in a time when people had to struggle to make a living and bring up a family. It made us resourceful. We learned how to work and not be ashamed of doing menial tasks. Basically the bringing-up I had as a child is always going to stay with me, and I have no regrets. I have had a good life. I have never missed a performance. I'm outgoing, and I love people around me. I entertain and cook a lot when I'm not working. But I'm a very private person and I'm pretty much alone except for a few very special people that I adore and love, who share my privacy. I love to swim. I love to walk. I love to fix things up around the house. I love antiquing, finding an old treasure and restoring it.

Some people say fucking saps your creative energy, but I don't believe that. I think it's a very healthy thing. A healthy sex life keeps you young and vital. And it should be frequent.

I don't mean three times a day. But frequent. Some of these sports managers tell their players no sex before the night of the game. That's a lot of bullshit. It's healthy to get your rocks off in a passionate way. Well, a lot of people have hang-ups sexually. I feel sorry for them.

Alice Roosevelt Longworth *Theodore Roosevelt's daughter*

Born February 17, 1884, New York, N.Y.

A black servant in a maid's uniform opened the front door of the elegant old brick home on Massachusetts Avenue, a few blocks from the White House, and led the way to the second floor, into a sitting parlor furnished in faded old furniture, threadbare carpets, photographs of her father, President Theodore Roosevelt, and his cronies, and mementos left by him—hunting guns, elephant tusks, sabers and a worn tiger skin. Presently Mrs. Longworth appeared, brushing back her wispy white hair, and with a lively smile sat down on a sofa next to a coffee table. She rang a little silver bell and the maid appeared with tea, which Mrs. Longworth served while lecturing herself with mock severity: "I must hold my shoulders straight." She wore a knit shawl over a simple dress, and a copper bracelet, which she said a friend had assured her would help her rheumatism and arthritis. She chirped merrily away for most of a long afternoon, paused for a time to chat with her granddaughter, Joanna, twenty-seven, and to pay, in cash, her three servants, it being Friday. "Poor darlings. They need their money," she said, struggling to extract the bills from the bank's packages. "The good bank put the elastic too tightly around them, goddamn them," she said. A few minutes later a gong sounded and she moved to an ad-

joining parlor. "Now the animal will be fed," she said as the maid appeared with a plate of zucchini and barbecued ribs. She ate the ribs, her favorite dish, and ignored the vegetables.

I NEVER FELT very romantic about boys. Let me think. I have no recollection. Must be hidden somewhere. Oh, no, no, no, no. I had no interest in boys. Only my father's friends. Sort of Rough Riders, you know. Military heroes. That was fascinating. Boys were totally uninteresting. My cousin Teddy Robinson—Joe Alsop's uncle, he would be—I saw his friends at house parties and things. But I never liked them. Never thought about them. I only liked those older ones. I probably had an Oedipus complex, a father complex, and these older ones represented him in some way. Something like that came into it. I had dismal female friends too. Oh, it was boring! I was a loner, you see.

I wouldn't go to school. Told the family I'd humiliate them if they sent me. And they believed me. I kept away and had a governess, so I learned as little as possible. I had a lovely time. Given the run of my father's library—oh, dear me, people don't read some of the best books now. Fraser, *The Golden Bough.* Anything they are discovering now, you can go to *The Golden Bough* and find it. Chesterton. Belloc. There were no pornographic books that I ever saw. I read a translation of Rabelais, and it was most entertaining. Awfully funny. Terribly funny. Chaucer. Boccaccio. Not very young when I read those, though; eighteen or nineteen, before I was married, anyway.

I had Bible lessons every Sunday, and catechism, the short one and then the long one. I read the whole Bible through twice before I was twelve. I was awfully proud of myself. It was sort of a stunt. I was taken to church every Sunday, the Episcopal Church just a way down the hill. The sermons were the dumbest things that ever were. "The Lord thy God is a jealous God"—sitting there planning bad things for you. It's awful to frighten children like that. The Christian God is a very savage God. Sheer voodoo, most of it. It was supposed to be stern and scary, but it didn't scare me. I paid no attention. I took out a book and read or something.

When my father became governor and we moved to Albany, the family said, "Now, my darling, it's time to be confirmed, and here we are in Albany, and our old friend Bishop Doane is here." He was marvelous, because he was dressed like a British bishop; he wore gaiters and a sort of three-cornered hat, you know, just like a character out of Trollope. And I said, "No. I'm awfully sorry, but I'm an unbeliever." I was fourteen then, and I was never confirmed. I had thought it all over and said to myself, "It's nonsense for me to be confirmed. I won't be confirmed." My father was a wholesome religious subject. He always went to church. But he was very good with me, because when I said, No, I wasn't going to do something, they didn't bother me. They may have been afraid of what I might commit. I was not doted upon. They kept away. There is a photograph of me taken at the age of two, and I look pugnacious and determined. I can't remember anything earlier than two. I was sent to live with my aunt when my mother died, and I stayed with her until my father married again. My aunt called me her "blue-eyed darling." But I was a bad darling, a rather firm darling.

I was an orthopedic case to begin with. If it hadn't been corrected I would have been on crutches. My ankles stuck out, like this, in dancing class. Then they stretched each leg.

My good stepmother took the exercise as a burden upon herself. Really conscientious. Stretched one Achilles tendon seven and a half minutes every day, and the other one five minutes. And it was just a bore for her. Nowadays they'd have someone come in, I suppose. I had a bill from the doctor's today. Really, what they charge for nothing! Simply incredible. I think the bill was seventy-five dollars, for one seance, and it said in parentheses, "Very long." All they did was to poke and prod me, told me what to eat and gave me the same pills all over again. Nothing done at all, you see. They don't take any of the heart tests. Is there a fate that I don't want to hear about, that I obviously can't bear: old heart! Well, let them say so, and let them say, "We can't do anything. Just be careful." But charging seventy-five dollars for one seance, and nothing! The way the medical profession is coining money off us boobs! Only in America! It would pay to go abroad and go to some nice German physician, preferably a Jewish one.

Lots of boys were around when I was a child, with their families. People came to tea. We played games, silly games. We all ran around in a circle, and then you said, "Sit down." And then someone sat down and banged the piano, and everybody sat down. Highly hilarious. All the children I knew had heard about sex. They told one another things, just as they do now. Snuffling around, just as interested. If you lived in the country, as we did at Oyster Bay, you see, you got accustomed to the sex of animals. We lived a rather simple life. Milk cows. Servants. In those days I would ring a bell and they would come. Now they sound a gong and I come. I had a lovely, delightful nurse who had been the nurse of my stepmother's little brother, who died when he was an infant. We rode carriages, *clop, clop, clop,* to the Long Island train, and all the men would be coming out of the club car, where they'd been having their drinks, and servants waiting for them with a horse and carriage.

I paid not much attention to boys. They were all right, but I didn't like them much. All those little "Grotties." All the little Groton and St. Pauls and St. Marks boys, nice little boys. One day I was just circulating about, came into my room—which had a marvelous closet, about as big as the bedroom—and came upon these two little boy cousins, from two rather prim families up at the top of the hill, doing curious sex searching in my closet. I was furious. I was outraged. They were hiding in the closet having experiences. It was funny to me. They were absolutely horrified. I expressed not my disapproval but my contempt. It struck me as rather silly. Most anatomy is rather foolish. They didn't dare explore one another where they lived, so they came up and found their way to my room. It was a dreadful picture. Terribly funny. Sex amused me. I can't be serious about sex. I find it very humorous. I think it's funny. Now people are so solemn about it. Tiresome. Boring, too.

One had to go to dances, and when one had to go, you did it. But I didn't bother about young men my own age. I was more interested in politics, on account of my father, and I had been in it so long. I enjoyed that. It was fun. I saw mostly older people. There was a lot of drinking, and a lot of them were drunks, too. All of my husband, Nick's, friends were sort of middle-aged drunkards, more or less drunkards. They all drank enormously. Most of them Harvard. They made a point of getting drunk. They thought it manly or something.

It was interesting to have the experience of living in the White House, but otherwise no particular pleasure. I liked the big parties, where there were all kinds of people, but it was not an attractive place. My first encounter with lesbianism was in the garden, the back yard, of the White House. Margaret Orsini,* who was the daughter of the Hungarian ambassador, said to me, "I must tell you something, Alice."

I said, "What? Go ahead and tell me."

She said, "Marina" (who was the wife of the Russian ambassador) "has been saying very nasty things about you."

I said, "I don't believe it. What is she saying?"

She said, "She says that Beatrice Wallace is in love with you."

Well, I wasn't going to let her know that I knew what she was talking about. So she cast a look of great scorn on me, and discontinued the conversation. I laughed so. I said to myself, "Well, what shall I do? Let her know that I know? 'Then it shall be a stinging blow, right in the face, a pistol shot, and a death's disgrace was in that pack of cards.'" I can't remember what ballad that was.

The family didn't particularly urge me to get married. They thought it was all right. There were some men who thought they wanted to marry me, but I wasn't very much interested in them. My father told me that a new congressman was coming in from Ohio, Nicholas Longworth, who curiously enough was Harvard and was in the Porcellian, and he thought he might amuse me. He was just the opposite of my father, except that he was Harvard and was in the Porcellian. Oh, those clubs had great sentiment. They all sat and had dinners, drunken tears streaming as they sang a song, old days of glory, baying at the moon. Nothing like that now. There was a lot of drinking. My stepmother did warn me. She said, "You know, your friend from Ohio is a very heavy drinker." Naturally I paid no attention. I didn't care. I didn't

---

* All of the names in this anecdote are fictitious, although the incident is real.

realize what it meant. That's the only bad thing. It was disgusting.

There was an enormous political junket to the Philippines, two senators and their wives, a lot of congressmen and their wives and friends of theirs, and they all went off on a Pacific mail steamer—old A. H. Harriman's line—and went on an inspection tour all over the Philippines, led by William Howard Taft, who was Secretary of War. It was just a funny American political junket. Nick was there, and I was along because I was the daughter of the President and I could do what I wanted to do. They all went back from Hong Kong, and I stayed on and went to Peking. I can't remember if Nick stayed on. We were more or less engaged by then. It was in the air. We had known each other two or three years.

I suppose it would be fair to say that I was never terribly in love. I was totally without sentimentality of any sort. I never thought about it. I certainly never brooded about it. It just came time to get married. More or less that. Got married. Like a friend. Nothing very exciting about it. I was interested in politics, so I thought marrying a politician would be much better than marrying someone else. I could not have married someone who was not in politics. And I preferred somebody who was not from the East, not Boston, or Philadelphia, or New York, which I didn't want particularly. Frightfully boring.

I hadn't kissed anyone when I got married, heavens to God, no. Nor afterwards either. I always thought it was a revolting habit. Now they act like a bunch of puppies in a basket. No, no, no, no. I don't know whether there was very much of that kind of thing in my time, but certainly not by me.

Just the other day something reminded me so much of my wedding. What was it? White House. People gathering. I remember looking out, and people were gathering, and I wasn't dressed. I wasn't excited. Oh, God, no, no, nothing of that sort. It was a very pretty party. All kinds of people there. An Episcopal ceremony. Could it have been Cottie Peabody? I'll have to remember. Oh, yes, it was Endicott Peabody, my cousin, who was head of Groton. Dr. Peabody. Heavens, I wasn't nervous. It was another big party, and I had been to big parties. It was a noon wedding. Everybody was married at noon in those days. Big reception at the White House, and then we started out on a wedding trip. My father had a motor, and a chauffeur drove us a few miles out into Maryland to Mrs. McLean's house—her son, Ned McLean (Ned's wife owned the Hope Diamond), they lent me the house. And then I went down to Cuba for a real wedding trip, went down on the train to Florida and then took a little boat over.

My expectation of marriage was nothing—just to weather it as long as I wanted to. Just more politics, that was all. Run every two years for the House. Father was in the White House. Then Taft runs, and my father and he split, and father runs again, and is beaten. And poor Nick. He lost. He took it very hard. It seemed nonsense to me to take it hard. He came back two years later, and he was Speaker when he died in 1931. That was as much as you can get from the House. I was interested in marriage, but not very emotionally. I was just built that way. Now they would put some psychological thing on it to dress it up. I suppose they'd say it was a father complex. Maybe so. We just got married. I had a baby. I can't say I was desperately interested in having a baby. It was an act of nature, that's all.

Now at ninety I have many of the afflictions of advanced old age. Janie, the maid, and the cat have me under complete control. I was really meant to be an old maid with a cat. Well, I've had great fun, and I'm still amused by looking on at things. I've had a very good time. All the things I learned as a child keep sifting up, things from the Bible and the British poets, the rhymesters. . .

I'm growing old. My legs are far from strong.
  I stoop and tremble like a chimpanzee.
My stories are interminably long.
  I laugh at myself continuously.
I talk about my mother's pedigree.
  I note a tendency to avarice.
These are the wages, O, Debaucheree.
  What is the use of going on like this?

Loretta Lynn *country music singer*

Born April 14, 1935, Butcher Hollow, Ky.

It was late morning on a hot, smoggy day in Los Angeles and the converted Greyhound bus with her name painted on the side had been sitting in front of the Universal Sheraton Hotel for an hour with its motor running before Loretta Lynn, the queen of country music, and her coterie—husband Mooney, short and stocky, wearing boots and a tilted-back cowboy hat, and her five band members—emerged and boarded. They were headed 250 miles north up the California coast to the Paso Robles County Fair, where she would appear that night, just a short hop for a troupe that spends two hundred days a year on the road. Ms. Lynn went straight to her private compartment in the rear of the bus, which was painted purple throughout. She had a pull-out bed, color TV, sophisticated recording equipment, which she uses when she writes songs on the road, a makeup table, and several closets filled with pointy-toed boots, shiny gowns, wigs and handmade lace underwear. The "boys" settled in with Mooney up front, where they played cards, drank beer, watched TV and napped on bunks stacked three on each side of the bus. Her long, dark hair hanging flat, her angular face unmade, wearing a simple cowboy shirt and jeans, Ms. Lynn looked very tiny and very young. She talked almost nonstop during the three-hour trip, ducking no questions, answering in a soft hillbilly drawl, and saying in the end that she liked "this girl talk."

I'D HAD MY PERIOD only three times before I got married at age thirteen. I had lived my whole life in Butcher Holler, Kentucky. My mother and daddy when they got married built a one-room log cabin, the last house in the holler. It had no running water, no electricity, and the toilet was way out back. Back in them days people papered their walls with movie magazines. The week before I was born, Mommy was laying on the bed and she had Loretta Young and Claudette Colbert papered up and she says, "Now if this baby's a girl, I'm going to name her after one of the girls." She said she got to thinking that Loretta was a prettier name so she named me after Loretta Young. And she's one of the actresses I want to meet some day. 'Course I was always called Lorettie.

Just like my song says, my daddy was a coal miner. Before that, he worked days hoeing corn for people for fifty cents a day and Mommy worked washing their clothes for another fifty cents. I remember the Christmas of 1944, when I was nine. Daddy had thirty-six cents. But he bought each of us a little something, me a four-inch plastic doll and my brothers little tiny plastic cars. We had corn to pop and a tree that we decorated with the tinfoil from Daddy's Prince Albert tobacco packages. 'Course I don't remember too much of this, 'cause I got mastoid when I was eleven months old. I was just learning to walk when I took this stuff, and they give me up to die three times. Mommy said I had real curly hair and they shaved me bald-headed and bored holes in my scalp, right behind both ears, which they stuffed with cotton. Every day that cotton had to be changed, so every day for three years they carried me, first one and then the other, twelve miles to the nearest town, Paintsville, Kentucky, and twelve miles back. I still remember them carrying me out of the holler in the wintertime, wrapped up in these old patchwork quilts Mommy had made.

This was a real kinfolks holler. My uncle had a moonshine still right on the hill where our house was. They all drank a lot except my daddy. I never seen him take a drink, but my mother said he drank when he was young. It was his first cousin that had this still and he got killed and as soon as he got killed my daddy broke up the still so nobody would find out. Nobody never knew how my uncle got killed and nobody cared. It was like the Hatfields and McCoys. One Fourth of July, my uncle had took his moonshine into town and sold it all so he took some moonshine from somebody else and they shot him and just left him laying on the hill. I was eleven and it upset me very bad because me and this uncle was very close. He was real mean but he was a good guy too. One of my brothers was named after him. He and another guy had broke out of the pen and were hid in our loft when this brother was born. My uncle's name was Lee and his friend's was Willy, so my brother was named Willy Lee. Just before he got killed, my uncle said, "Lorettie," he said, "when you grow up you're going to be a real pretty girl." I wanted to look just like Mommy when I grew up. Both of her grandmothers were Cherokee Indian squaws, and she was a Raimee Indian from Jennis Creek, Kentucky, about fifteen or twenty miles from Butcher Holler. Her skin was dark and her black hair was just as long and straight and beautiful as it could be. Every now and then she would sneak off and have a permanent, but Daddy hated that. And she never wore any makeup, but her eyes were round and just as blue as the sky. My husband's real old-fashioned about it, so I never wore any makeup either until I started singing on TV. That was the other thing my uncle said to me. He said, "Now Lorettie, I want you to sing every day, because while I'm running off the moonshine I always listen to you sing as you swing the babies to sleep on the front porch and it's company for me."

Five of us was borned in the cabin Mommy and Daddy built. There were two beds and I slept with all my brothers, some of us at the head and some of us at the foot. Then when I was nine Mommy had me three more sisters, and a year later we moved into the sixth house out of the holler, which had four rooms. Sometime after, I got my own little half-bed and I slept in the room with my mother and father. But, you know, I didn't have that bed but about eight or nine months before I got married.

Mommy made sure that all of us went to school. Daddy couldn't read and write very well, but my mother had a very beautiful handwriting and how far she went in school I don't know. But she could read. I didn't learn very much because the schoolhouse sat at the mouth of about seven or eight hollers and there'd be twenty-eight of us in the one room. There was kids that had never went to school that were seventeen and eighteen and couldn't even write their names. I hate to say this, but they were third and fourth cousins of mine. Also, during a year's time we'd have seven different teachers. When the teacher would try to make the boys give their lessons, the boys would just whip the teacher. So she'd quit and we'd get another. And I would cry because I'd get real close to the teachers. But I loved school. Not just school, but I loved getting away from home. I was the second oldest child and the oldest girl, so I always had to rock the babies and do the housework. I wanted to play. I had one dress and I would wear this dress to school for two or three days, then I'd go to bed and Mommy would wash my dress out and dry it and I'd wear it again. In the summertime we had no shoes. But when the frost got so heavy and our feet would hurt we'd have to have a pair.

It was wintertime when I met Mooney, my husband. It was the middle of December and it was very cold, and the window panes were out of the schoolhouse so all the kids had to gather around the big old potbellied stove. To raise money for new panes, we had a pie supper. It's kind of like a party where every girl who comes brings a pie or cake and the boy who buys her pie or cake gets to walk her home. So my husband had come to the pie supper. I didn't know him, because he was seven years older than me, but I went to school with his sisters and brothers. He'd been out of the army two or three months and he worked in the mines like my daddy and his daddy. Before the supper started we played ring around the rosey and of course I was in the middle of it, I was just a kid, you know, and he kept trying to get into the game and he was so small that we didn't take him to be over sixteen or seventeen. I was also real tiny. I don't think I was five feet tall and I was just as freckle-faced as I could be. My mother had given me one of those Toni permanents—this was the going thing—and my hair was just as curly and bushy. But I thought I was so pretty, you know. That night I had on my very first coat, what they called a teddy bear coat. It had little short fur that stuck out and was trimmed in red. I'll never forget it. That pie supper was the first time I ever wore it. I had on a pair of blue jeans, my permanent, my teddy bear coat and a red sweater that matched the red on my coat. The teacher let me make up the program so naturally I did everything—I was in the beauty contest and the cakewalk and I sang for everybody. I didn't think I could sing but I liked to, you know. So Mooney was kind of stuck on me and I was just a kid and I was flirting like kids do and when it come time for the beauty contest he made sure I won. I'd never had a boyfriend. There was one little boy in school, Granville Bowldon, that I'd had my eye on, but it was just puppy stuff. We all threw notes across the classroom saying stuff like "Roses are red, violets are blue, sugar is sweet and so are you." That's about as far as I ever had a boyfriend.

When it came to the pie bidding, there was another boy bidding real strong on my pie. His name was Flop Murphy— they called him that 'cause he had big ears—and he got up to four dollars and fifty cents. Then my husband said, "Five dollars and sold." He didn't wait for Flop to bid any more. I didn't care who won. I was so young and silly I didn't even realize what was going on. When it come time for us to eat the pie, my aunt took the first bite and said, "Loretta, why you've baked your pie with salt instead of sugar." We kind of scooted it back and nobody said a word. Mooney didn't say anything, but it embarrassed me to death and I wouldn't talk. I was so bashful. I know it sounds silly, but back in them days, when a stranger would come up the holler, all the kids would run and hide.

That night my husband walked me home. He had this jeep, but I'd never been in a car and I thought the jeep looked like something from Mars and I wouldn't get in it. So we lit some of those big pine torches like the Ku Klux Klan used to carry—we didn't have flashlights or anything that modern—and walked back up into the holler. I started running on in the house and he said, "Hey, come back here." I went back and he kissed me, the first time I'd ever been kissed. I didn't know how to do it. I was thinking, "Now is that the way I was supposed to kiss?" I was scared to death.

But I went on in the house just singing, you know, and woke Mommy and Daddy up. Mommy said, "What's wrong with you?" And I said, "Oh, nothing." And she said, "Who bought your pie tonight?" I said, "Doolittle Lynn." He'd been called Doo, short for Doolittle, since he was two 'cause he was so little. So Mommy said, "Oh, my goodness, Ted"—my daddy's name was Melvin but they called him Ted—"jump up, she says Doolittle Lynn walked her home." She went ahead telling me he was real wild and that there was no way I was going to see him again. Well, the next night he was at my house to see me, the next night and the next night, and one month later we were married. He kissed me on the tenth of December and on the tenth of January we got married.

They cried and cried. I was so young and they didn't want me to have a boyfriend. I told them a week before we got married we was going to. They thought I was kidding. I said, "He's wanting me to get married." Anything he said was all right with me. He was like a god to me and of course my mother and father didn't realize this, and naturally they wouldn't, me just a kid.

On the ninth of January he'd come to me and said, "Let's don't wait any longer. Let's get married tomorrow. I got a real good paycheck." I said okay. Everything was okay with me. It didn't matter. I didn't think nothing about it. I said, "But you have to ask Mommy and Daddy. And now don't ask them together," I said, 'cause I was real bashful. Daddy was out on the front porch. He'd go out there at night and just stand. So Doo went out and told Daddy he wanted to marry me and was it okay? And Daddy said, "I don't know. You'll have to ask Clurie." My mother's name was Clara Marie but they called her Clurie, like Lorettie. So he went into the bedroom and asked Mommy. And she said, "Well, I don't know. You'll have to ask Ted." This went on for like two or three hours. Here I was just sitting in the other room waiting for the answer. I said, "Wait till they start to go to bed, then go ask them together." So Daddy finally come in. He waited and waited till it got real late, but finally he had to come in, it was cold, it was the ninth of January. Finally they both said "Okay. But don't ever be mean to her or ever whip her or ever take her away where we can't see her." My grandpa, my mother's father, who was real Indian and had never said two words to me, said to Doo, "If you ever lay a hand on her I'll kill you." That was all he ever said.

I washed my hair right after Doo left, and curled it. I tore up a brown paper poke—they call them sacks today—twisted the pieces, then wrapped my hair around them and tied them. Next morning at eight when he come to get me it was still wet. I had to be the ugliest bride you have ever seen. I had on my aunt's dress. It was kind of bluish-green, straight, and came way down below my knee, real ugly, but them days we thought this was pretty. I had on Mommy's flat shoes and her coat. I guess Mommy felt I shouldn't wear my teddy bear coat. I don't know why, but I didn't. So we went to the hospital and had a blood test and three hours later we went to the courthouse in Paintsville. Daddy finally come over to town, but Mommy never did come. I didn't know Doo's real name till he signed the license. He'd kill me if I told you. His daddy's name is Oliver Vanetta Lynn and my husband's a junior so, see, I didn't tell you his name. That day Doo had on a brown sort of leather jacket of his brother's, an army shirt that he had dyed wine color, a brown pair of pants and brown loafers. He was a good-looking little boy. He couldn't have weighed over 150 pounds, but he was very muscular, real solid and real good-looking. All the girls were after him; he was real hot stuff in the holler. He looked like a little toy soldier, just as cute as he could be, and I never had no other boyfriends and I loved him. So we got married.

After we got our license we got in his jeep and drove back into Butcher Holler. He told me, "Listen, you're going to ride in the jeep with me else I'm going to drive and I'll hold your hand and you can walk." So I was finally riding in the jeep. We went home and Mommy had me two or three changes of clothes packed up in a brown paper poke and Doo's mother had got me my gown and a housecoat—the first gown and the first housecoat I ever had. Doo took me about sixteen miles out of Paintsville to the Chandler Cabins. First time I'd ever been out of anywhere; I didn't know the world was that big.

This gown my mother-in-law had got me was a big old round thing that I'd get if I was pregnant. Nothing sexy to it at all. But I thought it was the most beautiful thing in the world 'cause I'd never had one. So my husband says, "Get ready for bed." We were in the tenth cabin, the one on the end, and it had one of those big old reservoir things the heat comes out of. I had my teddy bear coat on and I was setting on this reservoir thing and I said, "I can't go to bed, I'm freezing to death, oh, I just can't go to bed." I guess it was my nerves—I've always been kind of nervous—but I really thought I was freezing to death. I was shaking all over. He'd been in bed for hours waiting for me to get into bed and me setting up on the reservoir. He had on his shorts and one of those little stretch vests with no sleeves in them, an undershirt, I guess. I'll never forget it when I saw him. It embarrassed me to death; I thought I was going to die. Just to see him in them clothes—I didn't think I'd ever make it. If anybody could have ever died of embarrassment it would have been me.

He finally throwed my gown out and said, "Get this on and get into bed. It's getting morning you know." Finally I went into the bathroom. I didn't know how to wear a gown, so I put it on over all my clothes. I come back in and he said, "You're supposed to wear the gown without your clothes on. Go pull your dress off." Well I went in and pulled my dress off and left my slip, my bra and my panties on. I come back in and he said, "You've got to have your other clothes off too." Mercy, I was in bad shape. I finally got everything off but my panties—there wasn't no way I was going to take them off. I think he kind of tore them off. I was crying and crying. When he started to spread my legs I went into a fit. I cried and I screamed. I thought you were just supposed to lay straight out and it scared me to death. Nobody had told me that thing would just go up and down. I thought it was just a little thing and it stayed one size. When that thing raised up, I thought, oh, my God. I'd never seen pictures or nothing. I couldn't figure out what was happening and he didn't tell me, so I just lay there. I really couldn't understand why I couldn't pee without it hurting me for a month later. I'd say to myself, "Why can't I pee without it hurting me?" I'd say that to his sisters, not to him, 'cause you didn't say things like that to a man. That was something really private. I couldn't tell him I was hurting and I was sore. Well I always said to myself, you know, why in the world couldn't he have been more gentle?

We stayed there for three days and I wouldn't leave the cabin. My husband couldn't get me to go out or eat or nothing. When we left we went to his folks' place and I wouldn't look at either of them. I wouldn't look at nobody. I stayed hid. And then I wouldn't go home for two weeks because I was so ashamed because I knew my mommy and daddy would know what I'd been doing. And my daddy, you know how I thought about my daddy. I just couldn't take it; I'd have turned fourteen different colors. My mother never said a word to me about sex. And not yet today we don't talk. I've often thought it must have been bad for her. They stayed to-gether and they were happy and they loved each other, but sex was for the man to enjoy and for the woman it was dirty. Women that did stuff like that were dirty, they were street-walkers. I mean it was to have children and that was it.

The Christmas before we were married Doo got me a doll and he said, "Now next Christmas you'll have a real doll." And next Christmas I had a real one, and the next one and the next one. I didn't even know what was causing them. When I was fourteen I was five months pregnant with the first and didn't even know it. My husband said, "There's something wrong with you. You'd better go to the doctor." He knew. I was so young and didn't know anything, and he didn't know how to go about telling me. So I went to the doctor and he said, "Well, you're pregnant." And I said "What's that?" And he said, "You're going to have a baby." I said, "Ain't no way I can have a baby." And he said, "You're married aren't you?" I said yes. He said, "And you've been sleeping with your husband?" Yes. He said, "Then you're going to have a baby." I said, "I can't be, 'cause that ain't the way you have a baby." My daddy told me he turned over a tin can and that's where he found me. You believe this stuff. You don't think your folks wouldn't tell you something so im-portant. And really they didn't mean to do it. It was just their way of life, but it can sure ruin yours.

When I was pregnant with the first one we moved out to Billingham, Washington, 'cause Doo's folks had lived there, and we stayed eleven years. It was my first train ride. Doo had hitchhiked ahead, so my mother packed me lunch for three days, biscuits with jam, hog meat and moonpies with that real stretchy icing, and gave me a note for the conductor to tell him I was pregnant. He sat me right by the bathroom and sneaked me food from the dining room and gave me a free pillow. I didn't have a quarter. Doo met me at the depot and took me to this room he'd rented above somebody's house. I had this little suitcase of baby clothes people had give me, and during the day while Doo was working as a mechanic I'd take them out and play with them just like they was doll clothes. I was worried sick that I was going to have that baby in the middle of the night and not know it and it would smother to death down there under the covers. When I come out of there sick there wasn't no way I could have slept through it. Doo carried me downstairs wrapped in a blanket and I was saying, "I'm going to die, I'm going to die." It took twenty-seven hours for that baby to be born. When they come in and told me it was a girl I said, "Oh, no, I didn't have a girl, I had a boy. That's what my husband wanted and that's what I had and I'm going to call him Jack." I thought you could have what you wanted. For a whole day I argued with the nurses and Doo was just as bad. He went and picked out the biggest boy and said that was his baby. When they showed him our little girl he said no, that wasn't it. So of course that really hurt me and I cried and cried and finally, I don't know if they told him to or not, but he came in and said, "That's okay, honey, that it's a little girl."

Ten months later I had Jack. Then Ernest. Well, when I had my fourth child I remember crying. I said to the doctor, "Operate on me so I can't have any more kids." And he said, "Honey, you should be having your first one, not your last one," 'cause I was only seventeen. So he said to come back in six weeks, and six weeks later I had a diaphragm and I used that thing faithful. How I got pregnant again I'll never know. My baby was about eight or nine and I'd started singing by then. I was so tired and I guess I just got my diaphragm in wrong. We were driving all over the country, hitting one little club after another. This was like three years after I'd started singing and I was having one hit record after the other. But if you had a number-one country song in 1963 you made only $150 or $200 a night, and you had to travel three hundred miles to each club and sing three and four hours a night with a different band every time. When we finally got to bed it would be four in the morning, and most of the time we'd have to sleep in the car 'cause we didn't have time to check in. I was so tired and I think that's how I got pregnant with my twins. When I found out I was pregnant again I thought my whole world had tumbled down. But I never thought about having an abortion. Once you're pregnant you're pregnant as far as I'm concerned. I wouldn't stop one of my own from having an abortion—I figure that's their busi-ness—but it wasn't for me. I was really tore up about it, and it wasn't till right at the end when I found out there was two of them that I wanted them. Then I was proud. Then I said, "I'm keeping them." My husband said, "Oh, no, these are mine. You're just the incubator," or whatever you call it. My girls are now ten and I tell them everything. They already know about babies. And the next thing I'm going to tell them about is men and about their periods. I said I'd never let a girl of mine go through what I went through.

Doo got me into singing in Washington. My four kids were in school and he got me a job working in this club in Wash-ington. I was always so bashful, 'cause having four kids one right after the other and not going no place, I was still drawed back into a shell where I wouldn't talk to anybody. We'd have these ten-minute breaks between singing, and I'd sit on the bandstand and drink tomato juice 'cause I didn't drink. So I would set there and I just wouldn't go to the bath-room because I knew if I went people would know what I was doing. My kidneys had gotten so bad from waiting that my back had been hurting and I was having to go to the doctor. What finally got me out of being bashful wasn't my husband saying, "Now get up there and sing." It wasn't this at all. One night I said to him, "I've got to go to the bathroom so bad I'm about to die." And he said, "Loretta, you're not bashful, you're just goddamned ignorant." When he said that it completely snapped me out of it. I thought, "So that's what he thinks of me." I got so mad that I went to the bathroom and all the way back I wiggled. And from that day on, I went to every table and flirted and danced and done just what I wanted to. He gets a little jealous now and then, a little bit on edge, but he don't say too much. I imagine he remembers the days when I wouldn't even move.

I was way up in my twenties, oh, Lord, I had four children and was already in the business, before the sex got better. For a lot of them years, why, all I was thinking about was letting my husband enjoy it. But I got tired of having kids and not enjoying it. I just knew it wasn't right. And he knew it wasn't right, 'cause he'd been with a lot of women who had enjoyed it. He couldn't understand, but he didn't hold it against me. He said, "Well, there's something wrong. Go to a doctor." I went to every doctor between the state of Kentucky and the state of Washington and they none of them ever helped me. They just told me it was in my head and they gave me shots and stuff. I had a doctor tell me one time that a woman way up in her forties had come to him and she'd never had an orgasm. He was an old-fashioned doctor and he said, "Well, there's nothing wrong with that. There's a lot of women who haven't." Here I'd went to him hoping for help and he's telling me that. That's the answer I got from a lot of them. I never heard nothing about masturbation. Only after my twins was born I heard about men jacking off, but I didn't see how a woman could ever do a thing like that. Finally a doctor in Nashville—I was twenty-six and we'd just moved there—told me about this little deelybob we women got on the outside. I didn't know anything about this little deelybob, and it's funny that my husband didn't know about it either. So we tried it; we'd tried everything. It didn't work right at first 'cause it all made me so nervous. I thought, "Oh, gosh, what's this, I can't take that too." And you know, the first time I ever did, we were in bed in our home in Nashville and we were just playing around, kissing and touching, it wasn't intercourse, and I just stopped right in the middle. It scared me completely to death. If you never have, you don't know the feeling, but isn't it something when you do the first time? So I worked and worked and worked trying to do it again, and three weeks later I did it again. And after that it was a lot easier. Really that little deelybob is too far away from the hole; it should be built right in. I think the doctors should operate on you and put it right there.

I think that what's happening today to women is good. I don't think God means for women not to have theirs too. He likes us women as well as he does men. Daggone right! And he made us with a brain just the same as he did a man and I think he made it a little smarter. Most women are told how dumb they are and I just don't like that. I know I'm not as dumb as a lot of people think I am. Men don't really want you to figure out nothing. They want to be the ones, and they'll push it just as far and as long as they can. Men are greedy things and they make women feel they have to perform some kind of service else some other woman will. And you know, they do get this service in these massage parlors. It's funny a man can dish it out but he sure can't take it. A man will go out—and he will every chance he gets—but when a wife goes out he can't stand it, because his pride is built up around her. A woman's got to take up for herself and I had to wait till I got old enough to take up for myself. Women are waking up. Then the husbands start waking up and finding out that everything they needed at home was there and they've been out trying to find it. And it's too late to worry about it. Every time I see that thing about "You've come a long way, baby" on TV I have to laugh to myself, 'cause you don't dare laugh in front of your husband, and I think, "Get on with it, kid." I'm for anything that works after missing out on all them years. You should be enjoying sex since when you became a woman and had your first period.

I've come a long way, but still today I've never sat on my husband's lap in public or not in front of my kids. Last year when I was doing the Dean Martin Show, the producer said to me, "Now when you get through singing just flop down in Dino's lap." I said, "I'm not flopping down in nobody's lap." My manager called me over and said, "Hey, you're talking to Greg Garrison, the producer. You can't talk like that." I said, "Let me tell you something. I'll walk out of this show if I have to sit in anybody's lap." And he said, "You won't have to, they'll tell you to." So Greg came over to me and said, "Honey, do you know how many women would love to sit in his lap?" And I said, "I don't care who'd love to sit in his lap, I'm not sitting in it." I done the show, but he changed the scene for me. I guess it's just one of them things that's pounded into my head. I can see there's nothing wrong with it, 'cause my husband will pull girls down on his lap and think nothing of it. My girls will bring their seventeen- and eighteen-year-old girl friends home with them and I'll say, "Doo, it looks terrible. I had four kids when I was their age." He'll say, "Well, now you're going back." I can't help it, it still affects me. I don't know if I'll ever get out of that or not. I just never seen my mother sit in my daddy's lap. 'Course I set in my daddy's lap; he rocked me till I got married, I was like a baby. But that was a different situation. Butcher Holler seems a long time, a lifetime ago, but I guess there's something I'll just always be stuck with.

Victoria Principal *actress*

Born January 3, 1950, Fukioka, Japan

It looked like a spread out of Glamour *Magazine: the lovely, single young woman in figure-flattering white T-shirt, tight orange pants and just a touch of mascara, showing off her newly decorated nest overhanging the Pacific ten miles north of Malibu, while in the kitchen chicken was frying and a homemade apple pie was baking. But when she sat down to talk, Victoria Principal was all candor and unblushing detail. Though her public relations man sat and monitored the entire interview, she never balked at a question or opted for delicate words. Neither did she try to sound brash and jazzy. It sounded like a familiar reminiscence that she had shared with a girlfriend or two, and a psychiatrist or two. For most of the day she anxiously awaited a phone call from her agent about an important movie part, and when it came, she flushed and grabbed a cigarette. The call was disappointing; there was no firm answer one way or the other. But she accepted it philosophically, and returned gracefully to the interview.*

OLDER GUYS LIKE to receive head but they don't like to give it. Even today, a man who's in his thirties or forties will immediately go to bed with you but it will be weeks, maybe months, before he'll consider giving you head. There's still that strange backlog of feeling that the genital area's something bad or unclean. I find that only younger men or men who've been married for a number of years can still indulge in intercourse during a woman's period. The married men have learned that it's fine. And the younger men, less stuck in preconceived male-female roles and more willing to talk about sex, have learned that it's not only fine but that in many cases a woman is really at her most lustful the week preceding her period or the first few days after the initial flow, when it's stopped being painful. Many times in the last few years I have found men, young and old, intimidated and unable to perform sexually at all. It's much more common than it's ever been. But I find that if I intimidate a man it's a man who doesn't make as much money as I do or who feels that I have experienced things, because of what I'm doing or whom I've known, that he could never duplicate.

I have always been involved with older men. By the time I was sixteen, I was dating men who were ten years my senior. My mother, whose ideas were sometimes a bit bizarre, preferred it that way because she felt an older man wouldn't put as much pressure on me as a boy who was just learning about sex, which of course wasn't true at all. I was going out with men who were much more sophisticated in their approach and to this day I can't relate to a man my own age. I'd probably say to him, "How's school?" My mother also asked that these men be wealthy, which seemed like a kind of selling out to me. I don't know where she got it, but she always used to say, "You can fall in love with a rich man just as easily as with a poor man and if you only meet rich men it will be much easier."

The only man I ever lived with was a superstar entertainer. I can't mention his name. He was 25 years older than I was and had been married a number of times. He had silver-gray hair. I was eighteen and had been living in New York for four months trying to be an actress. I always wanted to be an actress, I mean since the day I could walk or talk. At this point I was supporting myself by modeling and I was constantly pressured to put out, which turned me off, so I dated very little. I finally hit it as a commercial model, cosmetics not clothes, because although I was skinny I was only five feet six. I had to stay skinny to pay the rent, so I kept myself at 98 pounds by living on Tab and diet pills and I was sick all the time. To get the desired flat look I would tape my breasts down with ace bandages for hours on end and it finally hurt so bad I took shots to decrease the size of my bust. I was just obsessed with making it in my career and not giving in to the pressures and propositions that were handed out right and left. It really had become such a heavy thing with me that I was not, no matter what, going to go to bed with anybody who had anything to do with business. I was never going to get a part that way. I would hear stories about actresses who made it for a while and they'd say, "Oh, yeah, she was so-and-so's girl." And nobody was ever going to say that about me. Nobody was ever going to say that was how I got anything.

I don't remember ever being so exhausted in my life and I finally accepted a modeling assignment in Rome from a designer friend. We stopped on the way to see a friend of his who had a mansion in Switzerland. At this point I had no idea whose house it was, but I had my own bedroom and everything was kosher. The second night I was there my girl friend, who was also en route to Rome and who apparently was already involved with this man, introduced us. I disliked him instantly. But for the ten days I was there he pursued me relentlessly. Then he showed up in Rome and while still courting my girl friend kept after me. I was just repelled by him. He stood for a lot of things I didn't believe in. He was very wealthy and I didn't like the way he used it and I didn't like his way of life. Although he didn't flaunt it. Everything was too big, too broad.

Well, he finally got to me one night in a casino in Rome. I was being pressured from every direction to go to bed with somebody and was feeling a little like Joan of Arc. I was gambling and as I reached to pick up some chips I'd won, a hand reached and touched mine and, corny as it sounds, sparks flew. I looked at the hand, followed the arm and saw that it belonged to this detestable man and suddenly he didn't look so detestable. Within the next two weeks he convinced me that my place in life was next to him. I went back to New York to get my things. An affair had begun by that time.

No two people so unalike ever attempted to live together. Whatever he thought, I thought the reverse. His standards of morality were 180 degrees from mine. He'd fuck anything that walked; he lived for fucking and had no qualms about being unfaithful, which I couldn't begin to cope with. That's not the way it was supposed to be. And anyway I was used to being the one who broke things off. The first time he slept with another woman we'd been together only two weeks. By the end of our first year together he finally realized that I was on the level, that I hadn't been around very much, and he became a very considerate, gentle, loving man. But he continued to sleep around. He tried to hide it at first, then he became very open, then he began to hide it again as he began to care more, then when he realized he was caring more he became twice as blatant, to more or less deny that he finally cared for a woman. He has said himself openly that he loved me, that he has never said that to another woman. He doesn't trust women at all. He thinks we're only out for money or some kind of personal gain; he thinks everyone can be bought and sold. In my youth and ignorance I thought I could turn him around. I didn't want to be bought or sold. I wanted desperately to marry him, but he didn't want to marry me or anyone else. I just adored him and anything I could do to make his life better or happy was all I wanted to do, that and be an actress. That had never left me, and I was studying all this time at the Royal Academy of Dramatic Arts. He would say, "Don't worry about it. I'll take care of you. I'll get you a movie." And I'd say, "No. I'm going to study and I'm not just going to be an actress, I'm going to be great."

I was just obsessed with the man. I felt that I had run away from everything that I had ever known, from my parents, who were totally outraged, to live with this man, and I didn't know how to break it off. It was a very abnormal and in some ways masochistic affair. I led a very closed-in life. When he was away I stayed home because he didn't want me to see other men under any circumstances. And I had no women friends at all for fear he would try to fuck them. He tried to get me to participate in other things but to this day I can only relate in bed to one person at a time. It's not that I have moral hang-ups, it's just that you have to find what you like and I know that being in bed with someone you want is the most marvelous thing in the world and if you're giving yourself totally, then it's great. But a three-way is a stage production. He pressured me, but it was not for me. I did not like being in bed with someone else; I only wanted to go to bed with him. I was not unfaithful—other men did not interest me.

When I finally managed to leave, after three years and a nervous breakdown, I left everything he had ever given me except my clothing. Materially, no one could have been better to me. I had everything and anything I wanted and I learned how very rich and very unhappy I could be. I did not keep a single car, a single house, a single piece of furniture. The only jewelry I kept was the jewelry I had on when I left. It was my way of saying, "Whatever I gave you, you never bought." As a result, to this day we're still friends. I may be the only woman he respects.

The sex was good right up until the day I left. In fact, when we'd see each other later there was always that temptation—at least you know what you've got there. He never made me feel ashamed. In fact, he taught me a great deal about my body. He was the first person I was ever open with about everything. He was a friend, a kind of lover-father, and the father-daughter thing made it all right for me to talk about things that I would never have talked about. He provided the father I never had.

He was around, that's the perfect word for my father, he was just around. He was a career Air Force sergeant and his world revolved around his work and my mother. It was as though I had one parent, because my father was not involved in my upbringing whatsoever. If a decision had to be made I knew she would make it. If something had to be told to me she would tell it. I think he spanked me twice that I can remember. They were married when she was a few days from being twenty-one and he was twenty-seven. As she was expected to be, she was a virgin until that day, while my father, being 100 per cent Italian and in the Air Force, took great pride in not being one. She was of English descent and had been raised in Georgia, and where my father was open and affectionate, she was extremely reserved both verbally and physically. But the sex education was her department; he never said one word. When I was about seven and she saw that I was discovering the difference between men and women, she sat me down on the bed and said, "I'm going to explain to you what this is all about," which was very unusual for her. She didn't go into the graphics, into people getting together and procreating. I guess you could call it a synopsis, and I remember getting my locations mixed up and saying, "Well, babies must smell terrible when they first come out." Because of my mother's great reserve, it's hard for me to imagine my parents sexually. To this day she does not allow herself to be French kissed; she thinks that's not a nice thing. But they appeared happy and insisted that it was one for one and that neither had ever been unfaithful. My parents are still happy. They hold hands when they watch TV.

From the moment I could walk and talk and breathe I was obsessed with sex. From eight years old on, I spent every available moment thinking about sex. I was fifteen when *Candy* was published and I read it the second day it came out. The bizarre thing is that I never participated much because I had been so rigidly brought up to believe that you had to walk down the aisle wearing white and that you didn't sleep with someone before marriage because he would leave you and men forever after would not forgive you for having been in someone else's bed.

The first sexual thing I remember is when I was eight and we were living in London. I let a boy I kind of had a crush on see me in my slip. I thought that was very daring. At school the boys' and girls' bathrooms were separated by a wall that stopped a foot from the ceiling. So by putting one foot on the john and propelling yourself upward you could peer down into the other bathroom. That was the first time I saw what a boy looked like, and I was absolutely amazed that he should just casually stand there holding it as he went about his business. It was so unlike my own, but I wasn't shocked or repelled; I was fascinated. One day this little boy followed me to the bathroom, climbed up in the little space and said he'd like to see me with my dress off. I said that was a sin. He said, "I've seen other girls in their slips and nothing will happen and if you let me see you we'll go steady." Falling for the oldest male ploy in the book, I took off my dress and did a few turns. We went steady for months afterwards even though my mother made me give his bracelet back. He was the first boy to kiss me. We were transferred back to the States, to Puerto Rico, and the day the boat was leaving he came to say goodbye. I remember so vividly because I was sitting in the back seat of the car with my baby sister, who was asleep. And he said, "I want to kiss you." And I said, "But she's here," meaning the baby. He said, "It's okay." And he kissed me on the lips. It was so romantic, but for years I lived in dread of the day my sister would learn how to talk and would tell on me.

The next time I was kissed I was ten and was at a party at a friend's house in Puerto Rico on the base where we all lived. My mother would only let me go if she knew the parents were going to be there. I remember calling her from this particular party and asking her if I could kiss someone on the lips. She said, "Well, if you must, go ahead."

Because we all lived on the base together and went to school together, sex was pretty rampant pretty early. For a while there I was hot stuff. I was the second girl in my class to get a bra—I was thirteen, just beginning junior high—and that was a big deal. Shortly thereafter, growth ceased for a couple of years and I really could have given the bra up, but there was no way I was going to relinquish my first visible sign of womanhood. The big thing then was to wear a straight skirt, a very collegiate Bobbie Brooks–type shirt tucked in with a thin little belt, and bebops, which is your saddle oxford in patent leather. Some girls were allowed to wear heels, but usually only to church. I remember getting in terrible trouble for wearing lipstick, so I used to put it on outside in the morning and wipe it off before I got home from school. My big claim to fame was that Glen Roy Milstead and I were the first couple to actually kiss on the lips when playing spin the bottle at parties. Because I was always willing to take a dare, to try anything first, and because I did very well in school and had skipped a grade, I was considered both a great swinger and a loner. What my schoolmates didn't know is that while everyone else went way beyond kissing on the lips, that's where I remained. We'd have outdoor parties with big bonfires and there was a lot of heavy petting and touching under blankets. Some couples were even sleeping together. But I absolutely would not allow a boy to touch me and for a while even regressed into a pattern where I wouldn't kiss. I had become the vessel of my mother's teaching and an object of ridicule among my friends. I was afraid to go against what I'd been taught. But it began to come out in strange ways. I began to smoke. I got drunk for the first time when I was thirteen. My parents were away from home and I had a tumbler of bourbon with a peanut butter and jelly sandwich. Was I sick. I didn't get somewhat righted until I was fifteen and actually allowed to date, double dates only. My mother thought double-dating would inhibit any kind of sexual exploration, but it worked in the reverse. We'd double with a couple who'd been together for a year or two and they'd be doing things in the front seat we had no intention of doing, but we'd feel, "Well they're doing it so why aren't we?"

And then I met Ron. He was much older. My parents knew nothing about him, but every Wednesday when I was supposed to be going to the library he'd pick me up at the corner and we'd go parking in the back of the base for an hour and he would teach me how to kiss. He never touched me. He just taught me all the different variations of what you could do with your mouth and your tongue. Then he would take me back, drop me off, and I would walk home. And during those six months when my parents thought I was in the library, boy, did I get an education.

After kissing came touching. First we'd touch through the clothes. You'd let a boy hold your ribs and maybe his thumb would be touching the edge of your breast and you'd think, "Well, okay, tonight I'll let him." Then the next night his hand would go higher. When he reached your nipple you knew you had to make a decision. He'd either have to stop and start all over again at the ribs, or the next thing was to lift the shirt up and let him work through your bra.

The first time I let someone touch my breast I was fifteen. We'd been to get what was called a Friendly's Awful Awful milkshake and we were driving home along the main highway and he had his arm behind my back and his hand was on my ribs. And as his hand moved up I said, "This is it, this is the moment." And when his hand finally touched my breast my heart beat so fast and it was just the most marvelous feeling I've ever experienced. Every day after that, when he'd drive me home from school his hand would creep, very slowly, from my hip to my ribs and finally to my breast. This was all outside the clothes and it never went any farther. He was a beautiful blond boy named John something, and we went together for two months. And nobody, nobody has ever made my heart beat as fast as that first day when his hand crawled up my ribs and touched my breast.

When I was sixteen we moved to Massachusetts for a year and I met a boy named Tom Nevell. If anyone should have taken my virginity it should have been him. The first day I saw him he was walking down the hall at school and he had on a pair of white jeans and a navy blue shirt and I just saw his toosh. And I became a toosh freak from that day forth. I fell in love with that ass and I followed it to biology every day for two weeks and when it finally turned around the front looked just as good as the back. He was a rugged-looking sandy blond with green eyes and a lovely physique. It was love, for him too. Things progressed further with him than they had with anyone else, but there was still a lot of frustration. We'd go out in his red and white Chevy convertible and there was a lot of pressing up against one another and a lot of touching, even below the waist, but still all through the clothes. He just should have been the one. But there was still all that heavy stuff and pressure from home, coupled now with a new element of female jealousy. My body had really just happened the summer before, boom, it was all there. I loved it; I said, This is what I've been waiting for. It was all so new and I was all ready for flaunting it. So it was only natural for my mother to feel competitive. For years I said, "Mommy, will I ever have tits like yours?" Suddenly I not only had them but they were bigger.

Tommy and I broke up and I went out with other boys but it went right back to just kissing. There was just one boy, a man really—he was twenty—and with him I experimented for the first time touching someone with his fly open. It was just a one-time experiment. It was something I was curious about and it was easier somehow to do it with someone like this, who I didn't care that much about, than with someone I was in love with. There was some sort of process in my mind that I could do it without as much guilt and even if he didn't like me for having done it, it didn't matter because I didn't like him that much.

It was a month before my eighteenth birthday that I finally lost my virginity. We had moved to Florida and I was a senior in high school, but I was also modeling and doing commercials and entering beauty pageants—in fact that year I was Miss Miami in the Miss Universe thing—and doing whatever I thought would help me to be an actress. If that's what it took I was going to do it. My mother didn't mind the pageants and stuff, because there was some glory in it and she thought she'd be right there to protect me. But I was beginning to make my break, beginning to be able to look at things and for the first time realize where she was right and where she was wrong. She felt me trying to break away, and though she'd say she had no qualms about it, it must have been a very painful time for her.

So I was finally able to sleep with someone. I was walking down the steps at school one day and this beautiful blond boy, again, stepped out into the courtyard and the sun came out at that moment on his head and I remember stumbling down the steps and saying, "Who is that?" He didn't know it, but he got laid right then and there. I just felt, unh, there was Adonis. That was the one, whether he wanted to go along with it or not. I was ready. I had been ready since Tommy but nobody had come along. He looked a little bit like Tommy in fact and, as I got to know him, reminded me in many ways of Tommy. Very handsome and just exceptionally bright. I didn't know anything about him that first day I saw him. He could have been on the local garbage detail and he could have stayed there for the next ten years. It didn't matter to me.

He doesn't know it, but that day I set about pursuing him. The next month was spent in finding out everything I could about him: his family, where he lived, what he did in school, his grades, the girls he'd gone with, what he liked. And by the end of that month I was everything he'd ever wanted. I changed my hair and the way I dressed and joined a group because of him. By this time I knew his schedule cold and one day when I knew he'd be leaving a certain class I was standing right there. As he walked out I charged into him, practically knocked him over and dropped all my books. He picked them up and from that day forth he carried them. To this day he thinks he bumped into me.

It took him a week to ask me out. We went to a football game, which I detested, and on the way he pulled out a quart of Coke and a quart of bourbon, which I had no inclination to drink. I had on a brand new outfit—the tightest white jeans I could find and a white jacket—and somehow he spilled the entire quart of bourbon on my pants. We stopped at a gas station and I washed them in the bathroom sink, but I couldn't dry them and went to the game wet. On the way home we necked—no touching, no French-kissing. But when he kissed me I knew that the initial lustful look I had gotten was right on. This was the one. We had been going together four or five months when the day finally arrived. We had worked up to it with a lot of parking. It was only the last two weeks before the big night that there was any clothing taken off. Up until then it had been lifting something up or pulling something down, but the clothing was still on. And really we touched very little below the waist. It's amazing, but very little. And there was certainly no oral contact. That was not until a few years later in my sexual life. That was something,

God knows, my mother had never told me about. I was under the impression that there was only one position.

This particular night we were parked in his pale blue Chevrolet on some deserted road somewhere, and he thought we were going to fool around and then go home. I'm sure I caught him off guard. I remember him saying, "Are you sure?" I said, "For Godssakes, I'm sure." I don't remember what I was wearing; they all came off so fast. We were in the front seat. To have gotten in the back would have seemed too premeditated and I was still holding on to some vestige of propriety. It was very short and there was no particular pain or pleasure, no particular physical sensation. In fact, afterwards I thought, "Jesus, there's got to be more than this. If not, I'm going back to the other stuff because petting was a lot of fun." He was not a virgin but he'd only been to bed with a couple of other girls and he wasn't very knowledgeable. He did take care of the contraceptives, which meant prophylactics. There was no way I could have gotten pills, I thought, without my parents finding out. I think he had an orgasm and that was important for me. It had been deeply ingrained that sex was basically for a man's pleasure. But in fact, in the months following, my zeal far exceeded his; my curiosity was endless.

The guilt that remained was only for my parents. My mother asked me one day if I was having an affair with this guy and I turned bright red and she knew and started to cry. I remember saying how sorry I was and thinking inside, almost watching myself, that I wasn't very sorry at all. We were doing it now at every available moment, on the way to school, during lunch, in the park. The first motel we stayed at was off Highway One in Homestead, Florida. We'd planned it. We took the whole day off from school and carried luggage and wore wedding rings I'd bought at Woolworth's. We had our own eight-dollar cottage with kitchenette so I cooked to make it feel homey. That became our favorite, that and the Holiday Inn where we spent our graduation night.

The sex got a lot better. The first and only time I had an orgasm with him was about three months after we'd started. Only after it happened did I know the difference. I couldn't quite understand why I didn't have another, but I got a great deal of delight out of the activity anyway. We talked about sex fairly openly and he became very worldly about my time of the month. We decided to get married when we finished school. He wanted to go to college and wanted me to set aside the acting in order to work and put him through school. Some days I thought that would work; other days I knew it wouldn't. I guess I was in love with him, but not like the first one, not like Tommy. When a man takes your virginity it makes him very special, but marriage was not going to work. And as I said, my sex drive was much stronger than his and that worried me a great deal. He more than once said I made extreme and unusual demands on his energy and more than once insinuated that I hadn't been a virgin. All I could say was, well, I tried it and I liked it, but I was filled with terrible doubts and guilts. I thought that maybe I was a latent nymphomaniac.

Luckily the next man I had a brief affair with had a marvelous enthusiasm for sex that was absolutely contagious. Whereas my original lover had many hang-ups and guilts and reservations, this man—he was twenty-seven—was so natural and encouraging. In fact, the relationship was based on pure chemistry. It was just like finding your perfect tennis partner. He knew all about oral sex but there wasn't much of it. We took absolute delight in just pure fucking. I'm very grateful to him.

Then I moved to New York and within a few months began my tortured three-year affair. Since him, no one has ever paid a bill of mine or paid my rent or bought my clothes. Since him, marriage has never seemed very important to me. When I left him in London I came to Hollywood and it was like finding out what it was like to be single again. The first date I had in Los Angeles I went to bed with the guy. It was the healthiest thing that could have happened, because I needed to know I was desirable, just purely "I'm a person and I want you." And he was very kind and was actually not a bad first choice. For the next six months I went to every party I was invited to, I went out with every handsome available bachelor. Some I slept with, some I didn't. I was a real party girl and I was treated just the way I deserved to be treated. What I thought of myself was the way I was treated, and at that point I wasn't sure what to think. I knew that a man whom I had loved very deeply for three years had treated me like an employee, and if he thought that about me how could anyone good love me? I must be a bad girl. So I set out to prove what a bad girl I could be and yet at the same time what a good girl I really was. Finally I got with a very good psychiatrist and went into very heavy analysis, and he turned around my life and helped me come to terms with all those deep-down guilts. In my first affair the man had been rather laid back about sex, and in my three-year affair the man had been totally promiscuous, so there was a feeling that I wasn't a very good person and that the only men who could love me must be bad. I fell in love with another big blond Adonis, a sports hero, and that was another disaster. His problems and my problems just didn't mesh. The sex was very confusing. But the analysis saved me. I seldom go to parties anymore unless I really want to; I seldom find myself out with people wondering what am I doing there. I don't feel obsessed anymore about being with a man.

In fact, I haven't been involved with a man for months. I see a few people casually, but that's it. Now there is just an eagerness to enjoy life. Now there is a feeling that I don't have to pay myself back for anything. I'm not a bad girl.

Lou Rawls *singer*

Born December 1, 1935, Chicago, Ill.

When he is not on the road, which he is forty weeks a year, Lou Rawls lives not like a star but like a middle-class wage earner in a small, ordinary house in a "transition" neighborhood not far from the Ambassador Hotel in Los Angeles, where Bobby Kennedy was assassinated. He is divorced, and his mother and a full-time housekeeper help with his children, Lou Jr., ten, and Louanna, six, who sat watching television while Rawls had a can of beer beside his small back-yard swimming pool and chain-smoked cigarettes as he talked about his past. He wore a checked flannel shirt and a pair of powder-blue overalls, and despite his hard life on the road he looked considerably younger than his age. He spoke in a relaxed, resonant voice, and talked about his childhood with nostalgic pleasure, relating each segment of his life as a rich little story full of warm description and fondly remembered anecdote.

I DON'T THINK I ever saw my daddy over five or six times in my life, and my mama went out to Seattle during the war to work in the shipyards, so I lived with my grandmother in one of those one-room tenements in Southside Chicago.

Every Sunday we went to the Greater Mount Olive Baptist Church. Once or twice a month a professional group would come and sing at the church, and gradually five of us formed a little group and started singing around Chicago.

You were considered a man when you reached the tender age of ten and had to go to work. I worked in a grocery store and then later I rode the bus to Gary, Indiana, every day after school and worked in a steel foundry until midnight. On Saturday nights they'd have the local dance at The Warwick, and if you didn't go to The Warwick, then, Jack, you wasn't in it. You'd go over to the West Side and get you some pegged pants, a double-breasted jacket and one of those "Mr. B." collars, a wide necktie and a pair of imitation Stetson shoes that turned up and looked at you. Then you'd go to The Warwick, but you wouldn't do anything but go there and stand around the walls. I was about eleven and wasn't into girls yet.

What turned us on to sex first wasn't girls but old ladies. Old women in their thirties and forties. We would go to a church and sing, and afterwards the minister would designate some of the sisters to cook for us. I'd be sitting there eating that fried chicken and potato pie and they'd say, "You a fine young man. I just love little men like you." They'd have these big nice cars and they'd say, "Come on, I'll take you home," and they'd get you in the car and start feeling your thighs and saying, "Fine boy. Fine!" Then they'd maybe give you a little smooch.

Five of us—Sam Cooke was the leader—formed a religious group called "The Highway QC's," and we went over to Jewtown to get Skeets the Tailor to make us some uniforms. He said "Okay, boys, I'm gonna do ya'll a favor. I ain't gonna charge ya'll but $125 apiece for these suits." Man, we were sharp. Blue serge suits with four patch pockets and double-breasted coats. Then we got us a 1943 Chrysler and went down to the Bible Belt for a tour we'd made a connection for at the National Baptist Convention.

The first time I was scored I was thirteen and it was in this little bitty town of Tifton on the Georgia–Tennessee border. The minister of this little Baptist church where we sang said after the sermon, "Now ya'll know there ain't no hotel for these boys to stay at, so I want some of you sisters to volunteer to put them up." So I went home with this lady. She lived in one of those old shotgun houses way out on a country dirt road. It was just a bedroom, a kitchen and a hallway sitting up on stilts. It had one bed with an oil lamp over the head of it, and a great big potbellied stove to heat the whole house. This lady couldn't have been a day under forty, and she was fat, super fat.

She had these big patchwork quilts on the bed, so I said, "I'll just take one of those blankets and sleep down here on the floor."

She said, "Oh, no, no, no. You sleep in the bed with Mama."

The lady was nice. I'd wake up every morning to the smell of biscuits and ham cooking. We stayed there a week, singing at Tifton, Waycross, Valdosta—all those little communities around there. Finally it came down to the last night and she said, "Well, ya'll gonna be leaving tomorrow. I ain't gonna charge you nothing for the food and staying here, but you gotta be nice." I knew what she meant from the way she'd been squeezing and pinching on me all week.

So we got into the bed and at first I didn't know what she was going to do. Then this big fat arm just came over and she said, "Come here," and she pulled me over on her and I was

just buried in fat. She pulled my pajamas down so that my
little butt was sticking out. Then she pulled her nightgown up
and pulled the covers up on top of us. It was hot and sweaty
and she had me. She just kept hunching and going "Uh, Uh,
Uh" until finally she let out this one big yell and her arms flew
out. That was the first time she let me go since she pulled me
up there, so I rolled off, and pretty soon she starts snoring. I
think I balled a wrinkle, she was so fat. There wasn't any sensation for me, no orgasm or anything. I was embarrassed and
just felt like I was paying her for the food.

Losing your cherry wasn't any big thing with us, except
that *the* big thing was not to lose your cherry to some faggot.
You'll find more homosexuals in the religious field than anyplace else in the world and, man, I could name a few kids
that just got raped.

After we left Tifton, we went to Atlanta to sing, and the
first time I ever really got laid was in the back seat of a car in
the parking lot back of the auditorium in Atlanta. We were
leaving town right after the show but we had a thirty-minute
intermission and these little chicks started coming up and
saying, "Hey, ya'll are good! Ya'll gonna be just great." So
after the rigamarole dies down everybody starts pairing off,
and I'm taking my shot when one of the other dudes comes
over and whispers, "Hey, man, I'm going out and use the car.
If anybody looks for me, tell them you don't know where I
am." So the chick I'm with says, "Ain't you gonna go out
there, too?" So I said, "Well, yeah, yeah. I'm going." So we
got out to the car and he gets in the back seat and does his
number. So then I get in the back seat with this little chick,
and I ain't got sense enough—or maybe I was just scared—to
take my pants off. I just unzipped them and went chung,
chung, chung, chung, and it was over. She was a little teen-

ager and I didn't even know what her name was. There was
no courting or anything. It was "Okay, here it is." But it was
exciting, first of all because it was wrong—in the back seat of
a car during a thirty-minute intermission between singing
"Jesus Loves Me," which was like our opening theme song,
and "He'll Never Let Go Your Hand," which was our closing
song.

A few minutes later I'm standing up there singing in front
of five thousand people and I look down and there was white
all over the front of my blue serge pants. The dudes ribbed
me to death about that for a month. Every time I'd go on
stage they'd say, "Hey, Lou, better check out your pants."

After that, girls were always available, even when you
didn't want them. We weren't like the local boys. We had
two complete sets of clothes, and that made us bigtime. We
could change clothes. So we had the pick of the litter. All the
little girls would come up and say, "Ooh," and if you'd see
one you liked, you'd say, "Hey, come here. What you getting
ready to do?" and they'd say, "I got to go home with my
mama and daddy," so we'd say, "Okay, you come by tomorrow." We'd be staying someplace, and we'd smuggle them in.
We were just gonna be there for a minute, so it was hit hard,
get what you can, and go. It was like wham, bam, thank you
Ma'am—in the hallway, on the steps, on the kitchen table,
and there was no such thing as "I've got to satisfy this
woman." It was like self-preservation—jump on and get it
over with, and if in the interim she did make it, cool, and if
she didn't, well, hey, baby, next time.

Singing in the religious field, it was just hit the sheets.
Every town you'd go into you'd have a wife. You'd meet a
girl and start going with her, so you'd introduce her to the
rest of the dudes by saying, "That's my wife." Later on we

got more sophisticated and started saying, "That's my pin." When you said "my pin," that meant you were going to bed with her, you were pinning her to the sheets.

I'd heard people talking about getting head, and sixty-nine, but I didn't learn anything about it until I got into the pop music field. Sixty-nine was considered a no-no. It was dirty. And if a girl tried to do that to you, you'd say, "Hey, what you doing? Don't do that."

We never did mess with married women. That would create problems. There was enough single chicks, so why put yourself in the position of getting killed or run out of town over a piece of ass? It ain't worth it.

We finally got hip to contraception and started going into the bathrooms where they had those twenty-five-cent rubber machines, because after a couple of the cats kept getting a dose of clap we figured we'd better do something. I didn't get a dose of clap until I was in the Army down in Fayetteville, North Carolina, where there was this bunch of chicks who came up from South Carolina every payday. One of them fell in love with me and I went for it.

Blacks have always been portrayed as hot young studs who are always chomping at the bit, but this is only maybe 60 per cent true. This all goes back to slavery days, when the strong-looking young black was used for stud purposes. And so black men come along with the heritage that if you can't hump three or four chicks a day you must be a faggot or something.

The first time I went to New York City and worked at the Apollo Theater, I stayed at this hotel out at 125th and Seventh Avenue, the one where Castro stayed, and, man, it was like a bus stop. I would set up a time schedule. Okay, Ethel's coming at ten, Susie's coming at twelve, Margaret's coming at two, Jo Ann will be here at four, I gotta go to work at six, I'll be back at nine, and at ten Judy will be here.

My records were just starting to take off in '63 and I'd finished an engagement in Anchorage, Alaska, and had a couple of days to lay around, and got to thinking of all those chicks that had approached me but I had missed. So I figured I might as well clean the book, and in one day I screwed seven of them—a couple of orientals, three sisters and two Caucasians.

I can't see any difference between white women and black. Some might talk more than others, but when the lights are out it don't make no difference. I used to notice a great hang-up in black women about doing anything other than straight humping. But that has long gone by the wayside. Black women are getting more mature and sophisticated.

In the religious field, we didn't get into white women at all. The first time I got into that was on a tour with Sam Cooke. We were in Little Rock, Arkansas, at the National Guard Armory, and they put a rope right down the middle of the hall, white on one side, colored on the other. By this time Sam was getting pretty big, and somehow these white chicks got to him and made arrangements to meet up somewhere out in the woods. Sam said to me, "Come on and drive the car. You can leave me with them, go somewhere, and pick me up in about an hour." I said, "Hey, man, don't you know they'll kill you for that down here?" He said, "Aw, man, everything's all right." I was scared. I'd read about lynchings and stuff. I didn't do anything. All I wanted to do was get away, because I knew if we got caught it wouldn't make any difference whether I did anything or not. Anyway, I drove him out into this woods and these two white chicks were there in a pickup truck with a camper on the back. I left and drove back about fifteen miles to this restaurant and waited about an hour and then went back and picked him up.

The first white woman I had anything to do with, I married. I met Lana in 1960 when I was on a record promotion tour down in Houston at this club called The Sidewalk Cafe. I was twenty-two then and so was she. She was a typical Southern belle, blonde and blue-eyed, and we were really in love. When I left there I went to Cleveland to play the Theatrical Grill, and a week later she joined me. Her mother told the police I had kidnapped her. The police came to me and said, "Your name Lou Rawls?" and I said "Yeah," so they said, "You got a white girl with you?" I said, "White girl with me? Naw, man, what you talking about?" They were going to cite me for white slavery. Well, something had told me not to let her stay with me, so she was at another hotel four or five blocks away. We got married three months later. Twelve years and numerous show business incidents later, we decided we weren't in love. Sad.

The first orgy I ever saw was at the Waldorf Astoria in New York City, where these dudes came from all over the country for the convention of the National Association of Radio Announcers and Disc Jockeys. Different hospitality suites would open and around two o'clock in the morning, after all the straight people went home, the sex perverts would come out. So I walked into this hospitality suite and, wow, chicks were doing chicks, studs were doing chicks, studs were doing studs, and they said, "Come on in." I said, "Naw, I'm in the wrong room." I mean they were on the couches, on the tables, on the floor, just doing it. What turned me around was the dudes doing the dudes. I'd been running from that all my life, and I walk in and there it was right in front of my face.

I was about eleven and we were at this big religious concert in Chicago when a faggot tried to hit on me the first time. He kept patting me on the butt, until finally I said, "If you touch me again, I'm gonna kill you," and reached like I was going for a knife in my pocket. That cooled him off.

When I first got into this business there were a lot of young dudes who were just using their talent as a door-opener into the pimping business. They would go to a club and work, and get maybe three or four chicks, and take money from them and more or less become their pimps. I never could go for that, never took any money or even gifts. When I got married everybody was thinking, "Young black singer. White girl. He's going to put her into the street." No way.

There are a lot of stage-door Sallys and groupies and super-slick maneuverers who'll come around. The groupies don't want to brag about it. They just want to do it. The others come around in T-Birds and Cadillacs and diamonds and furs, and all they want to do is get laid so they can say to their friends next day, "Hey, I laid Lou Rawls last night." That kind of stuff doesn't do you any good. All it does is make people think you're trying to do something.

That doesn't happen with me anymore. I take care of myself. I don't age anymore. I stopped aging when I got to be thirty. It ain't no fun getting old, and you're only old if you think you are. I'm gonna die, but there ain't no sense in getting old to die.

You can't lay on top of a woman as long as she can lay up under you. All she has to do is jump up, wipe it out with a rag and keep on stepping. You can't even get up. If you get too carried away, you'll wake up one morning and there won't be nothing there. No voice.

Debbie Reynolds *entertainer*

Born April 1, 1932, El Paso, Tex.

It was not one of her better days. An electrical short had caused the mikes to fail during her main dinner show. She had a lingering cold. And there was the continuing pressure of painful divorce proceedings between her and second husband, Harry Karl. But Old Trouper Debbie Reynolds quickly showered, put on a blue turban and a soft, gray terrycloth robe, and emerged peppily into her garish dressing room at Harrah's in Reno, and ran briskly through a long string of between-show responsibilities. First she had to get her daughter, Carrie, eighteen, settled for the evening. A coltish high-school dropout who had just begun to sing in her mother's show, Carrie is Debbie's daughter by first husband Eddie Fisher. While attending to her, Debbie chatted pleasantly with a half dozen people who were waiting for autographs. After that, she sat down beside a man from the Nevada Department of Human Resources and quickly taped, unrehearsed and without a single miscue, three public service announcements urging people to volunteer as foster parents. Then she chatted briefly with her manager, her hairdresser and her music arranger while her matronly mother fussed about tidying up the room and monitoring the traffic. Finally Debbie sat down, ordered the No. 2 Chinese Special from the

hotel menu, with a glass of milk, and briskly responded to
questions for forty-five minutes. She answered each one rap-
idly and without any agonizing soul searching, rather as if
this was another responsibility of her job that should be done
in her accustomed efficient, good-natured, it-comes-with-the-
territory manner.

NEEDLESS TO SAY, I was a virgin when I married, like my
mother before me, and her mother before her. And that's the
only thing I ever heard; that's just the way it was supposed
to be. And all my girl friends' mothers taught their daughters
the same way. You didn't sleep around. Sleep around, why,
you weren't even supposed to be kissing. Holding hands was
a big thing. Today, of course, the moral values have changed,
and the girl who is a virgin is sometimes considered a nut.

I think that for young girls to have a number of men before they're eighteen years old is a terrible mistake. Because
they don't have a wonderful rooted love for one man. It's like
you walk by the candy store and you look at all of it, but you
can't have it. Having a different boy every week would make
me very unhappy with myself. The boys don't think much of
you. After a while you're just yesterday's newspaper. That's
not good for yourself. I wouldn't do it, and I've raised my
daughter Carrie the same way. I mean I'm her mother, and I
wouldn't do it. I want to be proud of myself.

But I was never brought up to think sex is bad, and before
I married, my mother had told me all about it and I'd read all
the books she'd bought or borrowed from the library for me.
My parents are just wonderful parents. They have lived their
lives doing for my brother and myself. There's not a time that

I felt insecure in life. I think that's because the one aspect my mother and father gave me most of all was common horse sense, which has stood me very strong in life. And also I didn't get thrown because I was raised with a lot of church-going and religion, and that belief has been very good for me.

I was born in El Paso, Texas, on April 1, 1932, in the middle of the Depression. My father worked for the Southern Pacific Railroad, so we didn't have a great deal of money. The area we lived in was very mixed, mostly Indian and Mexican. We were probably the second white family in the neighborhood. There were no paved streets and it was the desert right in back of our house. I remember as a child balancing on the railroad tracks and finding hobos and bringing them home to dinner. Nobody had any money, but Mother always had a big pot of beans cooking. In those days you weren't afraid to bring people home; people were really hungry and not looking to murder. Both my mother and grandmother were very religious. My father had his own form of faith; he never attended church regularly. In fact, it was always a laughing matter that if he walked into the church, the roof would cave in.

My father adored his mother-in-law, my grandma, so we saw them a lot and when things got really tough we moved in with them. I remember sleeping in my grandparents' house. There were five boys in the family, my brother, my mother's three brothers and a much younger child born to my grandmother very late in life. She thought it was a tumor; it turned out to be another son. Anyway, all of the boys and me used to sleep in one bed with our feet in each other's faces. And every Wednesday, Friday and Sunday we attended the red brick Church of the Nazarene. It was a very midwest form of the Hardshell Baptist—very hellfire and brimstone, very evangelistic, a lot of tent meetings. The ministers preached a very strong sermon, stuff like, "Live by the Ten Commandments or you're going to go to hell." But it never scared me, because everybody I knew who believed was fun. And nobody ever screamed at me as a child that if I didn't do something I was going to go to the devil. God was supposed to be a positive person, and you believed in Him because all the elders around you were so positive in their belief. They never discussed sex in church; you knew you just didn't ever mess around. They did say you couldn't smoke, drink, dance, play cards or do anything that young people like to do. And whether they said it or not, you were raised to be a virgin. A virgin is a good girl who meets the man she loves and marries him.

When I was seven, we moved from Texas to Burbank, California, and we immediately joined the Church of the Nazarene in North Hollywood. My mother and I were very involved in the church. I was like a young missionary. We'd both teach Sunday school classes and we'd go to all the evangelistic meetings and it was really a major part of our life.

I went to the local public schools, Roosevelt Grammar School, John Burroughs Junior High and Burbank High. My last two years of schooling were at Warners and MGM, which I didn't like at all. During those years, I didn't date very much at all. The boys weren't exactly running around looking for me. I was very tomboy and I could kick a football as good as they could and I really loved, idolized my brother and I loved sports and I wanted to be a gym teacher. I was skinny, little, blonde and funny—a Mad Hatter. I'd do any gag or shtick for a laugh. I was always voted Miss Personality in the school paper, that sort of thing. The boys always liked me, but they never dated me. I was their pal, their chum. Whereas the other girls had dates to go to football games and all of that, I had to take the bus and they thought that was funny. And my real name was Mary Frances, so my nickname was Franny, or sometimes Peanuts, and they thought that was funny. I was always very active and never had the time to sit around worrying about my hair and nails. I still don't. And I've never been much of a fashion plate. I get a headache as soon as I have to go shopping. I finally learned how to dress when I went to MGM, but it took them about three years to get me out of my paint-splattered jeans and T-shirts and tennis shoes. When I was in high school we didn't have any money and I had one skirt, one of those full, gathered skirts everyone wore then, one blouse and whatever shoes were on sale.

But the boys liked the feminine girls and the girls that would neck. And I wouldn't do it. Girls who would neck were considered very loose morally. I didn't want to do it. I think I was scared to death and so I wouldn't even face it. I pretended I didn't like it. How would I know that, when I hadn't even tried it? It was all in my head. I think anybody's frightened of something they haven't experienced. And as a young girl I was frightened of boys. They made me terribly nervous and I was uncomfortable around them because I had no relationship with them other than as another boy, tossing the football with them.

So in high school my four best girl friends and I started a club called the Non-Neckers Club. We thought that was very funny. And then one of our girls one night kissed a boy and we had to add another N—the Nearly Non-Neckers Club. We were probably around thirteen. I had my first kiss a little while later. We were at a boy-girl party and we were playing a game called Sugar, Peaches or Cream. It was the big game. A boy would go into a closet and say either sugar, peaches or cream and whatever girl was named sugar, peaches or cream would have to go in and kiss him. One kiss and they'd come out. Well, I would never play. I was always the captain and I named everyone else. But this one time they finally said I had to play. I was scared to death. The boy went into the closet. His name was Bob and he wore braces. Well, he picked my name, whichever it was—sugar, peaches or cream. I had to go into the closet. Have you ever kissed braces? Well, I was really not thrilled with my first kiss. I thought, "If that's what it's all about, I don't need any of this."

I had a girl friend whose mother had a friend named Captain Rogers who lived with them, and every time I'd go over there they'd be in bed together. My friend would yell, "Hey Mom, I'm going over to school and play ball." And the mother would say, "Okay, dear." I said to my girl friend, "Is he your uncle or something?" And she said, "No, he's my mother's boyfriend." She thought nothing about it, but I was shocked. I never told my mother because she wouldn't have let me go over there anymore. I mean, he'd walk around in his shorts and things.

There was one boy in high school who used to date me. His name was Leon Tyler and he loved to dance and he taught me how to dance and how to tap. We did little tap dances together and he took me to the school dances. He was as skinny as I was and silly-looking like me, so I don't think he would have had many dates either. But we got along great and I dated him right up until I married Eddie.

When I went into show business at age sixteen, the Church of the Nazarene asked me to leave because they believed that actresses were wanton, morally loose women. They told all these wives tales to my mother, but she didn't believe them. So I made the screen test and I wasn't struck dead and I didn't morally cave in in a half hour like they said I would. And I never had any problem with show business. I never had anyone chase me around desks or all those things you read about. I absolutely never, never did. Perhaps it was because I always looked so much younger and I truly was innocent and I guess it just stuck out all over me. So they knew that not only was I jailbait but I was also a little backward as far as my upbringing or experience was concerned. I mean Peter Lawford was not going to make a pass at me. Let's put it that way. There were all those sexy, voluptuous girls falling all over him and here I was, sixteen, weighing 98 pounds and still very tomboy. Just an amusing little kid—that's all I was.

I guess I started to look like a woman when I was around twenty. By then I was dating men like Hugh O'Brian, who was very sophisticated, and Tab Hunter. These guys would laughingly tell stories about me, that I'd drag my foot to stop the car, leap out the door, and be behind the screen door of my house before they could even get around the side of their car. I'd made a deal with my mother to leave the front porch light on so I wouldn't have to kiss anybody good night if I didn't want to. I'd go away for a weekend with one of them to water ski at Lake Arrowhead. I never thought it was wrong to go away for a weekend and I never thought anybody would ever be fresh with me, and they never were. Never. I wouldn't have liked that and they knew it. I didn't want to be nervous. I liked to have everything right aboveboard. A very funny young man named Arthur Lowe, Jr., called me and asked me out and I said, "No I don't want to go out with you because I understand that you're a wolf." There was a long pause on the phone and he said, "A wolf, are you joking?" And I said, "I hear that you're very fresh and I don't want any of that. I don't want any trouble. If I want to go to a movie, I want to see the movie, not neck. If I want to go bowling, I want to go bowling. Whatever we're going to do, I want to do that and not anything else and I understand that you're very fresh with women and I see no reason to go out with you." Well, he laughed and laughed and said, "Just try me. I promise to be very amusing and not fresh." I said, "All right, if that's a promise." I'd ask these guys why they took me out. And they'd say, "Because you're fun and we have a good time together and I enjoy you because you're so fresh."

I met Eddie Fisher at the studio. I was twenty-two and I was making a picture called *Hit the Deck* with Vic Damone, Jane Powell and Ann Miller. Eddie was a big name singer then—it was pre-Elvis, pre-rock, and he'd had I don't remember how many straight hits—and he was visiting Los Angeles and Joe Pasternak brought him down to MGM. We were introduced and he asked me out. I went with Mike Todd and Evelyn Keyes, I think that's who Mike was dating at the time, to Eddie's opening at the Coconut Grove. I was his date after the opening. And I had a terrific time. He was charming and he was a very attractive young man, maybe five years older than I was. Eddie was always a charmer, and very cute and a perfect age for me and in show business. He asked me to marry him on our third date. Then about a month later he gave me the biggest diamond ring I'd ever seen in the history of the world, something like eleven carats. The extent of my jewelry was a little tiny gold watch that I'd bought and was paying $48 a month for. The next thing I know he gave me the ring, and it staggered me; I was petrified to wear it. My mother loved Eddie. She had always watched his Coke Time show and was always saying to me, as I rushed in and out getting dressed for parties or what not, "Listen to this young singer, dear, he's so wonderful."

Eddie had been around show business a long time and had dated a great deal and I suppose he thought I was sort of from another world altogether. Now when I look back, having been in show business twenty-six years, I'm sure I really was an odd duck. We were engaged for a year and then we were married, at Grossinger's, because that's where Eddie was discovered, by Eddie Cantor. I was twenty-three, and I didn't even know what French kissing was. Believe me, I learned a lot. And it wasn't traumatic, because I was very attracted to Eddie. He was my first physical attraction. He had also had, I'm sure, many relationships, and he was very good with me, very bright with me. He did not mishandle a young girl of inexperience. I'm sure he could have scared me, but he didn't. He was experienced enough and an adult man and a very good teacher. That part of our relationship was not unpleasant.

Because Eddie was Jewish we couldn't be married in a church, so we had a small civil ceremony and the next day we left for some Coca-Cola convention somewhere with his manager and his press agent and his valet and his whole entourage. I had company all through my married life.

My concept of marriage was very old-fashioned. The man was the head of the house and handled everything. But that did not entitle him to adultery, not in my family, no. On my very first long trip, when I was eighteen, I went with Pier Angeli on a tour of South America and was introduced to a number of people with beautiful young wives—or so I thought. Later on they said, "Oh, that's his mistress. His wife lives somewhere else." I was shocked. Today nobody's a mistress. You're just a girl friend, and after a year or two he just walks out the door, looking for greener fields.

I'm still a very square person. I know I am. I've never seen a pornographic film. There was a scene in *Midnight Cowboy* where some guy let his drawers fall down and his rear end was exposed. I got up and left the room. But I do think I've grown up a bit. I now don't see anything wrong with having a relationship prior to marriage. In fact, I think it's healthy, as long as they truly love each other and are together with the thought of staying together. It doesn't have to be marriage, although I think young people marrying is still a wonderful thing.

I don't think it's right to raise children without marriage, without the wonderful roots and the security of the mother and father and the home life and the going to the park and the outings and the baseball games together. You can't have that if the kid thinks, "Well, I'm going to have a new daddy next week." There are times in life when you unfortunately have to give your children a new daddy, whether you like it or not. But that's out of your control. Both Eddie and Harry Karl, my second husband, were fine human beings. The end of one marriage was obvious; the second had to end in order for me to survive. Sometimes you have to fight to stay alive.

I don't have any sex life today. I'm just getting a divorce from Harry, and until I'm married I won't have any kind of intimate relationship with a man. When I'm divorced I'll be free. Between my marriages I was single for a year and a half, but I was never with anybody sexually. So I have had two men in my life, and I married them both. Right now I'm not interested in emotional relationships because I'm too drained. I've been working steadily for the last five years, and I want to be with my children. When they leave home in a couple of years, I'll be alone, and then I'll be lonely. But right now I wouldn't be involved with anybody. Because I can't have any more mistakes in my life. I certainly can control my emotions, because now I'm a woman, not a child.

Bobby Riggs *tennis player*

Born February 25, 1918, Los Angeles, Calif.

Still riding the wave of publicity that accompanied his tennis match with Billie Jean King six months earlier, Bobby Riggs was in San Francisco appearing as a publicity gag for a charity women's karate tournament. "Hey, Bobby," yelled a young black man who recognized Riggs on the street, "what you doin' in a girls' karate championship?" Riggs grinned mischievously and piped in a raspy voice, "I'm fighting the champion, and I'm gonna' kick the shit out of her, too." He had several bourbons with Coke while dining with four people from the tournament committee, and was up early next morning at the Mark Hopkins, dressed in tennis whites for an 11 A.M. press conference. He ordered up a huge room-service breakfast—grapefruit, eggs, sausages, pancakes, toast, English muffins, jelly, milk and coffee—and ate voraciously as he talked about his childhood and sports career, revealing more introspection than his public image indicated. His voice was hoarse and it had a kind of little-kid quality that helped give his chipmunkish face a look of innocence and naïveté.

You CAN'T MAKE EVERY TENNIS MATCH like it's the final for Wimbledon; you can't make every screw the same way. If you're going to come back for more then you may try hard to do more than your share. But if it's just something on the spur of the moment and you don't think you'll see the girl again, then sometimes you may not perform so well. Although for a guy part of the ego trip is being able to satisfy women. You like each one to tell you you're the greatest lay they ever had. Most guys need that feeling of satisfaction, and the really smart women, they give you that and tell you that you are. And okay, okay, so you tell them the same thing. That's part of the game, part of the fun of it. And I think that's the only right thing to do.

But women have never been terribly important in my life. They were always strictly incidental, strictly the extras and strictly for the fun. They were just the icing on the cake; they were never the main course for me. My big play was always the games, the tennis, the golf, the gambling. I was programmed to be a champion. As a child all I did from morning till night was run and play and jump and gamble, all day long, games, games, games, competitive, competitive, competitive, win, win, win. You see, I was raised in a family of seven boys and one girl, and I was the baby. My mother was just a plain-looking farm girl from Tennessee, a down-to-earth, Abraham Lincoln sort of person, very hard-working, very busy every day taking care of the house and having children and fixing dinner and washing clothes. And my father was already fifty by the time I was born in 1918. He was a minister with the Church of Christ, a very warm sort of a guy, a good handshaker, as preachers must be. He sometimes got out and played catch and ran some races with us, but mostly he was concerned with the church, mostly up on Cloud Nine preparing his sermons for the next week. And so a big part of my being brought up, a big influence, was by the brothers. They handled some of the authority but what they mostly handled was my whole athletic program. They taught me how to punch and jab and run and jump and how to shoot tops and marbles and how to go out, cut left, cut right, come back and catch a pass and how to swing a base-ball bat.

The earliest memory I can go back to is maybe when I was four years old, my brothers said to me, "Look, we want to have a little race; you're going to race the boy next door. He's a year older than you, but you've been trained by us and if you win you'll get to go to the movies with us, some-thing like Tom Mix. And if you don't win, why, we'll give you a kick in the ass." As I recall, this was probably John and Luke who were raising these things—they were the closest to me in age. They always loved to put me in games. They were constantly matching me up with somebody. I don't know why and they wouldn't know why. They just seemed to want to include me in things. And another thing was I lost my brother Frank when he was six and a half or seven. He was my next oldest brother, and one day at school he was halfway up the slide and the tardy bell rang. And he rushed up to the top and toppled off and hit his head. We lost him the next day. So he left me a gap there of seven years between me and my next oldest brother. When you're little that's a hell-uva difference, so they put me up against kids more my own age. And I guess because of Frank they gave me more atten-tion and love and affection than they normally would have. And we were all growing up in Los Angeles, a neighborhood called Lincoln Heights, so the weather was good all year around and we just played all the normal Southern California games. And I always had great incentive to win the games, it was the immediate thing, because I'd get a pat on the back from my big brothers.

One of my earlier memories is of walking behind my brother and one of his school pals—they were probably fourteen and I was seven and they'd take me every place, tagging along—and the guy made some remark like, "Hey, so and so is a pretty good football player." And my older brother said, "Oh, that guy isn't so good. Hell," he said, "my little brother can do it better than he can." My little brother can do this better, my little brother can do that better. And finally this guy said, "That little brother of yours must be something." And so, boy, I got turned on and had tremendous incentive and motivation to please my brothers. And they put me in every possible kind of contest, running races, running around the block, pitching pennies, and always against older, more experienced, faster and better competition all the time.

Then when I was twelve I started playing tennis. And as I say, I did everything in a competitive way. At that time my older brother John played a bit, and he took a terrific razzing from all the rest of the kids in the neighborhood because tennis was considered a sissy sport at that time. But I started playing at the local park and this really fine woman player got hold of me and worked with me for a month and then entered me in a tournament. I got to the finals and won a cup. Then the next time around I beat the boy that had defeated me in the first tournament and thereafter I was the champ of the thirteen and under division. I'm very proud of the fact that I've been the best tennis player in the world from the time I was twelve. And I've always been the best player of my age all of my life, and I still am.

Tennis was like Seventh Heaven to me. I'd always been doing neighborhood stuff and now I was winning cups and

getting my name in the fine print in the newspaper. I wasn't
one of those rich kids who took tennis lessons like he took
swimming lessons or dancing lessons. Not that my parents
were as poor as church mice. They were property-owners.
We had a nice two-story wooden frame house at 2840 Sichel
Street, brown, shingled, with four bedrooms, an attic and an
old shack out back that I put a ping-pong table in and used as
a neighborhood clubhouse. Basically I had a tremendous
boy's world; I had all the athletic equipment any kid could
want—a yard full of bats and balls and basketballs and foot-
balls. But I didn't have the bicycle and I didn't get the extra
dime for candy or popcorn at the Saturday movie. But, my
God, I didn't know the difference; I was delighted to get
the dime to go. So you see, it never took much motivation
for me to be good at tennis or anything else. I was so unso-
phisticated, so naïve in a way, the opposite of being blasé like
a kid who had everything.

I was so one-track-minded about sports that there really
wasn't any part of me for girls at that point. Oh, we talked
about girls the way boys do, about necking and smooching,
and wouldn't it be wonderful to grab somebody and feel her
up and that kind of stuff. But I could never bring it off. I was
not successful as a youngster, with the girls. I didn't have any
moral feelings about sex at all, because I was trying all the
time, but I just didn't seem to have the know-how, the knack
as far as girls were concerned. I was the type that felt the
straightest line was the best, but as you know, the direct approach isn't very good. Girls want to be romanced a little bit;
they want somebody to spend a little time with them and so
forth, and I just never had any feel for that. I do remember
hearing my brothers talk all the time, so despite my lack of
success I grew up knowing everything there is to know about
it. I was masturbating all the time from about five years on.

I guess technically you can say I lost my virginity at age seven. It was summer and we were out visiting family friends, church members, on their ranch. Their little girl was a year older than me, and she and I were supposed to be up in the hayloft picking up the chicken eggs. And she said something to me like, "Show me yours and I'll show you mine." I was barefoot—I hardly had a pair of shoes till I was twelve, and then only because you had to have them to go to high school—and was wearing overalls. So I took them off and she pulled her skirt up and I lay right on top of her. And we fooled around and she showed me how to do it. I knew what you were supposed to do anyway, because I'd heard my brothers. I actually put it in her—a kid is practically born with a hard-on, you know. But you have a dry run is what it is. The sensation was like a sting, like a little buzz. It didn't last too long, but I have a memory of screwing this girl at age seven. After that she wanted me to be up in the hayloft every afternoon, but as I recall, we had only three different afternoons. Somehow or other I get the feeling that she was taking the initiative in this more than I was, that she was engineering the thing. It shouldn't have been that way, because, Christ, I was anxious. But maybe when it came right down to it and I got somebody to take me up on it I was a little shy or a little bit backward about things. I know I was a little apprehensive about my parents showing up. I asked my older brothers about that years later and they said that it wasn't the big secret that I thought it was and that both families knew about it. I didn't see this person again for ten years, by which time she had grown up to be a very handsome girl. We met again in church and I looked across and our eyes met and she turned beet red. She remembered it, too.

Would you believe, after getting started at age seven and

liking it and wanting it and trying at every chance, that the next real time was ten years later? I was seventeen and I'd gone north to Berkeley to play in the Pacific Coast Championships. I played in everything, the men's singles, the junior singles, men's doubles, junior doubles, even the mixed doubles, I think. I was at Berkeley, and I got a call from a good friend of mine, also a good tennis player, who lived in San Francisco. He said, "Hey, Bob, my girl wants to come over and see some of the tennis. Can you get her a ticket?" I said, "Of course. I'd be glad to." This was Monday or Tuesday, and she came over around noon and I met her and gave her the ticket. Her name was Ramona and she was a beautiful Spanish señorita, Jesus Christ, really gorgeous, great figure, beautiful eyes, long black hair and perfect features. She was like twenty or twenty-one. I was only seventeen, skinny, with a crew cut; I don't think I looked like much at that time. So anyway, I played all these matches and for Chrissakes, when I walk off the court it's dark and she's still there. This guy was a good friend of mine, I liked him very much, and I wanted to be courteous so I invited her to dinner. And she said, "Yes, I'd love to." I borrowed a car and we went to Lake Merritt Night Club in Oakland—never forget it. They had a good band and we danced and I think I had my first real drink, a Tom Collins. I drank it like it was lemonade. She did too. And it got to be twelve o'clock and there was no way for her to get back to San Francisco. So I invited her to spend the night. I was staying in an apartment with my doubles partner, and he had a bedroom and I had one. So she stayed with me, and we just started making love, screwing, whatever you want to call it. She had a beautiful body and had had quite a bit of experience. This friend of mine was damned near thirty. So she was pretty sophisticated, but I don't remember her going down on me. Just straight screwing—that's the way I remember it. All in the bed except once in a while we fell on the floor. I know I didn't go down on her. Guys who would eat pussy, they were terrible or queer or something. And nobody would admit it if they did it. To this day I don't think any of my brothers ever have. There were all those old wives tales about it, that the snatch wasn't somehow clean and how could anyone think of putting their tongue on that, like your tongue might fall off or something. I was like that for a long time. But now I've gotten to the point of thinking it's part of the game and if you like a person and you have a feeling for them then there's nothing at all wrong with it. You know what they say: if you get over the smell you have it half licked.

Well, Ramona stayed the rest of the week with me. And after about three or four days, my friend called and said, "What happened to Ramona? She hasn't been home for four or five days." He said, "By God, I'll bet it was one of those—" then he mentioned two or three of the really good-looking, suave ladies' men we had at that time. But he was worried about her, so finally I got to be an Honest John. I said, "Walter, I've got to be honest with you. It wasn't any of those other guys. She stayed with me." "Well," he said, "did you, did you, um, screw her?" I said, "Yes." And he said, "How many times?" I said, "Well, the first night, fourteen times." He said, "Fourteen times, why . . . Christ." He was all shook up with one thing and another. He just couldn't get over it.

It really was fourteen. I remembered because I kept track by putting a pencil mark on a piece of paper after each time. We never stopped screwing all night long till it was like eleven o'clock the next day and I had to go play my first match. I've never forgotten it. That's the most times I ever did it in one night. Hell, I never have come close, never came

half as close. I don't think in my whole life I ever exceeded
three times again. That was the one time I went for numbers
and I don't know why. She was so beautiful and I just fell in
love. When I got back to Los Angeles she wrote me a nice
letter. Then I had a letter from her boyfriend saying she was
pregnant and for me to send money. He knew my address but
he sent the letter care of Perry Jones, the head of the Southern California Tennis Association. As a junior I was very
much under the jurisdiction of the Association, and Jones was
a czar and this guy was just letting me know that if I didn't
send money he would inform the officials. So I went to my
older brothers and they said, "Jesus, send her fifty dollars and
tell her to get some pills or go horseback riding or some
damn thing," something ridiculous. But I was scared and I
dropped it like a hot potato and never saw her again and
never heard from either of them again. I don't know what
she did about it—whether she was even pregnant or had an
abortion or what. I never heard any more about it.

So then I started playing in all the amateur tournaments
and the basic idea on the circuit was to see if you could fuck
some waitress in some restaurant in some town where we
happened to be playing. I was a real butcher, as the saying
goes. I just came on too fast. All I wanted to do was get laid,
and it was pretty obvious. I tried to fuck them all—nice girls,
bad girls, whatever. When you were training, though, you
were pretty careful. Like I never had a drink from the time I
was seventeen till I was well up in my twenties, and then
just on occasion. If I were going to get ready for a big event
and really try hard and be at my best, I would give up both
drinking and sex for a month before.

I never lost sight of my main goal, which was to become
the best tennis player in the world, so I just never got to be a
real ladies' man. And anyway I married early, when I was

twenty-one. She was twenty and a virgin and I fell in love
with her and finally had to cave in and get married in order
to get it. It didn't take me long to realize the fucking wasn't
everything. I wasn't completely happy. I wanted to stay out
and play gin and poker and different games, and I was late to
dinner and she'd raise hell about it. And the war years didn't
help. I was overseas in the Navy in the South Pacific all of
'43 and '44. Then I was on tour with Don Budge in South
Africa and around the world; and we had small babies and
somebody had to stay home and take care of them. So we
grew apart. But we stayed married thirteen years and I
would say that basically we were good pals and good friends
and she was very much part of my situation. I'm not a secre-
tive guy; I have no side deals. I never kept anybody on the
side or had girls or had affairs. I was not that interested in
girls and it always appeared to me that adultery would be
unfair, would be cheating, so to speak, if you really had an
alliance with somebody you were fond of. I'm not saying that
if I were out of town at a convention or something and somebody jumped into my lap that I'd turn down a good piece of
ass. I wasn't that moral or that strong. In fact that's what finally broke up my first marriage. I did develop another girl
friend, and my wife found out about it and wanted a divorce,
and she got it.

And then I married a lovely woman, a super-nice woman
and we stayed married for twenty years. We were very close
and my wife really understood me probably as much if not
more than I did myself. She's a very wise, very intelligent and,
I think, very fair girl, and finally she said to me, "Look,
Bobby, you're you and you do your thing. You love the tennis, you love the golf, you love to gamble. Wherever you go
you have a marvelous time." And she said, "You really in a
sense don't need me. I'm here, and it's more like you're living

in a hotel and I'm the housekeeper you come home to. I know you love me as much as you're capable of loving anyone." She questioned my capability as to how much I could love anybody. She had all kinds of patience with me for twenty years and gave me all kinds of time and all kinds of chances to make the adjustment, to be the kind of husband she would really like to have. I just didn't have it, and she realized it. She said, "I'm not getting any younger, and you aren't, and you're not going to change and I don't want you to change—that wouldn't be fair. So you go do your thing and I'll start over." She remarried a couple of weeks ago.

When we divorced a couple of years ago I was really quite shook up. I felt lost, I felt out in the world and all alone, I just didn't know what the hell it was. I had been married from the time I was twenty-one until I was fifty-five, that's thirty-three years, that's most of my life, and I thought, "My God, I've got to get another girl right away. This just doesn't seem right. Somebody's got to belong to me; I've got to have somebody." I have six children with the two wives and where they never played too big a part in my thinking it was still nice that they were there. You always had somebody nice to come home to, as the saying goes. And when I didn't have it anymore, I had that feeling of being lost or of longing or of missing something and lonely nights. Which I never had before, and it was a hell of an adjustment to make, very tough. It's taken me to just about now to realize that the single life isn't so bad after all and that when you want female companionship, it's available. And since my last divorce and since the publicity and notoriety I'm a hundred times more popular with the gals than I ever have been in my whole life. Finally I'm in the position where there's more ass around than I can take care of or handle. That's the irony isn't it? When I was young and looking for it and wanting it terribly it was nowhere around. Where was it? Where was it? Now they're around by the carload.

I'm in pretty good shape now; I haven't been hasty and moved anybody in. I guess I always thought the wife was supposed to be the mother and the homemaker and that she should maybe cater to the man more than he would cater to her. That's a little outdated. Now a guy's supposed to be thinking, How can I keep her happy and satisfied? But I think deep-rooted in me is the notion that a woman's responsibility is to keep the guy happy. And he in turn is going to try to respond and be pretty fair about things. That's what I always thought I was, pretty fair in consideration, in courtesy, in carrying out the role of the father, the husband. The man's role basically, I suppose, is to be the breadwinner and bring home bucks and be the head of the household and not cheat on her and be strong and give them the feeling of being loved. I always thought I was pretty good, at least about the money. Not having anything to start with and seeing other people who have it, I was always very concerned about economic security and I've always been very frugal, very unextravagant. No boats, airplanes, horses, big parties, fancy clothes or high overheads. I've never really had a vacation. Oh, I went to Europe on my honeymoon and I've been back to Wimbledon a couple of times. But that's it. For Chrissake, I've got too much money in the bank right now. I've got to spend some before I cash in my chips.

So about providing for them, I was good. But in my own particular case, I have the feeling that about the other stuff I never really matured. They say some men mature earlier than others, and I don't know if I've ever shown any degree of maturity when it comes to this ability of fatherhood and being a husband and a Rock of Gibraltar. I doubt very much whether I really matured past the stage of teenager, or a young twenty probably at the best. I just never wanted to get too far away from the game and the playing and the competition and the being on stage and getting the honors and the glories and winning the contests, the bowls, the check or whatever you were playing for. My life has been so one-sided in that direction that I think it's left me very short on other sides. I would say that I've been far from an ideal father or an ideal husband. But it doesn't mean that I didn't make a conscientious attempt. But it was like work for me; it didn't come easy, it wasn't natural for me. I guess you would say I must be a very selfish person. I tried to help my wife. We had a Sunday school for a couple of years together and we used to have them back to the house and I'd be games master for them, play tennis and softball with them and take them to see the Knicks or a table tennis exhibition once in a while. And I would go to the Cub Scout meetings. But these were attempts. I suppose a really mature person does these things naturally, but I'd have to think about doing the right thing, about not going out and playing gin and poker again tonight. It does give one a feeling of disappointment and regret a little bit that he couldn't measure up and that he was a failure in certain areas. I hate to think of myself as a failure particularly when it comes to being a father —and I really don't think I was. I get along very well with my children. I think they all love me and we have a good relationship and I love them, but we're not terribly close either. And I tried hard to be a good companion and a good pal to both my wives, and you know you don't last thirteen years and twenty years if you don't have a little something going for you. I mean, that's the record. But it hurts a person's ego and doesn't make them feel good when somebody says, "Look, this has gone far enough. Let's call a halt. I'd like to try a new ball game." And if you analyze it and consider all the evidence that's in, you realize that maybe the person is right about the thing. Well, okay. I would have to admit and take the rap that I probably am not very much of a person when it comes to a number of broad things.

Joan Rivers *comedienne*

Born June 8, 1935, New York City

Bustling about in a royal-blue floor-length gown, her short hair casually brushed, Joan Rivers was an hour away from the closing dinner show of another successful two-week engagement at the MGM Grand Hotel in Las Vegas, where she appears a half dozen times a year. Closing night meant, as it traditionally does, a round of casual gifts from the star to the musicians, stagehands and technicians, and she was parceling out ribboned packages to her quiet-spoken husband, Edgar, her daughter, Melissa, age seven, her manager and her publicist, for them to carry downstairs. Then she dialed room service and said, "Hi, room service, this is Joan Rivers. How are you? That's nice. What we'd like is one Diet Pepsi and two Frescas. Yes, that's all. Thank you." When the soda pop arrived, she plopped upon a sofa, kicked off her shoes, and sipped a Fresca while chattering with nervous intensity and cheery, self-mocking humor about her early years. She paused often to talk amiably with her husband or daughter, acting very much the fond family woman. Later, with her leading the way, they all walked out Indian file with their packages to the elevator.

Everything came late to me. I didn't kiss a boy until the summer between high school and college. Maybe that's because I wasn't good-looking. I was always fat, growing up. It took me a long time. Looking back, I think that by the time I was a senior in high school I was cute. But by then it was too late, if that makes sense. I really went through a very late transformation. Most of my high-school years I was 5′ 2″ and weighed 130 pounds. That's fat. And it was in the fifties, when everyone was wearing those big poodle skirts and stuff, which didn't help. I was not exactly the school Lolita. I had very few dates. I went to a private co-ed academy, Adelphi, in Westchester County, New York. It was a double-standard school—for rich kids and sports scholarship boys. And the sports scholarship boys were having some good time, because they were the jocks. And you were always in love with one of them, always in love with some terrific-looking Italian whose father fixed the school plumbing, in love with somebody who hated you. I went to more parties where they spun the bottle and I would go into another room and the boy I was with would immediately say, "Time's up." So when I graduated at age sixteen, I still wasn't kissed.

But that summer I went to visit a friend who had a summer home outside of Albany, New York. It means nothing to anybody, probably, but it was very pretty and in the country and one crazy thing led to another and I finally got kissed. His name was Jimmy Aberitus and he was in military school somewhere. He was like 6′ 4″ and weighed maybe 92 pounds. They had to put the buttons single file on his uniform. I met him at a tea dance or something. I went to everything. My friend Joan and I used to pretend we had infantile paralysis and that's why the boys wouldn't ask us to dance. We used to say, "They're not coming over because they know we limp."

Well the night Jimmy Aberitus kissed me in the foyer of my friend's house—we had been on a date and I'd had my lips puckered all night—I was hysterical, thrilled, just thrilled. I had wanted it so long. I was a little disappointed. I thought it was going to be just the best thing in the whole world, like when I was fourteen and Bobby Sherman held my hand for the first time. I could have been kissed at my senior prom, because I had a Williams man, Jack Brody, take me out, and he was on the track team and everything. But when we got to the door my mother opened it instantly and said, "Jack, give my best to your parents." And to me she said, "Would you please come in at once." Can you imagine? In my house, boy, you weren't alone for a minute with a boy. My mother was always watering the plants at four in the morning.

We were a happy family though. We're Jewish and we were brought up in the Jewish ethic, which is there's heaven and hell on earth, so be good to everyone now, but also enjoy life. My mother, especially, is from a wealthy family, so we didn't have to struggle. I went to private schools and had governesses. My one sister, who's three years older, went to Columbia Law School and is now a lawyer. You look around at what people went through—we didn't go through anything. I mean it was good, they really liked the children, my parents. And they tried to do their best. But they never once discussed sex with us. They were both very moral, moral in every sense, especially sexually. My father's an M.D. and he's practiced in Brooklyn and Larchmont and now in the city, and I swear to God I don't think he ever had an affair. They don't swear; they don't like off-color jokes. People will tell them a dirty joke and they'll both just sit there and go

Hmmm. They're not tight-assed but they're very conservative. My mother was brought up in an old-world Russian family. She was educated at home with tutors and literally was never alone with a man until she married. Her governess rode up and down in the elevator with her. You just wonder how these people survived, and if they ever had any fun. Anna Karenina did, and look what happened to her. Obviously a lot of my mother's puritanical background carried over into our household. Once either my sister or I said something about a penis and she said, "No! No! No! You mustn't ever say that." She was always saying to me, "Your camp counselors will tell you."

So I stumbled around a lot. My sister and I never heard any of those wonderful stories about the father planting the seed in the mommy and so forth, and in fact even she and I didn't talk. I guess I finally figured out what went on between a man and woman by the time I was ten. I found out how you have a baby because somebody grabbed me one day in the school bathroom and said, "You don't know where babies come from." And I said, "Yes, I do. They come from your weewee." And she said, "That's right." I was in shock. I had just guessed. I was only a second-grader and she was a fifth-grader. That's how I found out everything, from my girl friends at school—I mean just all the wrong ways. And consequently I came to sex with a lot of negative attitudes. I remember once in high school we found out a girl we knew was soul-kissing, the term for French-kissing in those days, and we were just disgusted. Yuck! The worst!

By the time I was a freshman at Connecticut College for Women in 1954, I was beginning to straighten out. But even then, kissing a boy was still a lot, as dumb as that sounds. And sleeping with a guy was considered really wild. One girl went away to Bermuda for spring vacation with her boyfriend and we were really in shock over that one. We just thought there was something wrong with her. Girls weren't supposed to have any physical desires. It's not until really recently that I've heard my female friends talk about their own desires. Back then we all lied and said we did much less with boys than we actually did. There was endless talk about how far we'd let a boy go. If you were going with a guy and you went to visit him at Yale for a weekend, you could sleep with him as long as nothing happened. There was a lot of that going on. My poor best friend in college—who shall remain nameless—was a very sexually oriented girl and I wonder, looking back, how she ever restrained herself. God, she always had a stomachache. I mean she just died, she'd come back from a date just dying. She'd sit in a car for hours with some guy just kissing and kissing and kissing, and she'd always come home with a stomachache. And you know, I don't think she was masturbating either. You just didn't think about masturbation then . . . or do it. I know it sounds incredible, but I didn't do it till much later, I swear to God. And we never discussed it; I never once spoke to my own sister about it.

During those years, I only knew one girl, a cousin of mine, who had to get married. And a couple of months later she had the baby. In those days you just said it was premature. I have this in my act. The kid's 11 pounds, 15 ounces at birth, with a full set of teeth and a cigar in its mouth, and the mother's saying, "Oh, we hope it will live."

Of course the worst of anything was abortion. We thought that was very bad. And you always heard those wonderful stories about somebody going into the bathroom with a coat hanger and stories about babies being flushed down toilets. I was always terrified of getting pregnant. I knew I could never go to my parents, so it would have been a bitch, I can tell you. In the late fifties a college-professor friend of mine had gotten a girl pregnant and they went down to Washington and they met somebody in a parking lot who took the girl away from him and threw her in another car and told my friend to come back four hours later to another lot. What that girl must have gone through! So four hours later he went back to the other lot and the girl was there. But if she'd been killed or died, he would never have seen her again. That was 1959. That's why I get so mad when everybody's fighting abortion. For God sakes, what they drove people to!

And so, with all the taboos and the fears, I got through school and nobody laid a glove on me. Not even close. I had some heavy petting sessions, but that was all. I was engaged to a guy my senior year, but he lived at home with his folks and four younger brothers. So when I'd visit him on weekends we'd sit in the den and do a lot of carrying on. But that was it.

The first time I slept with someone was a devastating experience. It was like "This is it!" It was like the biggest thing in my life, and it was with a guy I'd known since I was fourteen. By the time it happened I was twenty and a half, out of school and back in New York living at home and working as a fashion coordinator at a big store. My friend already was a graduate student at Columbia and had his own place in some not-very-good section of the city, which is, I think, probably the best place to be in love. It was a very big romance, we were destined for each other since we were fourteen.

We met again at the right moment. He was a friend of my cousin's and we all met for lunch one day. He was carrying a script under his arm—he worked at the Theater Guild part time. Well, that was it; he should have had me right there. I was very sophisticated, you know, out of college, black dress and pearls that day. But it all took many weeks, many weeks, though we both knew it was coming.

The day it happened he had been sick in bed, as a matter of fact—that old ploy. "Gee, I'm not feeling good. Come over and we'll eat dinner here tonight." But I knew, because I bought a new dress that afternoon before I went up to his place. It was a blue linen dress, empire, for which I paid around forty-two dollars, which was a lot of money then. God, when you think back, the underwear was so ugly: the panty girdle with the little hookies; the stockings all stretched and ugly hanging on the back of a chair; the nice sturdy cotton bra. Ugh! He had on his pajamas. I did get dinner, oh, yes, and then a lot of wine after dinner. Otherwise I wouldn't have gone near him. There were no candles on the table or anything like that. That wasn't his style; he was a poet. Just dinner and wine—we just knew. I kept thinking it was time and that of course it had to be him because it was going to be the rest of my life with him. And I was giving him the supreme gift that Joan Wallinsky could bestow on anybody. I was very dramatic about the whole thing, a lot of looks and no talk and all that junk.

Physically, it was like nothing. You read in the books, "She took to it like an animal." I just said, "Hunh, is it over?" The whole thing lasted about a minute and a half, including buying the dress. Now, I did think women were supposed to enjoy it, that I knew, that much I knew. I had read *Forever Amber* and *Gone With the Wind* and all of those, and I never for a second thought that sex was a woman's burden. And though it wasn't much the first time, I was not terribly disappointed because I was crazy about him, so it all sort of fell into place. I wish that for my daughter she should have the same kind of feeling. It was lovely. And I never regretted it. I didn't sit up and say, "Oh, my God." Afterwards, he lit two cigarettes in his mouth, literally. Then he yawned and seemed kind of bored, but I didn't understand anything about that or about somebody being good in bed or bad in bed. That came later when I had something to compare. At the time, it never crossed my mind. I mean, he got the supreme sacrifice: he was lucky, even if I never moved once.

The only bad thing I remember about that night is that I didn't have any cologne and that right before I left his place I went in the bathroom and put about a gallon and a half of his Old Spice all over me. I just figured you look different and you smell different and it's just different now and everyone's going to know. And when I got in the Westchester Rapid Taxi to go home, those poor people just must have died. But when I got home it was all okay because he called me and said, "Are you all right?" and, "I love you," and all that junk, which is very nice and very important. He just did everything right. It was all very romantic.

The minute we'd slept together I thought we were getting married. I mean that's it, right? I mean there's no question about it. And when you stop and think how terrific I must have been in bed, how terrific and frisky I must have been. The poor guy took off six or seven months later and joined the Army. He couldn't handle it and I couldn't handle it. The sex thing was driving us both nuts, and the guilts, and my parents hated him because they suspected something was up. They wouldn't let him come in the house; he had to meet me at the driveway. We had a real dramatic thing going, but it just wasn't going to work for the long pull. I'm a very explosive person, and he's crazier than me—still is. He still sends me messages. There were scenes when you'd jump out of a moving car and stuff like that. It's all very well and good, but somewhere in the back of my head I knew. Either he would have killed me or I would have killed him. I'm sure

I was not the easiest person then. I'm really very emotional, and that was a very bad period of my life. I was trying hard to be an actress and working as a fashion coordinator and I had no self-respect at all. I was struggling tremendously and trying to find out who I was, and I expected him to take over completely. I'd been brought up to believe that the whole thing was the guy's responsibility. What a terrible burden for both of us. And this guy just couldn't handle it, because he was struggling, too. So he took off. And within three weeks I was married to somebody else. It was just escape, not the solution to anything. That poor thing never even knew why I married him and it lasted only five months, five glorious months. The worst.

I really didn't have a good time with sex until after my first marriage. It was a very gradual thing with me, as I'm sure it is with a lot of ladies. I'm sure I do have a residue of anger at my parents about the sex, because I'm so careful to do it the opposite way with my own daughter, to tell her what she wants to know. It just would have been much nicer if it had all been explained to me and been told to me that it's terrific. And also, if they hadn't told me there were good girls and bad girls, and that if you slept with a guy you're not married to you're a tramp and now he'll never marry you. I mean they just got you crazy in our society in my day. Do you know that in all the years that I was between marriages, I never had the guts to go to a gynecologist and ask him for a diaphragm? Never! You were just embarrassed about any sexual feelings you had; they were all supposed to be bad. I had a friend whose mother kept her in pajamas when she was a little girl so she wouldn't masturbate. Now didn't the mother think the child could take down a pajama bottom? How stupid! How silly! But that was the whole era.

I don't know how I escaped it all finally. Mostly just luck.

261 : Joan Rivers

I never really, thank God, had anything like *bad* happen to me. I hate the term normal, but I never had a guy come out in high heels and my evening dress and lipstick or anything like that. And then the tremendous loosening up that's happened. But I think things have loosened up too much. Well, here we go, right? I just think it should be the most terrific, wonderful, exciting, electric everything, and that just doesn't happen if you're going to shack up with everybody who comes down the road. I'm convinced the kids today are missing something. When I went to *Love Story*—I mean you could vomit, right?—they all sat around me and cried. And all my friends who are into women's lib heavily, I think they're missing a lot, too. I know it sounds stupid, but part of the fun was the waiting. Somebody said to me that 50 per cent is the anticipation and the waiting and the playing the game and that whole thing back and forth. I must agree. I think it was wonderful.

Artie Shaw *bandleader, writer*

Born September 23, 1910, New York City

The rather fierce-looking round face, sharply accentuated by thick glasses and a thinning crew cut, did not look as if it belonged to the raciest bandleader of the Swinging Forties, a much-headlined sexual adventurer who was married seven times, including to Ava Gardner and Lana Turner. His cluttered apartment two blocks off Central Park in New York City spilled over with shelves of serious books, jazz records, intellectual magazines, tape decks and pre-Columbian artifacts— the den of an insulated, cerebral man. He sat chain-smoking Pall Malls in a leather chair, wearing brightly checked wool pants and a tan sweater over a sports shirt, with his feet, clad in bedroom shoes, perched atop a huge driftwood-and-glass coffee table. He talked in staccato bursts, monologues that might run on for ten or fifteen minutes, pausing only to get up and look for his cigarettes, not remembering that they were right beside him on a little table. He talked in a brusque, so-what-else-is-new manner and expressed a general bitter skepticism about life and the world—as he sees it, without much hope of survival. At one point, instead of rambling about himself, he rapidly read aloud several pages of an autobiography about his early life called The Trouble with Cinderella. *He wanted to see his interview before it was pub-*

lished, but only to insure, he said, that the writing was aesthetically suitable.

As I REGARD MY PAST LIFE and look at how I was raised and the way I've managed to grope my way through to some degree of sanity, I would choose a better way to do it if I had a choice. I would have started with a different set of parents, a different set of circumstances, and a different kind of world in general. But I don't feel bitter. Given that these are the facts and these are the circumstances, I did the best I could with the material at hand.

I grew up totally disconnected from my family. My father and I had no communication of any kind, and my mother and I had damned little communication, outside of biological. It's hard for me to talk about my father, even now. He was really a failure, a poor, pathetic man who had an adequate amount of strength but just wasn't able to make it in this American go-getter society. He grew up in Odessa, in Russia, came to this country and ran a saloon out West for a while, and then went to New York and met my mother. She was the typical Jewish lady who knew that society was composed of how much you have got and what you can spend it for. She was a seamstress, and she tried to make him into a tailor. But they were totally inadequate and couldn't make it. My father finally left home when I was thirteen, and then my mother in effect tried to use me as a sort of husband and tried to find a life through me. She had guilt working for her all the way, and it wasn't until years later, when I was about thirty-five, that I was able to fully understand that and not feel guilty.

By then I was going with Ava, and we were living this real fat-cat movie-star life in a house in Beverly Hills that's now worth about $400,000. We lived together until the social pressures made me and Ava get married. During this period my mother came out to visit us and stayed in Ava's apartment. We had some people over one night, Van Heflin and his wife and some other movie people, and it went on and on and finally it got to be about eleven o'clock, so I said, "Mom, I think it's about time for you to go home." She was really put out and was totally silent when I drove her home, so next day I said, "Aw, come on, Mom. Quit sulking like a child. I know you're not happy about what happened last night. Spit it out." So she said, "You're ashamed of me."

"It isn't a matter of my being ashamed of you," I said, "What it gets down to is that I'm your son, and as your son I owe you a certain amount of respect, a certain amount of filial affection and a certain amount of support. But I don't owe you my life. I'm not your husband." The word "husband" really threw her, because she got all kinds of incestuous overtones from it and said, "Oh, no, no, no, I never said you should be." But that incident finally snapped the cord with her. Christ, I had her around my neck for a long time.

I grew up with the usual dose of guilt about sex, the kind of lascivious, leering, furtive view of it as a dirty thing. I was an only child. When I was about seven or eight this older guy of about sixteen told me that I was born as a result of that dirty act, and I argued furiously with him that my mother and father wouldn't do that. He said, "Aw, come on, you stupid little kid." I never saw anything physical between my mother and father. For one thing, I kept as far away from them as I could. I do remember that when I first saw my father naked it was a weird, eerie feeling, because it was something you weren't supposed to have seen. I never saw my mother altogether naked. This was something you closed your eyes to and pretended you didn't see, even if you saw it, so my earliest brushes with sex were highly furtive and secret and therefore shameful.

If you played with your penis, and I don't mean in a masturbatory sense, you would be told, "No, no, no. Dirty, dirty." Masturbation was a shameful thing, something you didn't admit. It would cause hair to grow in the palm of your hand and stuff like that. A guy who was one of my closest buddies never admitted to me that he ever masturbated in his entire life. I finally figured out that either he was lying or there was something wrong with him. My first brush with it was before I could ejaculate. I must have been about eleven. I remember that there was a spasm, an exquisitely sensual and pleasurable sensation. Nothing came out, but I thought, "Jesus, this is something worth repeating"—or as the guy says "This sure beats pissing." I think this happened at a summer place outside of New Haven.

I was away from home and on my own playing with bands when I was fifteen. I was learning to play an instrument and that took all the energy, thought and cleverness I could come up with, so I was involved with and focused on that and didn't think about girls much. And anyway, there wasn't much time left over for screwing around.

By the time I "lost my cherry," as they say, I thought it was the kind of thing you had to do. I was constantly being indoctrinated with the notion that if you didn't do that, you weren't yet a man. I was fifteen and playing in Carmen Cavallero's band up near Northfield, Connecticut, when I began to take an incredible amount of ribbing about being a virgin. This was shortly before the band set out in a broken-down motor caravan to play in Lexington, Kentucky. There was another guy in the band who was also a virgin, and the constant ragging we got established a bond between us. After a while we made a pact that we would do something about our sexual ignorance as soon as we could, and the only place we could think of to do it was at a cathouse. About one-thirty one morning, after we finished playing a dance in Waterbury, Connecticut, he and I took off for town with five or six dollars apiece in our pockets. All of this is described, by the way, in my book, *The Trouble with Cinderella*. We didn't have the slightest idea how to find a cathouse, but we somehow ended up at one, I think after asking a couple of cab drivers. A colored man stuck his head out of the door when we knocked, and the man who brought us said, "I got a couple of customers." Through the door I could see this giant of a Negro gravely sharpening an axe on a stone he was holding between his knees. I was scared and wanted to run like hell, but my friend tipped the guide who had brought us two dollars, and we went into this dimly lit kitchen and started to negotiate the price. My friend did all the talking. I think they settled on five dollars. By that time I was feeling a little sick and not wanting to go through with it, so I told my friend to go first. He was gone an unbearably long time, and this huge man kept on sharpening his axe and never said a word.

When it came my turn to go I went through the door like a man being led to the guillotine. It was pitch dark in the room. I was as panic-stricken as I have ever been in my life. I groped around a minute and then I heard a woman whisper, "Hurry up, boy, let's go. Let's not stand around here all night, for Chrissakes." I don't remember exactly what I said, but roughly it was that I would pay her and we wouldn't do anything. So we just sat there in the dark for a few minutes and didn't say anything. Not one word was spoken. The only time I touched her was when our hands grazed when I handed her the money. Naturally I didn't tell my friend what happened. So the word got around that we both were no longer virgins, and the razzing stopped.

Later on that same week, we were playing at the Joyland Casino in Lexington and one night six or seven of us guys took this one skinny girl out into the woods behind the dance hall and there was a gang shag—they all screwed her right there on the ground. I couldn't bring myself to do it, so I pretended again. It was a dark night and there was a lot of confusion, so I was able to get away with it. I was disgusted with it and disgusted by the part I took in it.

We got back to New Haven and then went down to Miami with Cavallero and I got myself a steady girl. She was a chorus girl in the floor show in the gambling joint where we played. She was divorced and had a baby daughter. She lived quite a respectable life with her mother, and our relationship was completely innocent. Now and then between dance sets we would sit in somebody's car behind the club and neck and I guess I could have gone to bed with her if I had wanted to but going to bed with her never occurred to me. She was a, quote, nice girl, and going to bed with a nice girl was just something you didn't do. Remember, this was about 1925. After we went back to New Haven we wrote awhile, and then she went home to where she lived in the Midwest. I was wildly in love with her, but after a while I couldn't remember what she looked like, and eventually I couldn't even remember her name.

Not long after that I met a cute little girl at a dance hall at the Savin Rock amusement park just outside New Haven, where I had gone to listen to Barney Rapp's band. She had on a red dress. I owned a little Studebaker car called the Erskine, and we drove out into the woods. It was a summer night. I took the back seat out of the car and we lay down

on it, and that is how I officially lost my virginity. There was
no romance to it. It was very fumbly and embarrassing. She
just hiked up her dress and I pulled down my pants and we
went at it like two little animals. I don't think either of us
did it out of any sense of enjoyment. It was just a ritual. I
can't remember much of a physical sensation. I just thought,
"Well, it's over. Thank Christ I did it. I did actually screw
this girl. Now I can get on about my business and my life."
I drove her home and never saw her again.

I eventually left home in that car, left my mother and went
to Cleveland and started playing with another group. The
first time I remember having sex that was intensely satisfying was in Cleveland when I was about nineteen. There was
this woman of about twenty, a kept woman whose boyfriend
was out of town, and she picked me up at this place we were
playing. She got a couple of other girls. A couple of other
guys and myself went to this hotel where they had a suite,
and we went into an all-night bout of drinking and sex. There
was great sexual release, but it was all impersonal. I mean, I
was being used, and she was being used. There wasn't any
exchange of feelings between two human beings.

Also, somewhere along the line I had developed the Victorian notion that men were beasts and women allowed them
to "do it." Such a thing as foreplay in a sexual relationship
never occurred to me as a young man. It was, put it in, do
what you have to do, and take it out. You didn't think in
terms of bringing the woman pleasure. That was totally beside the point. I was astonished when I discovered that girls
actually enjoyed it too.

I have had to have a relationship with a woman in order
to enjoy sex. That's one of the reasons I never made it with
whores. It was too clinical for me. Fucking just for the sake
of fucking has no meaning to me. There's no sense to it. You

might well stick your cock in a knothole. That's been a running pattern through my life. I'm a very conventional man. One of the greatest problems I've had as a human being has been having sex in a society which says that if you want to have sex you do it within the conventions of a thing called marriage. So I got married. That's conventional. I got divorced. That's conventional. And when I was married I had almost no extramarital sex. And that's conventional.

I've never had the hang-up that I had to fuck a lot of beautiful women to prove what a man I was. I know a lot of guys might say that I did, when I would walk into a room with a Lana Turner or an Ava Gardner on my arm. But the truth is that I was a kind of male sex symbol. I used to hear Miles Davis say, "Man, I've got six bitches sitting at the table waiting for me." Well, I used to have bitches sitting around waiting for me, too. Don't forget, playing in a band, you're sitting up there on top of the stand, and if you've got two eyes, a nose, a mouth and a couple of arms where they belong, some girl will look at you and say, "Hey, you're cute." Women come to you. They used to follow me in cabs. Well, if you look around a roomful of women, all of them ready to make it with you, you'd be a goddamned fool to pick out the ugly ones. If there are pretty ones out there, they are the ones you're gonna pick. And if somebody says, "Why did you marry those girls, like Ava and Lana?" well, those were the girls I was hanging out with. If I go to a party and Ava Gardner's there and she likes me, it's not so strange to say, "Well, we'll make it." She was an incredibly beautiful girl. Same thing with Lana. I remember the first time we dated. We were riding around in a convertible on Sunset Boulevard and I was sitting there looking at her and, Jesus, she was breathtaking. Well, why not? Being goddesses was their business. There wasn't the sexual freedom in those days that we have today. A man who lived in a goldfish globe like I did couldn't live with a woman without it being shameful and scandalous, so you got married. I mean you took out a marriage license in order to legitimize the thing, and part of you said, well, if it doesn't work, what the hell. I hoped it would work, because divorces were messy and inconvenient, but I didn't go into it as any 'til-death-to-us-part bit. My marriages failed because they weren't marriages. It's that simple.

After we were divorced, Ava once asked me if we were all right sexually. I said that if everything else had been on a par with sex, we would never have separated. But obviously nothing else worked, and sex is a pretty frail reed to lean a whole relationship on, although without it, boy, you're in big trouble.

Now I have finally found someone who makes everything work for me. She's secure enough to be able to laugh at me. I don't threaten her much. At first I did, but then she began to see that it was a lot of bluster and that underneath it all I'm a sucker. We have real knock-down drag-out fights, but we build from them and go on. When I look back on my life, I marvel that I didn't come more crippled than I did. Somehow through this utterly complicated jungle path that I traveled, I managed to retain a pretty normal attitude about sex and women. And now for the first time I can see it is a distinct reality that a man can live with a woman in such a way that they augment and enhance each other as people, so that one and one becomes a little bigger than two.

Grace Slick *singer*

Born October 30, 1939, Chicago, Ill.

A rehearsal was scheduled that evening for the remnants of the old Jefferson Airplane, which (with performers such as Janis Joplin) had been the biggest American rock group of the 'sixties. Grace Slick and the other survivors of the group now called themselves "The Jefferson Starship." She had driven from Berkeley into San Francisco in her $17,000 Aston-Martin and stopped off at Enrico's, a sidewalk coffeehouse that flourishes amid a sprawl of failing topless clubs, porno bookstores and other strident tourist dives in garish North Beach. She wore a blue velvet jacket and jeans, and carried a huge leather bag, from which she fished a wad of fifty-dollar bills and ordered the first of three half-bottles of Mumm's champagne she would consume over the next two hours. She had let her black hair go "natural" and it framed her ruddy face in a bristly wreath. Her large dark eyes were ringed with heavy makeup. She talked bluntly about herself, and apologized for fear her story was too tame. Afterward she went with a small group to a nearby Italian restaurant, where she had two drinks but ate nothing. Out on the street a bent gnome of a black woman with wild eyes accosted her for a handout. After considerable badgering, Ms. Slick fished a fifty-dollar bill from her purse and handed it over, where-

upon the tiny woman glared at her and said, "Thank you, sir." A loud argument ensued, and Ms. Slick demanded her money back, without success. Finally she left to go look for her automobile.

JUST LET SOMEBODY TELL ME not to go out and get drunk or not to fuck some guy and that's exactly the first thing I want to do. Anytime people say, "Don't do that," then you know there's something good about it. So the most fun is to push a little bit beyond the rules.

My parents were lenient and to an extent indulgent, but they were very strict in another way. They'd give me physical punishment, which I really like a lot now and am very appreciative of; not violent, but very definite physical stuff. Like my father had a thing where he'd sit me in a rocking chair. It would start with him saying something like, "Don't touch that ashtray." So I would put my hand up close to the ashtray, and I'd keep moving my finger closer and closer, so that he had to watch. I would know he had to bend his head to watch me, and I'd keep moving my finger closer and closer, until I came just as close as I could without touching it. This would go on for a long time, and he was just as patient as I was. And when I'd finally touch it, he'd sit me in this rocking chair and sort of push me backwards and say, "Are you gonna do it again?" And I'd say yes. So he'd push my head backwards again, not hurting me, just enough force to make the rocker go. "Are you going to do it again?" As long as I could take it, I'd say yes. but finally I'd get bored and say, "I won't do it anymore. Let me out of this rocker."

That's what I like. I like that kind of punishment. I mean,

if you have a child and they're messing up, you say, "Don't do that, at all." And if they do it you say, "Don't do it again or I'm going to knock your goddamned teeth down your throat."

My father is an investment banker, a Republican, and very straight, but he is open to listening. He will very definitely tell me I am full of shit when I get through talking, but he will listen. He has worked in San Francisco since I was five, and we lived there and then in Palo Alto. He was pretty well-organized. Both my parents were. And I myself . . . well, sloppiness makes me nervous. If you don't put it back in a certain place, then you gotta do a really dumb, boring thing, which is look for something for half an hour. That's about as intellectually interesting as a turd.

My parents never did say, "Don't do this," about sex. They figured I would assume not to do it. Or that I already knew all about it in some way, which I did. I mean I knew that if you ball a guy and don't use something, you get knocked up. So you look out.

There was a sort of set of rules that you knew to go by. At Palo Alto in junior high, for instance, if you got into heavy petting with some guy that you were not going steady with, that was not considered nice. I went more or less along with what was going on. You'd mostly get into a station wagon, and if you had enough money you'd buy a six-pack, and lie around and neck in the back seat. When we were fifteen we couldn't drink legally, but we used to get sloshed, and, of course, our parents didn't want us lying around the house necking. So a car was cherished and prized. When you had a car, you could go anywhere and do anything, as long as you were home by twelve. I used to sneak our car out. It was a big four-door 88 Oldsmobile. I used to push it out into the street, turn it, open the door, turn it, push it a way down the street and then start it. So if they were to wake up, they would think it was somebody down the street leaving and not me.

I'd go out with girl friends to the Varsity or the Stanford to see a movie, or get the guys or something. We hung around drive-ins a lot, where the guys would hustle the girls and the girls would hustle the guys. You'd meet people there, and then go someplace else. Somebody's mother might be out for the night, and we'd say, "Hey, hey, hey, let's have a party." People would sneak booze from their parents, and it would be just basic kids sitting around. I didn't care for the popular music that was going on at the time. I was the only person who didn't get interested in Elvis Presley. I thought he sounded like he had adenoids or something, and the first time I saw him on television I thought he was repulsive and a bit lame. He doesn't bother me one way or the other now.

There would be some dancing, but I'm not a good dancer. I don't like to follow what somebody else is doing. After a while you'd turn off the lights and couples—everybody went steady—would sit around and neck. If you got your boob touched, that was a biggie. Everybody would get hot and bothered about that.

You'd go with one guy for a year, and then next year you'd go with another guy. Nobody impinged on anybody else's boyfriend. A whole lot of necking went on, the usual stuff, hand inside of dress, hand going into pants, dry-fucking. That's man on top of woman, and the action is the same as fucking, but you're dressed. It's great for the girl. Your position is straight up, so that you're hitting and rubbing exactly the area that you ought to be. It knocked me out. I had orgasms and loved it. I still like that.

Sometimes the boys would get off doing that. I had this funny time with a boy who was Catholic and we were in the back seat, one on top of the other, and he said, "We're gonna have to stop doing this." He thought it was wrong. And he wouldn't masturbate, a religion thing or something, and finally he got all clogged up and had to go to the doctor.

I never had any religion and I don't have any guilt about anything. I went to the Episcopal church for two years when I was about thirteen, because they had good skiing trips, but I don't like the idea of churches at all.

I didn't find out about masturbation until I was eighteen and going to Finch College. It was an accident. I was lying down on the bed, reading a book called *Peyton Place,* and it was a horny book. It was resting on my crotch and I was reading along and all of a sudden it got me off. I had gotten off with boys before, either dry-fucking or actually doing it, but I'd never done that before. I didn't know about it. For the next two weeks I went bananas with it. I had a roommate, so I had to lock the door a lot. I didn't realize I could do this. There was always a boy there before, and I thought they had to do it. Then I realized all it takes is pressure. I can do it to myself. There doesn't have to be a boy there.

I never touched the boys much. I didn't know that much. If I'd been given books on what to do to make them happy —but I didn't have any reading material. The only things I saw were these little books called "Tijuana Bibles," which had real crude cartoonlike drawings of donkeys fucking people, of girls sucking donkeys off.

I'd seen rubbers. The guys at school used to blow them up like balloons and shake them and go "ha, ha, ha," and we all knew what they were. And one day I walked into my parents' bedroom to ask them about something or other, and my old lady was lying there reading the paper and my old man was putting a rubber on. So I'd seen it before.

I got kissed first when I was nine years old. About nine o'clock it would get dark enough so that we thought our parents couldn't see us, and we'd play kissing tag. The boys would chase the girls and the girls would chase the boys, and if you hit somebody, you kissed them. I got tagged, and I thought, "Hey, that's all right. I like this game." There wasn't that much chasing of me when I was a kid though. I was real fat. Not a blimp, but tubby. I was blonde until I was thirteen. Then my hair turned black and my body came down so much they used to call me "Spider" because I was so thin. Overnight, puberty changed the whole thing. Most people start gradually, but mine was really fast. I never did get boobs though. I'm still waiting.

When I was thirteen and fourteen the big deal was to go to the movies, and the poor guy, for two hours his hand keeps moving closer and closer, down the shoulder, touching closer and closer, and then you might get the whole shot, and that was a biggie.

Fucking, until you got in college, wasn't particularly well looked upon. I didn't lose my cherry until the night I graduated from high school, Castilleja, old Castle A, which is a girls' school. We wore white crinoline dresses, and late at night, around midnight, we drove down to Carmel. I was out with a guy who lived in Carmel, and his parents were away, so I went with him and my best girl friend and her boyfriend down to Carmel and we stayed all night at this guy's house. I'd been seeing him about four months. I think I told my parents I was going to stay at my friend Diane's house. It wasn't planned or anything. We had a lot to drink and we were all kind of drunk. It took a long time, maybe four hours, because you weren't supposed to be doing it, essentially. So you had to start out slow and work into it. It was great for the girl, but a little tight on the guy. We started off with all the clothes on, and very slowly, very gently, little by little . . . it just had to be slow because it was supposed to be wrong, and that was enjoyable.

It was the first time for my girl friend too. It was weird, because at exactly the same time, without any planning to it, we ended up in the bathroom together, half-crocked, and we looked at each other and went, "Hey, hey, hey, so that's it, huh? That's the biggie, baby. You got it."

She said, "Did you like it?" And I said, "Yeah, that was all right. I think I'll go back and do it again."

I don't think he knew I was a virgin, because I didn't bleed. I thought I was going to have to get up in the morning with a hangover and change the parents' bed, but nothing—I didn't bleed, and it wasn't painful at all. I was horny and I enjoyed it a lot. Balling is always good, and sometimes it just knocks your brain out. The first time you ball somebody is always excellent.

He was blond and very strong looking. I like strong men, Germans and Japs, 'cause I'm so mean, and those are the only guys who can stand me.

Germans and Japanese are strong fuckers. They don't give a shit. I married a German guy, Jerry Slick, and the only reason we split up was that we were actually physically separated; I was with a rock and roll band and he was off doing cinematography. Paul Kantner, my old man for the last few years, has got a big German jaw, all massive and kind of structured. He's very relaxing, very kind, and he fucks like a bastard. But he doesn't give a shit. I can tear his ass off and he doesn't care, because he thinks he is the best race in the world. He isn't intimidated by anything I do at all. What he thinks is, "You're a jive-ass chick," rather than, "Oh, my God, is she strong and unsexy." He thinks "You're so goddamned strong. Watch me fuck you." And he does it. Well, a small retiring chick is gonna have different desires and different guys, but I obviously need a guy who is gonna damn near kick my brains out.

Except for Orientals, which has happened in the last couple of years, I've never done that thing where you look across a room and go *bam* on a guy. I had a girl friend, Sally, and she said she balled my old man, Paul, four years ago or something, before I did. She said, "We did a thing at the Whisky-a-Go Go, where you're across the room and you see somebody and go 'All Right!'" I never do that with a guy. I have to meet him and talk to him for a long time, not about ancestry or any of that shit, but just, you know, communication. I've never seen anybody across a room that I'd like to just screw. How the hell would I know he wasn't gay?

The only jock I ever dated was at the University of Miami. I went out with a football player for a solid year. He was the kindest man I've ever met, but not bright at all. I loved his ass, but there wasn't much going on above the eyebrows. I had been at Finch College for a year, and I went down to Nassau on an Easter vacation, and loved the sun, so I decided to go to Miami U. Mostly I went to college just to see places I hadn't seen. I think college is a bit lame.

Miami U. is where I first smoked dope. The school was totally divided at the time. This was 1959. There were the Caucasians, and they had the Student Union. And there was this thing called "The Snake Pit." That's where the Jewish kids were. "The Snake Pit" is any area you can find where there is a lot of traffic, and you sit in the middle of it and smoke dope. I kept seeing these jokers lying around laughing, people climbing all over them to get to class, and I thought, "Hey, that's great." Then I noticed that their cigarettes looked funny, all screwed up, like they'd been carrying them around in their pockets for seven days. I like smoking dope for writing songs and balling, but that's it. I don't take any speed at all. I like champagne, and I know what my tolerance is: half a liter every hour and forty-five minutes. But every now and then I skip it and get blasted. I don't like a whole lot of booze with balling, 'cause it makes you kind of stupid. A girl can fuck all night, just keep going until she gets tired. But it's not quite that simple. You gotta wait for a while, because if you can get a guy off six times a night, that's amazing. I hate to put myself down, but that's difficult, very difficult. I don't like balling every night. I think that ruins it. If I had hamburger every day for a year I'd be damned sick of it. I like to wait a couple of days. I prefer to ball approximately twice a week, really well, and have the whole thing good, instead of knocking it off every night. I like to be plenty excited.

I don't have any girl friends who haven't fucked Paul, but I don't want to screw everybody that comes into the room. I never got into that. We got a big house over on Fulton Street with a big water bed in it, and nothing is ever planned, but something will happen, there will be a party, and there will be a lot of balling. If there is swapping it is genuine. I mean we have all known each other for ten or fifteen years, and we all like each other.

There was a kind of acid made about eight years ago, Sunshine, and that I liked, 'cause it was in pill form and you could break off a little and snort it, or you could take the whole thing and get wired to the teeth. I don't take it anymore. You can't get that goofy when you have a three-year-old trying to stick a wet finger into a wall plug. But if I saw Sunshine again, I would definitely try it. I've got only a small sense of moderation. I've got this vague idea that I can do damned near anything, and it hurts for about twenty-four hours and then the body always comes back. As excessive as I might be, I've got the idea that this body will not die.

I was all in the middle of the Haight-Ashbury free-love-culture era, but the thought that everybody in the world ought to get together and love each other never occurred to me. Unfortunately I had read ancient history, and I knew that certain people are gonna be friendly and get along together and be gypsies or rock and roll musicians, but some people are gonna knock your brains out. We had a good time singing about it, but I never thought that everybody was gonna be able to do that. A lot of crap was written about that. Because of what was written about Haight-Ashbury, people probably think I smoke dope from the time I get up in the morning until I go to bed. I don't smoke that much marijuana.

What I've developed in the last couple of years is this peculiarity about Orientals. I keep trying to hustle Japanese guys, but without much success. They generally do not like my style at all. If I can get one to look at me with some appreciation from a distance, I feel great. But I'm not diminutive or retiring, which is their concept of women. I'm 5′ 7″ and 5′ 10″ if I put on shoes. What's exciting to me is the fact that they aren't interested in me, which is a little weird.

Dr. Benjamin Spock *pediatrician*

Born May 2, 1903, New Haven, Conn.

After a long day's work on a magazine article and a quick dinner, Dr. Spock returned to his motel room overlooking the Columbia River in Portland, and telephoned at 9 P.M. to say he was ready to be interviewed. He wore a conservative dark suit, a striped shirt with a rounded collar, a regimental tie, suspenders, long black socks held up by garters, and old-fashioned shoes—all from Brooks Brothers. He had a halo of close-cropped gray hair, thick eyebrows partially obscured by a pair of heavy-rimmed glasses, and a deep suntan from sailing in the Virgin Islands, where he and his wife, Jane, keep a thirty-five-foot ketch. He stretched his youthful 6′ 4″ frame on a sofa, hands folded across his lean stomach, and sat in one position and talked for almost three hours. His conversation was graceful and precise, so vividly descriptive and detailed that long passages needed virtually no editing. He had a way of underscoring words with a slowing and a rising of his gentle voice. He spoke with great feeling and at times bitter resentfulness about his childhood, the memory of which seemed still so painfully fresh that when he recalled it, his face changed and he looked like a child. At times he would stare absently across the river, lost in reverie, and then a few minutes later erupt with a deep belly laugh or a chuckle as he resurrected anecdotes from his youth.

IN MY ADOLESCENCE and early adulthood I wanted to rebel and shuck off the excessively heavy conscience and stern morality taught me mostly by my mother. I wanted to be a man of the world. I felt that to be educated reasonably and to be decent was enough of a moral guide. But as the decades went by, it became clear to me that I never did succeed in freeing myself from my mother's morality. This was brought to light by my rather accidental involvement in the opposition to the war in Vietnam, and the intensity of my indignation against Lyndon Johnson for breaking his promise not to send any Americans to fight in an Asian war, and then, two years later, for trying to throw me and four others in jail for telling the truth about that war. So, yes, I ended up just as moralistic as my mother would have liked me to be in the beginning.

It is ironic that my mother thought of herself as a rebel against the sternness of her mother, of whom it was said that she once locked a child who had misbehaved in a closet all day while she went shopping. It seems plausible to me that my mother was influenced both by her mother's sternness and her father's waywardness. He was a dashing person, one of the youngest colonels in the Northern Army during the Civil War. But he deserted his family off and on, and that was something not tolerated in a person from a "respectable," if not distinguished, family. My father was a self-made man who worked his way through Yale and went on to have a responsible career as counsel to the New York, New Haven and Hartford Railway. My maternal grandmother originally objected to his attentions to my mother, feeling he was not from the right social drawer, but my mother was not dissuaded in the slightest. My father was no pushover, but he was relatively quiet at home, very reserved, and he was not one to argue with my mother. He left the discipline of the six children largely to her. Our parents devoted their lives entirely to us (Mother gave up card games, at which she was sharp, from the birth of her first 'til the maturity of her youngest), loved us, were proud of us. But it was very difficult to be a child in that particular Spock family. My mother was not only moralistic but very opinionated and very, very sure of herself. As far as any of the six of us could remember, she never changed her mind on anything, no matter how hard we pleaded. She could be a very jovial person with outsiders. I remember that the children of the Adams family, who lived two doors from us, said they envied us for having such a delightful and amusing mother! She was a great mimic and storyteller and could rock people in their chairs. But with her own family she was grimly stern, and I, being the oldest of the six, felt that I took the full brunt. My sisters thought I was her favorite. What I disliked was her control. I went away to boarding school for two years, from sixteen to eighteen, to Phillips Academy, Andover, and the big excitement was to come home for Christmas vacation. There'd be a dance almost every night in New Haven, nothing like the debutante balls in New York but still, for New Haven, fun. I was fascinated with girls then, though terribly shy with them. One vacation I did something my mother didn't like and she said, "No more dances for you." This was within two or three days of the beginning of the holiday, so ten dances had to be declined. I felt so outraged that I and my sister Marjorie—whom I called Hildy—sneaked up to the next dance and met some of our friends outside on the lawn of the house. This was the only time I was ever openly defiant of my mother. Her friend Patty Foot heard about it from her son William, and she in a mean way told my mother, "I hear Bennie and Hildy went to the Stoddards' dance." Well, we were in terrible disgrace with my mother. I remember that ten days as the blackest period of my whole childhood, when I was most in disgrace. You couldn't argue with Mother. If you did, that would only make the penalty more severe. We weren't allowed to see any of our friends during that holiday. We were under house arrest. But for us the punishment was not as uncomfortable as the overwhelming sense of guilt. That kind of discomfort has stayed with me all my life, with my conscience always asking, "Are you sure you're right? Have you done everything you possibly could? Have you done the right thing in the treatment of your patients?" I have been a severely conscience-bound person all my life.

To my mother sex was a major area of sin, and we were all brought up with a horrible fear of sexual wrongdoing. My mother was always telling us, "If you don't want to have children who are deformed you mustn't do anything impure." And then, "You mustn't touch yourself." That was the key phrase, "touch yourself." She never got any less delicate than that. You had to stay pure for the pure person you were going to marry.

At times when she suspected we were not accepting her prohibitions strongly enough there would be very grave talks. She would come and sit on the side of the bed, after I'd gone to bed, or take me into the den, and say, "Now Bennie, you will keep yourself pure, and I hope you will keep pure thoughts. You do want to have normal children and be worthy of a fine wife, don't you?" And I would say, "Yes."

It was always made clear to us that we mustn't associate

with disreputable types, children less moral than we. They might want to get into sex play. When I was little we summered at the Connecticut shore, and once, when I was about four years of age, a girl a year older at the beach suggested that we undress and show ourselves to each other. Instead, I immediately went home and told my mother. The next summer a farmer's son suggested sucking my penis. But again, being the good boy that I was, I rushed home and told my mother on him.

We were made to feel guilty about everything. If I broke a window I dreaded its discovery, the disapproval and the possible punishment.

When I got to my teens I was extremely bashful with girls, but fascinated with them. When I was about fourteen, my mother gave me a more explicit talk on sex (my father was much too reserved), about how a man and a woman fall in love and get deeper and deeper in love, get married, and how the husband's weewee goes into "a special place" in his wife. This all had to do with pure love, and certainly not before marriage. I remember my mother driving me downtown in New Haven, and as we went by a street corner where people were waiting for a trolley car, I involuntarily turned my head to see what a girl on the corner looked like. Mother said sternly, "Bennie, that's disgusting!" She had a contemptuous phrase for girl watchers: "Men who look at girls as if they were horses." In other words, purely carnal, that a man could imagine making some kind of advance to such a girl. I don't really know why she thought of horses as being objects of lecherous gazes. Perhaps because they were all flesh and no soul. At a time when most young women had turned to flesh-colored stockings, my sisters had to stay in black stockings. My mother told them that to wear flesh-colored ones was to invite men to look at them as if they were horses. And they couldn't wear makeup until they left home—this in the Roaring Twenties.

My mother was really quite handsome. She started out with very dark hair that turned prematurely gray and then white. Her skin became more and more tanned as she got older, and she had flashing gray-green eyes. My father was a rather serious, perhaps slightly stern-looking person with sandy hair. Somebody at the time compared him with Calvin Coolidge. The most intimate thing I ever saw between my mother and father occurred when I was about ten. My mother was upset about something and Father was talking to her in the den. She was in a nightgown, having just gotten up. My father was sitting opposite her, and he reached over and patted her on the knee. I thought this was embarrassingly intimate. Their kisses were brief and birdlike, nothing more.

In their adulthood, my own two sons reproached me for not having shown physical affection for them. I was surprised and totally unprepared for this and said, "But my father never showed me the slightest physical affection." It never occurred to me to show any toward my sons. In the neighborhood I grew up in, I never saw a father being physically affectionate with his son, or his wife.

It wasn't until I got to Andover at sixteen that I heard dirty stories, and I can still remember the first ones, fifty-five years later. Though they weren't very funny, they were branded into my memory. One went: "What goes in hard and dry and comes out soft and sticky? Give up? Chewing gum." The other was about a man who was in the upper berth of a sleeping car, and there was intercourse going on between a bride and groom in the berth below. And this couple used the word "turtle" to avoid a vulgar word. Finally the guy in the upper berth said, "Please stop. Every time you turtle I mock turtle, and I'm swimming in the soup." When I went to Andover, 1919 to 1921, everybody had to be in the dormitory at eight P.M. The dormitory master went around checking, and you were in terrible trouble if you got caught out. Everybody dressed very conservatively, three-piece suits, white Brooks Brothers shirts and snap-brim felt hats. In the summer, for a dance, you wore white buckskin shoes, white flannel trousers, a blue jacket and a rep tie. I was ashamed when I went to Andover with collars that didn't button down. I felt like an outsider, gauche.

Any Spock who went away on vacation or a visit or went to college, as my sister went to Vassar, had to write my mother twice a week. Furthermore, you had to tell her everything you had done every day, who you did it with, and what kind of people they were. Once when I was slow in writing one of my semi-weekly letters I got a telegram saying, "write or come home." I didn't doubt that Mother would remove me.

She made me live at home my first year of college because she said I had lost my idealism at Andover. This was because I had written her about going out on a Sunday afternoon with some other Andover boys to call on a couple of girls, from a respectable enough family, though they weren't so prim. One of the girls had given me dizzying compliments about my attractiveness, obviously trying to stir a little advance from me, which she didn't get because I was too scared.

I was fascinated with girls and thought I might like to know some fast ones. But if a girl was just a bit too seductive in manner—I don't mean an invitation to go what's called the limit; I mean just an invitation to get a little friendly—it scared the hell out of me. I was as bashful as a bashful girl. I'm sure I had a standoffish, haughty, frightened manner.

I realized years later that my mother was a jealous person,

and that I told her about the compliments of that girl just to provoke her jealousy. It obviously alarmed her greatly. All during my adolescence and youthful years Mother would say to me, "Bennie, why don't you like wholesome girls?" I hated that word and vowed I would never pay attention to her kind of girl. She meant somebody who was very open and unseductive and brought up with only the highest ideals, you know, like one's little sister, nothing held back, nothing mysterious.

From the age of twelve until the age of sixteen I worshiped from afar a girl who was a year older than me. She sat two rows in front of me in Center Church Sunday school in New Haven. She was dark-haired, with sparkling eyes, and somewhat mysterious. She lived with an uncle and aunt, and I assumed that her parents were dead. I invited her to dance once at "The Christmas Frolic," a big, wholesome dance at the Lawn Club in New Haven, where people from the age of four right on up to grandparents played games and danced. I was electrified to see her there and spent a couple of hours wondering whether I would dare ask her to dance. Her name was Marta, not Martha but Marta, which I thought was very romantic. Finally I got up the courage to approach her, and said, "Aren't you Marta?" What a question, when this was the person I'd dreamed about for four years. We danced around the room once, but in my inner turmoil I couldn't think of anything more to say. That was the only time I ever spoke to her, although I faced her and was watching her all the time every year during rehearsals for the Sunday school Christmas play.

My next love was a girl whose father had died. Peggy was her name. She was very pretty and very shy, and I worshiped her mostly from afar, from the age of sixteen to the age of twenty. I was able to invite her to the Yale-Harvard football game and the Yale Prom. She consented to come, and looked beautiful. I was totally excited but I couldn't think of much to say to her. And I couldn't think of an excuse to see her at any other times than when I was offering her an invitation to a game or the prom.

Then I met Jane, the woman that I married, and fortunately I didn't have this degree of inhibition with her. I met her when I was twenty and she was seventeen, and it was immediately possible for us to talk, talk, talk. She thought that I was interesting as well as attractive, and she was the first girl to take me seriously. My sophomore year I was on the junior varsity eight-oared crew, which unexpectedly beat Harvard. There was a dance afterward at an elegant summer resort near New London, Connecticut, where I first met not Jane but her fifteen-year-old sister, and gave her a great rush, thinking she was an older woman of twenty-seven. She didn't have much to say, but she smiled in an amused kind of way and didn't seem to mind my attentions. She invited me to visit her and her family on the Labor Day weekend, and that's where I met Jane. Her father had died three or four years before. I proposed marriage to her on the second night of that same weekend.

So I later thought, Marta was an orphan, Peggy's father had died, and Jane's father had died. There is a strong presumption here that I was scared to death to get interested in a girl that had a father anywhere around. It tells something about my relations with men, about my severe inhibition of sexuality, and that underneath my resentment and fear of my mother was an even greater awe of my father. In 1933, at the age af thirty, I went into psychoanalysis, for professional purposes. I complained bitterly for weeks to the analyst about my mother. But my dreams showed it wasn't my mother; it was male ogres that were terrifying me. And my associations showed that my father was the person I was really scared of. Freud would say that any boy's afraid of his father to a certain degree and that this is where the incest taboo comes from. At about the age of three and four a boy dreams of marrying his mother—and sometimes says so, openly. Around five and six he realizes his mother is married to someone else, which stirs up, in his unconscious, fierce feelings of rivalry with his father and fear of his father. This anxiety eventually compels him to suppress his sexual interest in his mother completely, and in other females to a lesser degree until adolescence reverses the trend. The stricter the family and the stronger the repression, the slower the reawakening. Anyway, a Freudian would say that the pure chance of a guy falling in love with a succession of three girls who didn't have a father would be not more than one in ten billion.

By the time I met Jane, the sum of my physical contact with girls was almost nil. From the age of fifteen on, I had forbidden carnal thoughts, and the only outlet for them was nocturnal emissions. I can assure you there was nothing else. I felt guilty about the nocturnal emissions too. I mean I thought it was disgraceful for that to be found on my pajamas. I had finally gotten up the courage to kiss Susan, the girl next door, who was one of my sister's friends. It was a weekend on the shore at Bradford, and Susan and I had been swimming and were sitting on the dock. She was plump and womanly and appetizing looking, and I got up enough courage to give her a quick little peck. There was certainly no body contact.

Jane was an attractive, sophisticated, educated woman who was used to being taken seriously in conversation. The kids' conversations in my family were never taken seriously. If we tried to talk about anything a little bit serious, my mother would accuse us of being pompous or laugh at us.

And here suddenly I was talking to someone who thought my ideas were worth discussing. It took four years of courtship before Jane would marry me. When I first proposed to her, she was going to Miss Walker's School in Connecticut and she said, "I've got to grow up and look around for a long while." We had an on-again, off-again romance in which I kept wanting her to commit herself to me and she always said no. After two years I called off the quest in disgust. Jane later said she was sorry we had called it off, and when she went abroad for a year with her mother and sister I wrote her ardent letters. We were finally married a year after her return, in the summer after my second year of medical school.

In our courtship we were very proper. Love, though it had its physical side, was predominantly a matter of idealism, shared idealism, shared interest in literature and doing good. We had long, earnest conversations. I was halfway through medical school, so I knew enough about sex from the anatomical and physiological point of view. But physical sexuality was only a subordinate part of our relationship. Sex as fun? I would never have used that word. I would have thought that was vulgar.

My mother's morality was ten times as heavy a threat as is desirable. There's no need of making a person impotent until the age of twenty. I mean the only time as far as I know that I had erections as well as ejaculations before then was in dreams. This is a severe inhibition. It's probably significant that of the six Spocks of my generation, only three married.

It certainly would never have occurred to me to get involved in an impromptu sexual situation. I would not have thought of this as appropriate. I dated only two women prior to Jane. I danced once with one of them and I took the other one to two Yale proms. Jane and I got married in 1927, and we have lived a deeply satisfying life, not without the usual

292 : **The First Time**

strains. My physical, sexual adjustment was average, normal. Extramarital sex was always out of the question, by my standards.

I've been a goodie-goodie all my life, but I don't have regrets about the way I was brought up. I was very resentful during my adolescence and youth. But obviously what I've accomplished in life has been largely a function of, the result of, this rather complex, artificial and ridiculously inhibited kind of childhood. I'm a product of my childhood. The fact that I'm a pediatrician is an expression of the fact that I was the oldest of six kids in a child-centered family. The fact that I had particular ideals—in the way I practiced pediatrics and in the drive to write a good book on child-rearing for all parents—was a product of my strict idealistic upbringing. The fact that I became an opponent of the war in Vietnam was an expression of this moralistic upbringing. So there's no point regretting it. I've had a very good life. We've raised two fine sons and I'm known as a friend of parents and children around the world. It all happened to work out this way, so why monkey around with it?

People, young people particularly, say that sexuality is a perfectly simple instinct that's meant to be enjoyed. I say, sorry, that's a gross oversimplification. I'm a Freudian and Freud says that sexuality in a human being is never a simple thing. All poetry, drama, literature, painting, sculpture and architecture are expressions, sublimated expressions, of partially inhibited sexual drive. I believe that in the process of evolution sexuality has become partly spiritual in human beings and that man is partly a spiritual animal. And in most societies since the beginning of history monogamy has been the ideal. Human beings have been unfaithful in large numbers, but this does not destroy the ideal, which is born anew each generation. And marriage will persist, I believe.

Hubert Prior (Rudy) Vallee *singer, actor*

Born July 18, 1901, Island Pond, Vt.

Every Sunday Rudy Vallee has a few loyal friends up to his big pink stucco house on a mountain overlooking Los Angeles, to play tennis, drink, and eat a few half-dollar-sized hamburgers, which Rudy cooks on a hibachi beside the pool, empty and strewn with leaves, and the tennis court, which is cantilevered over a cliff. Usually wearing a baseball cap and tennis outfit over his paunchy middle, Rudy serves cheap California champagne in paper cups, sometimes mixed with orange and grape soda, which he buys in gallon plastic jugs at the Von's Market in the valley below. On the occasion of our visit, as he cooked he played a cassette recording of a recent personal appearance he had made in Honolulu, in which he sang only a few songs but told a string of gamy jokes. When it got dark, Rudy, his wife, Ellie, and his coterie went inside, sat down before the living room fireplace, and hauled out a stack of big black scrapbooks, which contained hundreds of photographs of girls he had dated. He would recall the name of every one of them and what each was like as he turned the pages. He also described how he had outfitted several well-known actresses with tailored black satin dresses. Finally his wife said, "Rudy, why did you have black satin dresses made for them?" Rudy roared, "To get a hard-on,

294 : The First Time

for Chrissake, what do you think?" Of all the interviewees, he was clearly the most uninhibited—a man who had lived long and lustily, with no embarrassment whatever.

I NEVER FELT that physically and facially I was anything of a lady-killer, but I had a great reputation for being a cocksman. I wasn't, really, because fucking wasn't the most important thing to me. I was always in search of romance. Kissing. Hugging. Just to be with her. Not to be *in* her, or even to dry fuck her. I can't stand unattractive women. Phyllis Diller makes me sick. I love beautiful women. Just to be with a beautiful woman and look at her. I loved it. Loved it. Loved romance. Always have.

Terry Moore told me once that Howard Hughes asked her, "How does Rudy get all these women?" I had taken to two women that he liked. One of them was Mary Brian, who I met when I was at Yale and started dating when I came out to Hollywood in 1929 to make my first movie, *The Vagabond Lover*. That's why I can never play a Howard Hughes hotel in Las Vegas. I'm writing about all of that now, in my third book. Walter Kane, who does all of the booking in the Hughes hotels, was my buddy. We were in the Coast Guard together. He wanted to book me over there and started to make the arrangements, but then he told me, "Rudy, Howard says, 'No Vallee.'" I wrote and said, "Howard, I never meant to hurt Mary. I was in love with somebody else at the time. Please don't hold that against me, because there are bets that I will never play Las Vegas again. Howard, I want to prove to these bastards that I can play and do a good job. Please."

But I never heard from him. I don't think he will ever for-give me.

I used to be goddamned well-hung. Obviously I can't name her here, but a great movie beauty of that day liked it. I fucked her twice in one night, which was unusual for me. Once was normal for me. She was living down on Wilton Place in an apartment with Illona Massey. We'd been danc-ing at the Grove, and when I drove her home I parked and we got over in the back seat and fucked. Then we went into her apartment. I sat down on the sofa and she came walking out in a minute stark naked. My mouth dropped open and she must have known what I was thinking, because she said, "Yes, I know. I'm flat." She lay down on the carpet on her stomach and said she wanted to do it in the Viennese fashion.

It was always the romance that I liked. The dark, exotic Arabian Nights type was my ideal. Back in my Yale days, as I went to the post office one morning, Murray the newsboy had his pile of papers and magazines stacked up and there, staring at me from the cover of *College Humor,* was a crea-tion by Rolf Armstrong—a gorgeous brunette with a pile of beautiful black hair falling around her shoulders, a sensuous mouth, parted lips and eyes that promised pools of sex.

Then one night in 1929, when we were shooting *The Vaga-bond Lover,* I took Mary Brian to the Blossom Room of the Hollywood Roosevelt and there on the dance floor I saw, fa-cially at least, the girl of the cover come to life. I made no at-tempt to conceal my interest, and Mary calmly told me, "Her name is Fay Webb, and her father is chief of police in Santa Monica." I felt something like a heel, as I knew I was making Mary unhappy. But I had never promised Mary anything, never told her I loved her, nor had I ever made passionate love to her, as she definitely was not the dark, Arabian Nights type that was my ideal. I subsequently learned that Fay Webb was under contract to MGM for fifty dollars a week, which enabled Louis B. Mayer to look to Chief Webb for favors for anyone from MGM who got into trouble. I called her and asked her if she would have dinner with me that night, to which she readily assented. After that day's shooting, she and I repaired to my bungalow, where I pulled her into my arms, not, however, before having four or five Alexanders, which I had learned she liked. But it ended in violent embraces. Nothing more. Later I phoned her father and asked if I might take Fay with me to the Santa Barbara Biltmore to stay overnight, and I assured him he would have nothing to worry about. I think he rather hoped I would compromise her so that I would have to marry her. True to my word, we stayed overnight at the Biltmore, and nothing happened—nothing until we were married.

My last night in Hollywood after shooting *The Vagabond Lover*, I invited all the crew of the picture to be my guests at the Coconut Grove. These were the days of Prohibition, but I was able to secure enough rye, gin and bourbon, and of course my mother and father were with me that evening, as well as Mary Brian. I had met Fay Webb, but I felt obligated to spend my last night in Hollywood with Mary Brian, who I had met years before at Yale. As we sat eating and dancing, the maître d' came over and said Florabel Muir, M-U-I-R, of the New York *Daily News* would like to interview me. I was rather angry and said it was a hell of a time for an interview, when I was playing host to fifty or sixty people. But being the stupe, S-T-U-P-E, that I am, I said, "All right, bring her in." Now Florabel Muir, who had a face as close to that of a horse as I've ever seen on a woman, approached our table, accompanied by another woman, and I sat them down. They enjoyed a five-dollar dinner and began drinking my liquor, and she proceeded to ask me a lot of stupid questions, including how did I feel about going back to New York. Although I was going back to the Brooklyn Paramount Theater and the daily grind of doing four and five shows a day, I had already resolved that someday I would make Hollywood my home. I should have seen that this horse-faced Irish cunt, c-u-n-t, was a bitch of the first water, not to be trusted, with no scruples. A few days later, her column in the *Daily News* came out, and she quoted me exactly as saying that the thought of returning to the Brooklyn Paramount Theater made me sick. And here I was supposed to come out on the stage of the Brooklyn Paramount and tell them how thrilled I was to be back. I had become known as "Brooklyn's Boyfriend." And *The Vagabond Lover* was so bad that it damned near destroyed me, and I wound up with less than $20,000 out of it.

Here's a picture of Mary Smith*, the one girl I was really hung up on. She was great in the hay. She wore everything I wanted her to wear. Black satin and high-heeled shoes. She had two abortions by me. She was marvelous, but she didn't really love me. I had her followed, and I had a friend who was a locksmith and we got into her apartment in Hollywood and found her diary and photographed every page of it for two years. There wasn't one kind word in it about me. She started it by saying, "Guess who I met today. The Great Vallee!" She made fun of my white knees when we went to the beach.

I never touched my first wife at all. We got married in New York in 1920, on a Saturday morning. She made me marry her. She loved me so much that she just swept me off my feet. We would ride across town and she would stick her

* A pseudonym for a well-known actress of the twenties.

head out the window and yell, "I love Rudy Vallee!" We went together for a week and then got married, and on our wedding night I said, "Leona, I just can't go through with it."

Don't ask me how, but I screwed for the first time when I was about six years old. I don't remember much about it. We were all so young. There were four or five of us, and we all went up to the icehouse near the beaver pond behind Valentine School and screwed this girl. I don't remember much about her except that she wasn't very attractive. How the hell four or five of us happened to gang up on her that afternoon, I don't know. Hell, she invited us. There was no raping or anything. It was all very sweet and gentle and relaxed. I was so young that I didn't even know why we were doing it.

Then when I was about eleven, I fucked this girl named Rosie who used to come into my father's drugstore where I was working. I was in her, but I don't remember that it was a helluva thrill. In fact, I had masturbated three or four times by then, and I thought that that was more fun. I knew all about rubbers and everything because we sold them in the drugstore. My parents were Catholic, but they weren't strict and they never talked about sex at all.

Losing my virginity didn't mean a damned thing to me. I thought dry-fucking was actually more exciting. You know, just rubbing your prick against them until you came.

I never felt guilty about a goddamned thing in my life. What the hell is there to feel guilty about? I never did a thing to hurt anyone. I never understood why anyone would feel guilty about sex. I never wanted any children. You know why people have children? Vanity, pure and simple: look what I created. But if I had any children, I would explain sex to them in simple, graphic terms. That it's a thing of pleasure. And if you don't want children, be goddamned sure you don't have any. And if you don't want a disease, be careful.

No quoting from the fucking Bible. The Bible is the worst goddamned thing we have in this fucking world today. How can people be so stupid as to believe in the Deity? I'm seventy-three, and I say it's a lot of horseshit. If it makes you a better person to believe this horseshit, then embrace it. But I don't need it, for Chrissake.

When people have asked me about having kids, I said, "Another Rudy Vallee? God Forbid!" Then they say, "Well, what about all the things you have accumulated? What are you going to do with it all?" I say, "Fuck it. Let it burn. Who cares?"

I'm supposed to be a ham, but there's no vanity in me whatsoever. Fuck the applause. If I didn't need the money, you couldn't get me to perform. I've had it, up to here. I never made any real big money, despite all the movies and the fact that my Fleischmann Hour radio show was on the air for ten consecutive years. And a lot of people got rich out of the Villa Vallee nightclub, but I didn't. I worked there for a whole year for nothing. I'm so fucking stupid.

But fuck all the wealth if you're not feeling well. I've got good health. I've got a lovely wife, who I love and who loves me. So I'm one of the happiest guys in the world, though I still have to work my balls off.

I have no fear of dying whatsoever. I enjoy life very much. And if it happens tomorrow, no regrets. Just let it be quick. I've had seventy-three years of the best of everything. The finest of food and liquors. Beautiful women. What else could I want?

Irving Wallace *writer*

Born March 19, 1916, Chicago, Ill.

Workmen were pounding and sawing away on a six-room office suite he was adding to his meandering French country house in Brentwood, an expensive neighborhood two miles from the ocean in Los Angeles, but Irving Wallace carried on calmly with his carefully structured writing schedule: 11 A.M. to 6 P.M., six days a week, with thirty minutes off for lunch. He sat behind a huge desk in his study, at work on a new novel, making notes in a neat, tiny hand while placidly smoking a pipe. He had a manila envelope prepared, containing a thirteen-page biography and a photograph, asked what The First Time *was about, grasped the idea instantly, and responded with a well-constructed chronology of his youth. At the end he graciously suggested several other potential interviewees, was full of meaty advice and encouragement, and said he'd like to help any way he could.*

WELL, UNIQUE among writers, I grew up in a place called Kenosha, Wisconsin—fifty thousand people, Midwest, you know, on Lake Michigan between Chicago and Milwaukee, a largely industrial town. And it still is. But now it's a real

300

sex-freak town, all the bottomless places and so on. But in those days it wasn't that way.

When I was going to junior high school there, I remember in manual arts class, of all places, somebody showed me a picture of a nude grown woman. You know, a frontal shot. He pulled it out of his pocket and said something like, "Look what I've got." Wow! That blew my mind. I was so young— beginning of junior high, must have been about twelve or thirteen. Then came a whole rash of Tillie the Toiler comic books and things like that, the dirty Tijuana-type things where all the men were twenty inches and all the women were lying around naked. Very leering—the furtive part of an education.

My parents came from Europe as children (my father had a store) and whenever they'd talk about sex or something they felt was a little off, they would speak in Russian so I couldn't understand. Then I'd know something forbidden was being discussed. Well, my mother, dear woman, she'd had a miscarriage before my sister was born that she kept secret from her own relatives for years, because that, of course, meant that she'd been going to bed. That was the atmosphere. I don't know how I thought I was conceived. Immaculate conception maybe.

No. I remember that as a young kid I thought children came from breasts. I mean that babies came out of breasts. I don't know where I got that idea. I was just a young kid. Nobody ever sat down with me and talked about sex the way I did with my kids years later. Then one of my older cousins (he was going to a military academy) explained to me one day where babies came from. I couldn't believe it. You put it in, the man puts his in the woman, between her legs, and then after a certain period of time a child is born, comes out. I was stunned.

Sex just wasn't talked about openly at home, although my father was a liberal progressive in other ways. He voted for Battlin' Bob LaFollette and so forth.

I will say that in all the time I was going to high school, I never got laid. None of the fellows in my crowd did. Not one. No, wait, that's not right. One of my classmates was going with a girl and they started, as they said in those days, "sleeping together," but then they got married while they were still in high school, and they're still married.

There was always, like, one so-called bad girl in high school. Somebody had fucked her in the auditorium once. Or in the balcony. Or touched her or felt her. She was one of the girls who swung. No, "swung" wasn't the expression. She "put out," or she was "hot stuff." But that was one girl out of maybe twelve hundred kids. But neither I nor my closest friends ever got laid. And it wasn't because there weren't girls. There were a lot of gorgeous Lithuanian and Polish girls in this town, but they weren't putting out.

On a date you could go just so far. You'd go down to the beach and you went in swimming in the evenings and then you'd have bonfires and then you'd go back to the car. If you could put your hand under a girl's suit and touch her breasts, that was a great achievement. Later on, you might get down to touching her vagina. But that was it. You had to have an automobile. If you didn't, you were cooked. Where would you go? So you would be in the car, and the dialogue would be something like, "I love you, you know, and I can't keep my hands off of you," and then she'd say, "Don't go any further. I really can't. Don't touch me there. I'm getting too excited. Let's stop and have a drink or something. Please don't."

I didn't carry prophylactics in high school but I did for a while in college, or right after that. Wait a minute. Of course. Now I remember, way before I went to college I carried one folded in my back pocket. Finally it just wore out and rotted. And then it became a good luck symbol and I didn't want to throw it away. So I had to get a new one. I look at my kids today—I have a son who's twenty-five and a daughter who's eighteen and just graduated from a private high school in Vermont—well, I went with my daughter when she was fitted with an IUD two years ago. And she talks to me about her affairs, at least up to a point. I didn't feel happy about it the first time I learned she was involved, but then I decided it was healthy and natural at her age. Now we talk about it at great length and it's a lot better. Oh, my, she's so clean and unguilty and outgoing and beautiful.

Our son was caught between two worlds. He was on the cusp at eighteen, he just came in on that new era, and I think he started sleeping around the first year he went to college. But he had to free himself, become independent. He was living with one woman, whom we adored, for three years, quite openly. They kept house. And we can discuss it. My son and I talk about women.

We used to talk about women a lot when I was a kid too, but it was either overly romantic or quite the opposite, a leering kind of thing. We had no other frame of reference. It was all a little furtive, sex was, a little dirty and a little guilt-making.

I was in the Army, for example, with Ronald Reagan. He was my superior officer the first year. Nice, affable guy in those days, we thought, but a little uptight. And now I understand that when Reagan or Nixon, they have these committees report on obscenity, they always get back suggestions they don't want, so they turn the reports down, the idea being, you know, "We've got to keep the women of this country clean," not only keep the country Number One, but the women clean. And remember, to them sex is unclean.

And the Strom Thurmonds and all those fellows in Washington who are setting the moral tone. They really think sex is dirty. Of course I understand that, because we all did once. When we grew up it was a secret thing, and if you didn't do it to have children then there was something wicked and dirty about it. The word was always dirty. And that's crap. I mean, Jesus, Henry Miller was over here one day—grand man! grand fellow!—and he was the first one who understood what was going on and came right out with it in his early banned books, but we couldn't accept it then. When Miller came over, my children were here and they adored him because he just came right out and talked so cleanly and honestly about sex. Not dirty-old-man stuff. It was a pleasure.

God, that's the only part of my life I'd like to rewrite. Not the rest of it, the rest is fine. But that part of it, to have grown up in that repressed atmosphere, which those dummies on the Supreme Court are still trying to move backwards into, and they can't succeed any more, only technically. It must be marvelous to grow up where sex is normal and open. People say to me, "How can you believe that? Hell, if it's all open, there can't be any romance, any titillation, any build-up." I reply, "There still is romance. But it's just healthier. And the sex becomes a natural part of the kissing and petting and foreplay, and becomes the natural final pay-off, and then there's oneness. Much better. Much healthier."

When I was sixteen or so, I had just begun to hear words I had never heard before, like muffdiver, a whole new vocabulary. I never knew any young man in those days who'd ever gone down on a woman. Or would admit it. People wouldn't admit to masturbating either. You'd get pimples if you did it. Or your penis would fall off. It was really a horrifying thing. And a woman masturbating—you didn't even mention it.

Now, in the course of my work, if I'm in New York or Paris or so on I'll take a woman out for a drink to try to get some material, and I've heard more in the last couple of years—say, women in their twenties, they say, "I didn't have a guy around so I just went home and masturbated." Just like that. Even that took a little getting used to, for me. I remember sitting in the Plaza bar one evening and a woman was telling me, "There's just been nobody lately, and I felt that way the other night so I just went home and masturbated. What's wrong with that?" I said, "Nothing. Fine."

On this whole sex thing, a writer has a double problem. A number of us out here in Los Angeles who've been married and writing for some years agreed that marriage is inhibiting because if you have an affair on the side, get involved with some woman, eventually you're going to use that material, as most writers do, and you have to be pretty careful in terms of your wife and identification and people putting things together. And so you're inhibited about it and there's a kind of dishonesty. But it doesn't inhibit me. I just write, whatever I think about and can remember. And if it's true or not true, my wife doesn't ask me where I got it.

When I wrote *The Chapman Report* the women in my neighborhood were all very young then, some married, some not, and, well, they used to talk to me. I have a kindly face and I listen. A lot of writers don't listen. But I listen. So I heard all of this stuff and I said, My God. I wasn't even writing a book yet. I'd written one novel, but I'd never written anything that had made it. But I didn't just want to write a book about three or four women in the neighborhood. Then one day I got the idea for *Chapman Report*, and I wrote it. What I did was make a list of eight or nine women I knew, and what I knew about them (some fact, much of it perception), and then I cut off their names, blended some of the women together, and then made up some character background and story to make it work. Well, when the book was published, two things happened. A young woman walked up to me in Beverly Hills and said, "You son-of-a-bitch, I'm never going to speak to you again. You're writing about me, and everyone knows it." And I said, "What are you talking about?" Because I hadn't used her at all. I didn't know it, but she was married and was having an affair with a Hollywood director, who she later married. And one of the female married characters that I had created was having an affair with a director. But I didn't know about this girl's affair. And another one I used, at one time in her life before she got therapy, she was a nympho. You don't run into too many of those; that's a male sexist joke. But that was the way she got it off, sleeping with everyone. She once slept with a whole band, very sad and pathetic. Anyway, this woman I did actually write about. She was the one who was played by Claire Bloom in the movie. And one day, after the book was a big success, she dropped by our house, very pretty, married, and brought the book and asked me to sign it. And I did. And she said, "Why don't you write about me sometime?" Blind. Blind.

So I write about it and use what I hear and what I may have experienced. But it's very difficult for all writers with wives, unless you don't give a goddamn about the sensitivity of your wife. A couple of times early on, my wife would make cracks. I'm not going to say whether it's true or not. I'm just going to say, always, this stuff is stuff I've picked up, I've heard, I've found out, or I met this woman on the Riviera and here's what I heard. Indeed, it may be all fantasy, creativity. Nobody knows. Some guy was out to get an interview for *Esquire*. He wanted to know if once you've made it, is it easy to get women, if you had a lot of affairs. I said, "This is

not an area we can talk about. Norman Mailer can talk that
way, but I can't. I love my wife. And even if I had an affair
I wouldn't discuss it."

And I'll tell you something funny. After I got my first big
best-seller, it got a lot of publicity all over the world. Now,
I'd been freelancing when Art Buchwald was a stringer in
Paris for the *Herald Trib*. We knew each other, and I used to
go to Paris to write for *Colliers* and so on. Art had just begun
to make it when my first big best-seller came out, and here I
was getting all this attention, and Art and I went out to
breakfast one morning in Paris. We were alone, without our
wives, and Art looked at me and said, "Jesus, you know, before, when we wanted all these broads, here we were, two
unattractive guys and nobody gave a damn about us, and today—is it true with you?—you can have anybody, the whole
Copacabana line. They're all name-fuckers, you know. And
now you've become absolutely beautiful. You're a party conversation piece. They can go to bed with you and say you're
lousy. It doesn't matter what. I mean you've slept with them.
But we married and went public. Isn't life horrible? Before,
you wanted it and couldn't get it. Now you can get it all, but
you can't have it." He was moaning all morning about it.

I believed in the double standard until possibly ten years
ago. I don't any more. I mean I would be unhappy if I knew
my wife had an affair. But that wouldn't be the end of it, because there must be a reason why that happened, and if she
still loves me, then that's it. It certainly would be a downer
for me in terms of ego. I have some hang-ups about the
whole thing, but I'm shaking them, at least intellectually. I
don't know if I turned around completely emotionally. For
example, the first time I heard my daughter—found out inad-
vertently my daughter was sleeping with somebody, well, I
blew my stack. And she said, "Well, what do you want. What

is it?" And I said, "Well, wait until you're eighteen." And she said, "What is this numbers game?" Of course she was right.

When I was young it was a bad thing to get a wife who wasn't a virgin. When I look back, it's just incredible, but I felt that the woman you marry should be a virgin. But I've analyzed it, and I think the real reason for wanting to marry a virgin was not that you were getting something used, but that you were afraid to have your performance compared to some other guy's. If you got a woman who'd slept with other men, she could assess you, and maybe you weren't up to standard and weren't all that good, you see. It's often a very unconscious insecurity. There was insecurity in terms of how good you were. You had no way of knowing if a woman was enjoying you enough—I mean that feeling of being tested. It had to do with those inhibitions. But we've learned a lot. And everybody's different, and all their demands are different, and the pleasures are different, and what you do is different. There are just no rules. But in those days there were rules, although they weren't written. For instance, there was no thought that a woman's orgasm was as necessary and important as a man's. I mean, women didn't speak up and say, "I want to come" or "I have to" or "You owe that to me; I don't care how, but come on, I've got to be satisfied." The rule was that it was a one-way street, generally. Sometimes you'd meet someone a little more sharp and they'd say, "Well, I haven't come yet" or "Come one, keep going, I'm almost there."

I think a part of that corruption and inhibition when I was young came from reading. Because the books lied a lot in that sense. They generally over-romanticized love, made it seem perfect, and somehow when you got down to flesh with flesh it was never as perfect as the thing you'd read about in those books. The unrealism and the closedness of literature, the fakiness of so much of it, the idea that everything was perfect, really confused a lot of guys, confused a lot of people. Because now you can read books and see that guys fail, that it could be great to go down on someone, sixty-nine or something, that everything works and it doesn't matter whether it's one minute or sixty minutes or whatever. People who are reading the new realism don't have this whole goddamned Hall-of-Fame standard any more.

And guilt. Later on I had no guilts. But there was always an idea lodged in our minds—my peer group—that if you screwed a girl she was not as good as another girl. That was crummy. Or there was another thing that went on, which was if I was going out with somebody and liked them very much and was able to go to bed with them, there was a guilt feeling that I should marry that person. That took a long time to get over, a long time.

In those years I went steady with about three girls for quite a long time, really attractive young women, and it was only waist-up petting and endless kissing and roaming around and feeling, but not even any effort to get more.

Right after high school two male friends and I formed an expedition and went down to Honduras in search of material. I was about eighteen and was writing for newspapers and magazines. We got to the Mexican border, Nueva Laredo, and we all decided (I was the virgin of the three) to find some women. We walked down the street, and there were the Mexican women standing outside beckoning. So there was a very pretty one, and I went to her bedroom and got laid. It wasn't physical relief, because the first time wasn't that great. It was the idea! Relief, people could always get it by masturbating. That was no problem. It was the idea of connecting with a woman for the first time. No more mystery.

The love-making didn't last very long, I assure you. It cost two dollars. I felt like a man—you know, the old-fashioned thing. I'd gotten it up, and it was with a woman a little older, and she was attractive, and I knew there was more to it and I'd have to learn a lot. But it was the first time and I felt like a terrific hero. Oh, boy, what an evening!

Mae West *entertainer*

Born August 17, 1892, Brooklyn, N.Y.

The living room of the capacious apartment she has lived in since 1932, not far from Paramount studios in Hollywood, like the rooms in her Santa Monica beach house and her San Fernando Valley ranch house, is done all in white: a white piano with several white-framed photographs of herself and a white nude statue of herself on it; white carpeting; white furniture; several white-backed Mae West scrapbooks; dozens more white-framed photographs of herself on the white walls; and a white-framed Rubenesque nude portrait of herself, done in 1934, that hangs above the white sofa. Presently a dark-haired and enormously muscled man of about forty-five, obviously a weightlifter, entered the living room, exactly like a bit player in a high school play, and said, "Miss West will be with you in a few minutes." After fifteen minutes she appeared, wearing a white pants suit, her platinum hair piled and swirled like a frozen custard. Her conversational voice was exactly like her famous performing voice, and was still peppered with pure Brooklynese, e.g., "apernt-ment" for appointment, "orkester" for orchestra. Her memory was remarkably precise, and her stories were full of rich, amusing detail. She was frank and unashamed about her life, but was careful to an almost Victorian degree about the words she chose to describe the most earthy incidents, and occasionally when she felt herself becoming too vividly descriptive, would point her finger and say, "Don't use that."

I'VE NEVER BEEN without a man for more than a week since I was thirteen years old. Sex and my work—which has all been about men and sex—have been the only two important things in my life. I needed a lot of men, and I've had a lot of them. I was liberated quite early, before anybody even used the word. I thought to myself, "If boys can do it, why can't I?" It made me angry that men had this privilege and women didn't. It wasn't fair. My mind told me I had just as much right to do it as they did.

I was tricked into getting married—I did it because I was scared—and I never had the slightest interest in having children. That was the last thing I would want to do. What did I need that for? I had to concentrate on myself. And I'm still concentrating on myself. I needed a lot of men because I had to find out how they thought, for my writing, you know. I was never interested in women. I don't think I've had two girl friends in my whole life. I never cared a thing about politics, or music, or traveling, or parties, or reading. I'm too nervous to read much.

I never had one of those love affairs you read about, where the woman could die because she feels it so strong. I liked some of them more than others, but I didn't love any of them that much. Of course, you don't have to be in love for the sex to be good. Two guys stand out in my mind as the ones I liked better than the rest. I went with them a couple of years each. I thought it was love with them, but then I realized it was just habit. I'd just gotten used to them. So I got rid of them.

One of them was Italian, very handsome. It took me a long time to get him out of my system, about two years. The sex thing was terrific with this guy. I got used to it and I wanted it all the time. I wanted to do it morning, noon and night, and that's all I wanted to do. My mother didn't like it. She had ambitions for me. She said I was only interested in myself and not in my career. She was right, and when I realized that, I got rid of him. It almost killed the poor guy. He started to drink. He would come around to our house looking for me, and my mother would say she didn't know where I was. He would cry and cry and say he was going to kill himself.

When I got rid of one guy I'd find another one right away. But I wouldn't go with a lot of guys one or two times. When I found one I liked, it always lasted a year or a year and a half. I never start with anybody unless I am sure that's what I want. I don't like any of these guys who are going to give me a lot of trouble. If they can't be cheerful I get rid of them. I had this one guy once, a former Mr. America, almost six foot, and I thought at first he was going to be fine. But I didn't know his mind. I mean, I had lots of affairs with him, but I didn't know him well enough to talk to him, you know? After a while he started sitting around sulking, and what did I need that for, you know? I got rid of him fast.

When I was growing up my mother wanted me to have boyfriends, but she didn't want me to have any special one. If she saw me liking one more than another, she would point out some fault that he had, and then I would see it and switch to another boy. We had a brownstone in the Bushwick section of Brooklyn. My father was an athlete, a boxer, and then he had a big detective agency in Brooklyn. He was the one who started these night patrols. He was Catholic and my mother was Lutheran. They weren't terribly strict, but they were very narrow-minded. My father was out every night working, so I didn't see him very much and I could stay out until ten o'clock and play with the boys. I always liked boys better than girls, and I always had a lot of boys after me.

I started going to dancing school when I was eight years old, and then my father built me a good-sized stage in the basement, all white, with a white curtain and everything, and I had a dancing teacher who came to the house and gave me lessons. I started exercising when I was twelve. My father exercised all the time and lifted weights—he was the Brooklyn champion—and that made me want to do it. Of course, I used lighter weights than he did. But I have exercised all my life, and I still use the dumbbells every day. I missed all the usual children's diseases. When my brother, who is dead now, or my sister would get measles or something, the doctor would say, "She'll be next." But I never had anything. I've never had an operation of any kind, and I only get a cold about once every ten years, and then I catch it from someone else.

I never smoked or drank. I don't like it. I saw a lot of other people who drank, and what it did to them. I figured it might hurt my looks. I've taken good care of myself. As far as sex is concerned, I don't see any change in myself except in my thinking. I mean, you don't want to use all of your energy and vitality in bed, not if you want to do something else.

I never used bad language, and I never liked to listen to dirty stories. We didn't have to go to church every morning and night in our family, but we were very proper people. Sex was an embarrassing thing in our family, and to this day I don't discuss sex with my sister, who is five years younger than me and lives on my ranch in Sepulveda.

I knew all about sex quite early. I knew what a man was and how it worked and everything. You heard things on the street. I knew that if you do it before you go through your changes, you're safe. So I was afraid to wait for the changes. I figured I had better go ahead and do it. And even at that time a girl felt like it was old-fashioned not to do it, that she was doing it to be modern. I started thinking about the fact that men could do anything they wanted to, but women were supposed to wait until they got married. I thought that was unfair and unequal, so I said to myself, "Gee, I'm not going to wait until I get married." I wanted equal rights, and I wasn't afraid, because it was before my changes. They didn't come until I was about fourteen.

I was well-developed before that though. My music teacher would hold me on his lap and kiss me and kiss me, and just go crazy. But he was afraid to go any further because I was so young. I was thirteen, and he must have been about twenty-one. He had been an actor and a dancer on the stage, and he was very good-looking. It happened one night on the stairs in our house, in the vestibule. I had been in this amateur show at the Royal Theater and he had walked me there and back. It was winter and I had on my fur coat, and I was standing on the stairs one step above him. He was afraid, so I told him I had done it before. I wanted to see what it was like. I lied to him so he would do it. I felt ashamed to say I hadn't done it. He said, "Are you sure you've done this before?" and I said, "Sure, a couple of times."

My mother and father were upstairs, but they couldn't tell what was going on. If one of them opened the door and came down the hall upstairs, I would have been able to hear them.

And they wouldn't be able to see anything because I had my fur coat wrapped around me. The underwear was that long kind with a string tied at the waist and a slit down the front that folded over. That was pretty convenient.

It hurt the first couple of times, but I wasn't frightened. What was there to be frightened of, for God's sake? I felt right doing it, and after the first couple of times, it felt good.

I was always careful about not getting pregnant, and I never had any trouble about it. Back then you used a little silk sponge with a string on it. You wet the sponge in warm water and then put it in and it worked fine—you just pulled it out and washed it. Women ought to use them today. They worked pretty good.

I was a brazen kid then. Not too fresh though, although I would sometimes give my father an attitude. There was a music teacher in Brooklyn named Professor Watts, and he put on the Knights of Columbus amateur show. He had a twelve-piece orchestra, and I had never sung in front of an orchestra before, so my father said, "Let's put her in it, and if she gets stage fright, we'll forget the whole thing." I wasn't frightened at all. I was just worried about where the spotlight was. I sang a song called "Moving Day." I had a rough voice and a certain way of moving, and after a few seconds I knew I had them in my hand. After that I did a tap dance. I got the gold medal that night.

I got married between sixteen and seventeen. He was very good-looking, a good bit older than I was. He was an acrobatic dancer, almost six foot, so he had a pretty good body. He was on the bill with me in this show and he kept staring at me and finally asked me if I would do an act with him. I told my mother and father about it, and they came to see him dance and liked him. Then he came to the house three or four times and finally my mother and father said I could do an act with him. They had him investigated and found out he was all right. He was Lithuanian, but he had a family, sisters and everything. He looked like Gene Kelly, sang jazz and ragtime, and was a great acrobatic dancer.

There was an opera singer of about forty who was in the show with us, and she talked me into marrying him. He bought her a suit and a hat, a lot of clothes, to get her to help him. There were a lot of guys hanging around my dressing room, and she would see me kissing them hot and heavy, so she started talking to me about getting married. "You need to have a husband," she said. "Something may happen to you one of these days, and you won't be married, and then what will your parents think?"

She kept on talking to me about it. She kept saying something might happen, but if I got married I'd have somebody to blame it on. Getting pregnant was a great disgrace in those days. I had a very beautiful close relationship with my mother, and I never wanted to do anything to hurt her or my father. So when this opera singer kept after me, and told me I could get married and still see other guys, that sounded okay to me. If she had said, "You've got to marry him and be with him forever without having anybody else," I wouldn't have done it. There were too many others around. I had a whole band one time. Joe Schenk was the piano player, and he brought them around to the house and we would go down to the basement. I had him, and then the trumpet player, and then the drummer.

I was just fickle. I liked all kinds of men. Big ones. Short ones. I never had any special type. I always saw something I liked about different ones. Their eyes. Their shoulders. Their hands. But I never fooled around with married men. It isn't fair to wives. The guy I married was very sexy-looking. He was in love with me. I liked him, but I didn't love him. I

finally agreed to marry him after he promised not to tell anybody we were married. I didn't want to do anything to hurt
my mother. We were on the road with this show and got
married one morning in a town in the Midwest. We never
lived together as man and wife. I had my own hotel room,
and in those days you had to leave your door open if there
was a man in the room, and the house detective would come
along every now and then and look in.

It only lasted four or five weeks, until we got back to New
York, and then I thought, "How am I ever gonna get away
from this guy?" I got him the lead in this show that was going on the road for forty weeks, and I got rid of him fast.
Maybe I was lucky I was married. I'd have married that Italian if I hadn't already been married. I didn't want to go
through a divorce and all that mess, so in a way I saved myself. I didn't want to hurt my mother, and she never knew
about the marriage. She had passed away when I finally got
a divorce after I came out to Hollywood in 1932. My husband
passed away in 1954. He was always in love with me.

I used to try out parts and material on my mother. She
knew what was good. Finally she said to me, "Mae, I've been
watching you. You can write your own play." So I wrote a
show and got a director and we started rehearsals. I had an
unusual way about me, the way I moved around, and this
director kept watching me and finally he said he had directed
so-and-so and she had this quality and he'd directed such-
and-such and she had that quality, but, he said, "you've got a
quality I've never seen." But he wouldn't say what it was.
Finally I decided I'd better ask him, so I said, "Okay, what
have I got?" And he said, "You've got SEX, SEX, a low sex quality." And the way he said it, it sounded better than a high
sex quality.

He kept saying, "You don't drink, do you? Don't ever

drink! You're gonna set the world on fire. This play reeks with SEX, SEX, SEX." Everybody kept using that word sex so much that I just decided to call the play that, and that was the title, "Mae West in *Sex*." It was a sensation. Sex was just a word in the medical books when I first used it in a show. We packed them in at ten dollars a seat when three-fifty was the top price everywhere else.

I brought the censors on in Hollywood, but I saved the industry—Paramount and seventeen hundred theaters. When I got out here the movies were doing so bad, during the Depression, that you could fire a cannon in the theaters. My pictures broke all kinds of records, and I made a lot of money in Hollywood. I made $500,000 a year for several years, when the income tax was three per cent, and then five per cent. When Garbo was getting $75,000 a picture and Gable $50,-000, I was getting $300,000 to star and another $100,000 for the story. But I've spent a lot of money. I used to play the horses pretty bad, and then I owned a string of horses. I've got a lot of property, but I don't like to talk about my investments in public.

I've got a public waiting if I ever want to do another picture. I'm still writing, still working. I feel about as young as I ever did. I don't have a wrinkle, and I've never had a facelift. I never felt guilty about sex. There's something wrong with people who do. I did what I was supposed to do. Fate—there are things that happen, things that are supposed to be. I haven't had all the men I want. Not yet. I still see one every now and then that I want.